Regulating Political Parties
European Democracies in Comparative Perspective

REGULATING POLITICAL PARTIES

European Democracies in Comparative Perspective

Edited by

Ingrid van Biezen & Hans-Martien ten Napel

Leiden University Press

Cover design: Suzan Beijer
Layout: CO2 Premedia

ISBN 978 90 8728 218 9
e-ISBN 978 94 0060 195 6 (e-pdf)
e-ISBN 978 94 0060 196 3 (e-pub)

NUR 754

This book is distributed in North America by the University of Chicago Press (www.press.uchicago.edu).

Printed and bound by CPI Group (UK) Ltd, Croydon, CR0 4YY

Table of contents

INTRODUCTION

Regulating Political Parties: European Democracies in Comparative Perspective

Ingrid van Biezen & **Hans-Martien ten Napel**
Leiden University

The increase in party regulation

The question of how parties are, and ought to be, regulated, has assumed increased importance in recent years, both within the scholarly community and among policy-makers and politicians. Given the traditionally private and voluntary character of political parties, the state in liberal democratic societies would not normally intervene in the regulation of their behaviour and organization. But in recent years the legal regulation of parties has become more and more common, to the point that party structures have now become 'legitimate objects of state regulation to a degree far exceeding what would normally be acceptable for private associations in a liberal society' (Katz 2002: 90). In that sense, parties in contemporary democracies are to a growing extent managed by the state, in that their activities are increasingly subject to regulations and state laws which govern their external activities or determine the way in which their internal organization may function. Even in countries such as the Netherlands, where the regulation of parties has traditionally been relatively non-existent, the issue is assuming increasing importance. This can be demonstrated, for example, by the impending review of the party funding law and the recent court cases around the question of female representation within the Political Reformed Party (SGP). Both these cases are addressed in the present volume.

The increased importance of the law in describing, prescribing, or proscribing the operational activities and functions of political parties implies that the state is assuming an increasingly substantive role in the management of, and control over, their behaviour and organization. This raises important questions and concerns, ranging from the motivations inspiring specific regulations to their effect on the parties and the party systems and the underlying conceptions of the role and place of political parties in modern democracies.

Surprisingly, however, despite the increasing relevance of state regulation of political parties, this phenomenon has hitherto received relatively little systematic and comparative scholarly attention, from political scientists or lawyers. Thus, a recently published handbook on comparative constitutional law acknowledges that '[p]olitical parties and party system dynamics are ... critical to understanding how constitutions work, and why they may not, in spite of well-intentioned designs'. It is added, however, that '[u]nfortunately, much of the recent literature in comparative constitutional law has paid little attention to the multiple ways our basic constitutional structures are conditioned by political parties and party system dynamics' (Skach 2012: 875; see also Pildes 2011: 254-264). Hirschl has advocated the idea of incorporating the social sciences in general, and political science in particular, in the comparative study of constitutions (2013; see also Von Bogdandy 2012).

Until such time, however, except in Germany, the 'heartland of party law' (Müller and Sieberer 2006: 435), the subject of party law tends to be a neglected aspect of research into political parties, with discussions limited to passing references and lacking a comparative dimension (Avnon 1995: 286). The very few existing comparative texts are generally not available in English (e.g. Tsatsos 2002). In addition, while some comparative work has been published on the financing of parties, this is not generally written from the perspective of party regulation more generally that is adopted in the present volume (e.g. Nassmacher (2009).

The current volume aims to address part of the gap identified above by discussing the various dimensions of party regulation, in the Netherlands as well as in Europe and in other regions of the world, referring to both conceptual issues and recent empirical findings. It is based on the papers presented at an international symposium held at Leiden University in June 2010, organized by the editors. The symposium brought together national and international scholars from the disciplines of law and political science to discuss the regulation of political parties, in the Netherlands and elsewhere, from an interdisciplinary and comparative perspective.

This volume is embedded within a larger, EU-funded research project (Re-conceptualizing party democracy),[1] which investigates the changing conceptions of parties and democracy in post-war Europe through a focus on public law and involves, among others, the development of a comprehensive database on 'The Legal Regulation of Political Parties in Post-War Europe'.[2] Within the framework of the volume, some of the empirical results emerging out of this research project are being published for the first time.

Outline of the volume

The volume provides an overview of the practical and theoretical dilemmas of state regulation of party financing and party organization (Chapters 1 and 2), and the historical patterns of party regulation and constitutionalization in the Netherlands and other European democracies, as well as the European Union (Chapters 3, 4, 5 and 6). In addition, several case studies and focused comparisons shed light on prevalent instances of party regulation and judicialization, such as the Dutch courts compelling the orthodox SGP party in The Netherlands to end the practice whereby women are denied passive voting rights (Chapter 7), the consequences of legal bans on political parties (Chapter 8), and the practices of regulation of ethnic parties (Chapter 9). Furthermore, the comparative reference is extended also to include an analysis of practices of party regulation in Latin America (Chapter 10).

The volume opens with a chapter by Richard S. Katz on 'Democracy and the Legal Regulation of Political Parties'. The chapter has two related objectives. The first is to argue that evolving standards regarding the legal regulation of political parties are excessively weighted in favour of the expressive functions of parties (articulation), at the expense of their governing functions (aggregation). The second is to argue that this bias in favour of expression is based on a vision of democracy that, whether seen as a throw-back to the pre-democratic era of the cadre party in the 18th and 19th centuries or as being in the vanguard of a move to a post-partisan nirvana in the mid 21st century, essentially assumes away politics.

The second chapter, by Ruud Koole, deals with 'Dilemmas of Regulating Political Finance, with special reference to the Dutch case'. The chapter explores the dilemmas faced by governments when introducing or changing the public financing regime for political parties. It concentrates on the importance of ideological considerations for the variation of political finance regimes, most notably general views on the role of the state. It presents two such opposing perspectives on the scope of state involvement, which are subsequently used to construct a typology of rationales of political finance by confronting these general views with recent calls for more transparency in the field of political finance.

In Chapter 3, entitled 'Lessons from the Past: Party Regulation in the Netherlands', Remco Nehmelman provides an historical overview of the development of party regulation in The Netherlands. It discusses the desirability of special legislation on political parties, and focuses on the question which minimum standards of regulation should be adhered to such that the principle of democracy is guaranteed. In addition, the question is raised whether lessons can be drawn from the past discussions on regulating political parties.

In the following chapter, 'The Constitutionalization of Political Parties in Post-war Europe', Ingrid van Biezen shows that political parties in contemporary democracies are increasingly often accorded formal constitutional status. The chapter explores the temporal patterns of party constitutionalization and reveals their connection with moments of fundamental institutional restructuring such as democratization and state building. It furthermore reveals the different dimensions that lie beneath the constitutionalization of political parties in old and new democracies, and discusses the different models of party constitutionalization in light of the underlying conceptions of party democracy.

Chapter 5, by Fernando Casal Bértoa, Daniela Piccio & Ekaterina Rashkova, is entitled 'Party Laws in Comparative Perspective'. This chapter provides an overview of regulation by means of party laws in post-war European democracies. The chapter presents a qualitative and quantitative overview of the content of party laws in terms of the range and magnitude of party regulation, thus mapping the changes in regulatory trends over time. The chapter furthermore addresses the question which aspects of political parties are regulated most intensively and most frequently, and whether there are significant differences in the evolution of regulation between different groups of countries. The final part of the chapter supplements the quantitative examination of party regulation with a qualitative case study on the peculiarities of the party law of Spain.

Chapter 6 by Wojciech Gagatek is called 'Explaining Legislative Conflict over the Adoption of Political Financing Law in the European Union'. This chapter proposes an organizing perspective leading to the identification of sources and dimensions of the conflict over the adoption of party law in the EU. It then discusses the legislative procedures that led to the adoption of Regulation 2004/2003, which governs political parties at the European level and their funding. Finally, the findings of this research are discussed by analysing the role of and divisions in the European Commission and, subsequently, the European Parliament (EP).

Chapter 7, by Hans-Martien ten Napel and Jaco van den Brink, is dedicated to a case study of 'The Dutch Political Reformed Party (SGP) and Passive Female Suffrage'. The chapter first analyses the two – partially conflicting – judgments of the highest Dutch courts in this case, the Council of State and the High Court. Then, the authors discuss the case law of the European Court of Human Rights (ECtHR) in order to determine to what extent the ensuing admissibility decision in the SGP case corresponds to the Court's conception of democracy.

'Will it all end in tears? What really happens when democracies use law to ban political parties', is the question Tim Bale asks in Chapter 8. An earlier comparative empirical investigation by the author of the consequences of recent bans on 'extremist' parties in three self-styled European democracies (Turkey, Spain and Belgium) found that those consequences were not as dire as predicted. In this chapter Bale attempts to answer the question whether the three countries still defy the predictions that bans will make no difference, that they will make things worse, or that they will put existing achievements at risk. Or, upon reflection and a return visit, did the fears of the critics turn out to be justified after all?

Chapter 9, by Ekaterina R. Rashkova and Maria Spirova, looks into 'Ethnic Party Regulation in Eastern Europe'. The political integration of national minorities is one of the most challenging tasks facing the new EU member states. This chapter focuses on one form of political representation – political parties – and studies how legal arrangements in the region encourage or discourage the existence of ethnic parties. Focusing on the experiences of Bulgaria and Romania the paper argues that regulatory arrangements are important in but not key to achieving meaningful political representation.

In Chapter 10, 'On the Engineerability of Political Parties: Mexico in Comparative Perspective', Imke Harbers and Matthew C. Ingram examine how public law provisions regarding political parties have changed over time in the Mexican case, and how the extent of regulation has grown to the present day. Looking ahead, the authors demonstrate that party regulation has increased steadily since the 1950s and that it has had mixed effects on political contestation, cleaning up elections while simultaneously generating an electoral landscape that is markedly unfair and biased in favour of major parties.

Patterns of party regulation

On an overview of the various chapters, one is first of all struck by the apparent increase in party regulation that has taken place in recent years. The chapter by Casal Bértoa, Piccio & Rashkova clearly demonstrates that this trend is visible throughout Europe. It also holds true for the Netherlands, a country that has traditionally known little, if any, specific party regulation. As Nehmelman notes, Dutch political parties have for a long time been dominated by civil law and their own statutes. Today, however, it is not just the Electoral Law that contains references that specifically concern political parties, but also the Act on State funding for political parties, while the Media Act has certain sections guaranteeing their (cost-free) use of the public broadcasting media. Recently, moreover, a new Dutch law on party finance was adopted by Parliament, 'a combination of a subsidy law and a transparency law' as Koole characterizes it in his contribution to this volume. The SGP case might have led to further regulation, although, as Ten Napel and Van den Brink point out, this has not materialized in practice. Still, Nehmelman believes the time has come to include a specific Constitutional provision to guarantee the free shaping of the political will of political parties. Such a reform of the Constitution was proposed as early as in 1950 by the Dutch State Commissioner Van Schaik, but is perhaps even more relevant today, given the way in which Dutch and European courts apply in particular the principles of non-discrimination and of secularism. Van Biezen also notes that the Netherlands is one of the few countries where the judicialization of party politics has not yet affected their constitutional enshrining.

Secondly, it is interesting to see that the objectives of such party regulation tend to differ. As Katz argues in his chapter, the common justification for an increase in party regulation, used for example by the Venice Commission for Democracy through Law, is that states must protect and improve democracy. Another important reason given is that parties perform a number of crucial functions in the realization of democracy. Regardless of the exact objective, however, the volume also contains a clear warning, in the sense that it is clear from the various chapters that the objectives of the regulations are not always achieved. For example, according to Harbers and Ingram, the Mexican case illustrates that even extensive and detailed regulation is insufficient to guarantee responsible party government, and thus casts doubts on the idea of the 'engineerability of political parties'. In the case of ethnic party regulation in Eastern Europe, the effects are often also indirect, as the chapter by Rashkova and Spirova illustrates.

Thirdly, there appears to be a trend towards regulation not just at the systemic level, but also at the level of individual parties. Although historically regulation started at the level of elections (the systemic level), increasingly also the units (parties) have to subscribe to the basic principles of the constitutional and political system (see also van Biezen & Piccio 2013). Thus, it is possible to discern a trend in the direction of a more militant democracy, a subject that Bale investigates for Turkey, Spain and Belgium. Bale concludes that we would be mistaken if we were to suggest that the consequences of party bans are always and everywhere malign. An intriguing question is whether the same applies to the regulation of internal party democracy, German style, which equally appears to be on the rise.

All in all, the developments as documented and analysed in this volume to a large extent point in the direction of a developing interpretation of political parties from, originally, essentially private into essentially public entities (cf. Persily and Cain 2000; van Biezen 2004; Webber 2012). In the process, the more public the parties become, the more regulation they appear to invoke. Dutch professor on Constitutional Law and former Judge of the Court of Justice of the European Union, A.M. Donner, suggested in a contribution to the annual Dutch constitutional conference in 1982: '*Let us postpone as long as possible the official recognition of the party system (in the Netherlands), because in its nature Law just brings regulation, and he who regulates, restricts.*' According to Nehmelman, who uses this quotation in his chapter, although by nature the law may indeed just bring regulation, regulation entails not only restrictions but also guarantees. The precise ways in which the law constrains or facilitates political behaviour, however, remain to be investigated in more detail.

At this stage, what seems clear is that the more parties become regulated, the more public they become. The contributions tie in, therefore, with current debates within the academic community on the changing nature of political parties, whereby recent processes of party organizational adaptation are seen to reflect a gradual strengthening of their relationship with the state (Katz & Mair 1995; see also Gauja 2008). As the legal regulation of parties through public law can be seen as one of the ways in which the link between parties and the state has acquired increased importance in recent years, this volume will no doubt be of interest to scholars concerned with such processes of party transformation, e.g. regarding the cartel party thesis. Party regulation leads, as Van Biezen puts it in her chapter, to the transformation of political parties into integral units of the democratic state.

It is quite possible that this development will lead to a further withdrawal of citizens from existing party-political structures. In terms of political participation this can hardly be regarded as a positive outcome. In so far as this risk becomes more imminent, this volume thus not just documents and analyses but also contains a certain warning against taking the regulation of political parties too far. Perhaps the EU can serve as a model in this respect, because – as Gagatek demonstrates – at least since the Tsatsos 1996 report the subsequent drafts and proposals for a political financing law have become less and less strict, to arrive in the final version only at a model of financing political parties. On the other hand, should ours indeed be a time of 'expressive individualism' (Taylor 2007) or 'radical pluralism' (Gauchet), both party discipline and party ideology may soon belong to the past (Vogelaar 2012). In that case increasing party regulation will at most be a supplementary explanation for the decline in organized political participation.

Notes

1 The research project Re-conceptualizing party democracy is funded by the European Research Council (ERC_Stg07_205660). Their financial support is gratefully acknowledged.
2 The online database can be found at http://www.partylaw.leidenuniv.nl.

References

Avnon, Dan (1995). 'Parties Laws in Democratic Systems of Government', *Journal of Legislative Studies* 1/2: 283-300.

Biezen, Ingrid van (2004). 'Political Parties as Public Utilities', *Party Politics* 10/6: 701-722.

Biezen, Ingrid van and Daniela R. Piccio (2013). 'Shaping Intra-Party Democracy: On the Legal Regulation of Internal Party Organizations', in William Cross and Richard S. Katz (eds.), *The Challenges of Intra-Party Democracy*. Oxford: Oxford University Press, forthcoming.

Bogdandy, Armin von (2012). 'National Legal Scholarship in the European Legal Area—A Manifesto', *International Journal of Constitutional Law* 10/3: 614-626.

Gauja, Anika (2008). 'State Regulation and the Internal Organisation of Political Parties: The Impact of Party Law in Australia, Canada, New Zealand and the United Kingdom', *Commonwealth & Comparative Politics* 46/2: 244-261.

Hirschl, Ran (2013). 'From Comparative Constitutional Law to Comparative Constitutional Studies', *International Journal of Constitutional Law* 11/1: 1-12.

Katz, Richard S. (2002). 'The Internal Life of Parties', in Kurt Richard Luther and Ferdinand Müller-Rommel (eds.), *Political Challenges in the New Europe: Political and Analytical Challenges*. Oxford: Oxford University Press.

Katz, Richard S. and Peter Mair (1995). 'Changing Models of Party Organization and Party Democracy: the Emergence of the Cartel Party', *Party Politics*, 1/1: 5-28.

Müller, Wolfgang C., and Ulrich Sieberer (2006). 'Party Law', in: Richard S. Katz and William Crotty (eds.), *Handbook of Party Politics*. London: Sage.

Nassmacher, Karl-Heinz (2009). *The Funding of Party Competition: Political Finance in 25 Democracies*. Baden-Baden: Nomos.

Persily, Nathaniel, and Bruce E. Chain (2000). 'The Legal Status of Political Parties: A Reassessment of Competing Paradigms', *Columbia Law Review* 100/3: 775-812.

Pildes, Richard H. (2011). 'Political Parties and Constitutionalism', in: Tom Ginsburg and Rosalind Dixon (eds.), *Comparative Constitutional Law*. Cheltenham, UK: Edward Elgar.

Skach, Cindy (2012). 'Political Parties and the Constitution', in: Michel Rosenfeld and András Sajó (eds.), *The Oxford Handbook of Comparative Constitutional Law*. Oxford: Oxford University Press.

Taylor, Charles (2007). *A Secular Age*. Harvard University Press.

Tsatsos, Dimitris Th. (ed.) (2002). *30 Jahre Parteiengesetz in Deutschland: Die Parteiinstitutionen im Internationalen Vergleich*. Baden-Baden: Nomos.

Vogelaar, Maarten (2012). It's the Personal Inspiration, Stupid! The Future of Christian Political Engagement in a Disenchanted Political Order. MA-Thesis Philosophy: VU Amsterdam.

Webber, Gregoire C.N. (2012). 'The Polycentricity of Political Financing', *Public Law*, 1: 310-327.

CHAPTER I

Democracy and the Legal Regulation of Political Parties

Richard S. Katz
Johns Hopkins University

By the early 1950s, democracy had achieved near universal recognition as the best available form of government, or even as the ideal form of government in a more absolute sense. At that time, the commitment to democracy was in many cases more rhetorical than practical, and in any case there was considerable dispute as to exactly what democracy means in terms of institutions and practices at the practical level (McKeon 1951). Are 'people's democracies' or 'guided democracies' really democracies at all (Macpherson 1966)? Are 'majoritarian democracies' and 'consensus democracies' equally democratic (Lijphart 1999)? What is the proper balance of functions and activities between elites and ordinary citizens (Bachrach 1967)? Does democracy require that the distribution of citizens among demographic (ethnic, cultural, gender) groups be mirrored in the distribution of political offices (Pitkin 1967)? Should or can democratic participation be limited to those who are juridical citizens, or even among those who are citizens, to those who are in some sense loyal to the state as currently constituted or who satisfy some non-trivial standard of competence?

One thing that all of these questions have in common is that at some level the answers have implications for political parties and party systems. Moreover, as the definition of democracy has been elaborated explicitly to exclude the 'sham democracies', and to make explicit accommodation for the various 'democracies with adjectives' (Collier & Levitsky 1997), it is increasing obvious that, as Schattschneider observed, 'the political parties created democracy and that modern democracy is unthinkable save in terms of the parties' (1942: 1)

The debate concerning the definition of democracy and its optimal institutionalization of course continues, and questions concerning the optimal nature and role of political parties have played a large role in that debate. Increasingly over the last half century, however, the debate concerning political parties has also moved into the realm of law. As van Biezen (2008) has shown, provisions concerning political parties have become part of the constitutions of a growing number of countries. Even when parties are not explicitly recognized as having constitutional status, many aspects of their structures, finances, and practices have become the subjects of statutory or administrative regulation. Obligations concerning states' responsibilities both to foster and to regulate political parties have found increasing prominence within the corpus of international law (e.g., 'Document of the Copenhagen Meeting of the Conference on the Human Dimension of the CSCE', June 1990 - Copenhagen Document).

The increased legal regulation of political parties,which in earlier times were regulated, if at all, simply as another form of private association, commonly is justified on the grounds that states must protect and enhance democracy. This often has been taken to imply an obligation to regulate or constrain the influence of all organizations in which considerable social or economic power is concentrated, a category into which political parties clearly fall. Even more, however, regulation of political parties has been justified by the recognition that parties perform a number of crucial functions in the realization of democracy, with the implications that, on the one hand, regulation of parties is justified by their particular importance, and on the other hand, that regulation is justified because parties play a role that effectively makes them semi-state rather than purely private entities.[1]

Among the functions of parties in modern electoral and representative democracies are the recruitment, selection, and presentation of candidates; even in the absence of formal restrictions on independent candidacies, as a practical matter a party nomination is virtually a prerequisite for election. In most countries, parties dominate political campaigns, defining the issues (both which issues will be prominent and what positions with regard to those issues will be presented to the voters), providing most of the actual propaganda, and receiving the lion's share of media attention – and even where, as in the United States, control of campaigns is vested in, and media attention is focused on, candidates as individuals rather than parties as organizations, it is still candidates *as the nominees of the major parties* that matter. Between elections, parties play central roles in the organization of government. This is, of course, particularly obvious in parliamentary systems, but it is hardly restricted to them. Between elections as well, parties provide important venues for popular discussion of political issues and the formation of public opinion, as well as structures through which the politically engaged citizenry can communicate effectively with their elected representatives. And at election time, parties are even more prominent in providing opportunities for politically engaged citizens to act collaboratively.

This list of functions can be both extended and elaborated in greater detail. Moving in the direction of greater generalization, however, and adopting the vocabulary of the functionalist paradigm, one can identify two particularly important complexes among these functions. On one hand, parties play a central role in performing the function of interest articulation: through their manifestos and other propaganda, they do this as 'speakers' in their own right; through their organizational structures, they provide mechanisms through which interested citizens can 'speak' for themselves as well as providing 'megaphones' by means of which other interest articulators (e.g., unions or trade associations) can make their voices be heard more effectively. They express, or facilitate the expression of, the desires and demands, the aspirations and the fears, of citizens and organizations. On the other hand, parties also play a central role in performing the function of interest aggregation (putting forward comprehensive proposals in their manifestos and later crafting compromises in the process of coalition formation) and then (at least to the extent that one accepts the appropriateness of a principal-agent understanding of democracy[2]) acting, and being held accountable, as the agents of the electorate in the process of governing. They decide which mix of desires and demands the government will attempt to satisfy and which will go by the board; in short, they determine who wins and who loses. Neither the individual party format, nor the party system format, that is best suited to the performance of one of these complexes of functions is best suited to the performance of the other; some compromise is necessary.

In this paper, I have two related objectives. The first is to argue that evolving standards regarding the legal regulation of political parties are excessively weighted in favour of the expressive functions of parties (articulation), at the expense of their governing functions (aggregation). The second is to argue that this bias in favour of expression is based on a vision of democracy that, whether seen as a throw-back to the pre-democratic era of the cadre party in the 18th and 19th centuries or as being in the vanguard of a move to a post-partisan nirvana in the mid 21st century, essentially assumes away politics.[3] Since the claim of 'excessive' weight can only be made relative to some standard, I begin with the second argument.

politicians, if only because party discipline imposed by the party leader or caucus would be equally inimical to rational deliberation.

If, as this ideal assumes, legislative assemblies are made up of rational and public spirited men and women open-mindedly seeking the commonweal, then effective representation requires that all reasonable arguments be brought to their attention. Obviously, this is most likely to occur if those arguments are espoused by individuals who are members of the assembly, but even in the absence of such members it may be reasonable to suppose, as Canadian Supreme Court Justice Frank Iacobucci did in the case of *Figueroa v Canada (Attorney General)* [1 S.C.R. 912 [2003]], that the arguments of defeated candidates and the opinions of those who voted for them will be 'taken into account by those who ultimately implement policy, if not now then perhaps at some point in the future' (para. 44). Thus, not only debate in parliament, but also debate in the context of election campaigns, and presumably also debate within a party's membership organization, contributes to the rational identification of the public interest, and so should be as free and wide-ranging as possible – and since parties are the principal articulators of contending views, the range of parties participating in a campaign should likewise be as broad as possible. Indeed, the value of elections is seen to lie at least as much in the campaign as in the ultimate choice made on election day. While equality of citizens is, of course, important, equality of opportunity or standing for the various view points to be expressed is even more important.[7] Moreover, even if the campaign is about policy, the choice made on election day must be about popular confidence in the would-be representative and the granting to him or her of a 'general power of attorney' – to listen to and participate in debates in parliament, before using (in Burke's words) 'his unbiassed opinion, his mature judgment, his enlightened conscience' to reach a decision.[8]

The alternative view might be identified as responsible or parliamentary party government (see Katz 1986, 1987). Debate is important for identifying and testing ideas, and for informing citizens regarding the proposals of their would-be governors. While such debate may lead to changes of opinion, either among citizens or within the governing elite, however, there is no illusion that unanimity is, in most cases, either theoretically possible or indeed even desirable. There are real conflicts of interest and values that will not be obviated by either intellect or good will. Legislation ultimately is about the aggregation of preferences rather than the weighing of arguments, and parties, rather than being united by a common view of the public interest are united by sharing, or speaking for, the same bundle of particular interests, even if each party finds it politically advantageous to call its particular bundle the 'public interest'. In contrast to the Burkean trustee, who is trusted by the electors to do what s/he decides is right after hearing the debate and evaluating the arguments, the responsible parties representative is delegated to pursue the aims that s/he, or more accurately that his or her party, promised, and on the basis of which voters made their choices of whom to support. Election campaigns are important because they inform the voters of the programmes espoused by the contending parties (and may indeed induce some voters to change their partisan preferences), not because they lead the voters to abandon their underlying interests or values in favour of a previously unrecognized common interest, or because they lead the parties to adopt 'better' (as opposed to trying to find more popular) policies. Ultimately the primary purpose of an election is the making of a choice among parties, each of which, it is assumed, will put its programme into effect (albeit modified to reflected changes in conditions over time) if it achieves a parliamentary majority, or failing a majority, will try to advance its programme to the degree possible in coalition with other parties.[9] Simply, in the holistic view, elections are about individual expression; in the party government view they are about collective choice, and not just choice of a local representative but choice of government, and thus also of policy, whether directly through the election of a coherent single party majority or indirectly as the result of coalition negotiations among a number of cohesive parties.

In the holistic view, the juridical legitimacy of parliamentary decisions flows from the delegation of the authority to decide to members of parliament by their constituencies, but the more substantive legitimacy of decisions flows from their acceptance as being 'right' on the basis of the arguments adduced to support them. As the name implies, in the parliamentary party government vision, the representative is the party as a collectivity. The legitimacy of parliamentary decisions flows from the fact that the parties are enacting policies, that at least the broad outlines of which have been substantively approved by the voters.[10] There are no 'right' or 'wrong' policies– only policies that are preferred by more rather than fewer citizens, and that are more or less effective in achieving the aims of the coalition that supports them.

In the holistic view, democracy is primarily about reason and process, because it is argued that the deliberative process will help decision makers to 'find' the common interest. For the responsible parties view, democracy is about outcomes, primarily in terms of policy. In fact, in greater detail there are two versions of what I am calling here the responsible parties view. From the perspective of what I have called elsewhere 'popular sovereignty democracy', it is about maximizing the likelihood that the policies best identified as the will of the people – defined as a majority choice – are enacted; that is, the question is what policies are *enacted*. From the perspective of 'liberal democracy', it is about preventing the enactment of policies that will excessively work against the interests of some groups (Katz 1997); the question is what policies are *avoided*. In either case, however, both the intellectual or moral capacities, and the preferences, of citizens (at least as they exist on election day) are taken as given, and the primary focus of citizen activity is electoral choice to put the right parties in office (or to prevent the wrong parties from being in office), and secondarily to engage in activity between elections that signals to the parties what policies will be rewarded or punished at the next election. In both cases, parties are assumed to be coherent, and to be pursuing strategies that are largely dictated by the exigencies of the pursuit of office (see especially Downs 1957; Schumpeter 1950). That is, this view is associated with the idea that parties are primarily associations of office-seekers and office-holders.

In sum, then, we have two complexes. The first complex combines the primacy of the expressive functions of parties and elections with the idea of democracy as an instrument of moral, intellectual and community development; belief in a unitary public interest to be discovered through rational deliberation; and the notion that parties are appropriately understood as associations of citizens. The second complex involves the opposites: the primacy of the decisional functions of elections; a pluralist or partisan (one might even say a 'political' in Finer's terms) view of interests; the idea that parties (re)present alternative comprehensive programmes; and an understanding of parties as being primarily teams of professionals.

Regulation of Parties

Against this background, what can we say about the legal regulation of political parties? At the risk of some oversimplification, these regulations can be classified under three main headings, although in practice the regulations are generally more interconnected and overlapping in intention than this classification might suggest. The first concerns the regulation of parties as organizations, and addresses questions of membership and internal structure and decision-making (in particular, the choice of party officers and candidates and the formulation and adoption of the party's programme and rules). The second concerns the regulation of parties as contestants in elections, and addresses questions of campaign practices (including campaign finance), the allowable content of party programmes, and qualification for a position on the ballot as well as any other rights, privileges, or obligations accorded to parties in elections that are denied to (or not required of) individual citizens or other organizations. The third concerns the activities of parties in government, and addresses questions of patronage and other possible abuse of state resources for partisan advantage, requirements for the formation of party groups in parliament (and the advantages that accrue to them), and restrictions on party switching by MPs during a parliamentary term.

Parties as Organizations

With regard to parties as organizations, legal regulations appear to be based on some combination of three models. The first, the oldest, and the most prominent in the academic literature, sees parties primarily as organizations of candidates for office or of those who already hold office and organize in some way to coordinate their activity and maximize their influence, or perhaps a bit more broadly as organizations of candidates and/or office-holders plus their supporters. This model clearly is associated with the second of the two complexes discussed above. While it may lead to regulations concerning party activities outside of formal elections, especially those regarding the raising and spending of money, in this model these generally have been directed at politicians as individuals rather than parties as organizations, which indeed the law may not recognize at all in countries using a candidate-centered electoral systems; in list PR systems, parties must be recognized in the guise of lists of candidates, but extra-electoral organizations need not be recognized. This model effectively precludes state regulation of the internal decision-making procedures of the party. While it does not preclude the party adopting rules and having them become legally enforceable in the same way as the rules of any other private association, the default would be, as Jack Brand described the traditional constitution of the British Conservative Party (analogizing to Czarist Russia): 'autocracy, tempered by assassination'.

In the second model, rooted in the model of the mass party of integration (although not necessarily tied to all of the sociological and ideological assumptions on which that model is based), parties are understood/defined as associations of citizens who work together on a long term basis to advance their collective interests and to secure the election of their preferred candidates. In structural terms, this reverses the dominant/subordinate roles of party members and candidates/officials. To use a sports analogy, in the first model, party members (to the extent that such a category is recognized as extending beyond candidates or elected officials at all) are the organized boosters or 'cheerleaders' for the party team (Mayhew 1974), or perhaps they are the equivalent of the season ticket holders; those making decisions for the team may take the fans' preferences into account – after all, loss of its fan base can be economically costly for a team – but the fans do not decide who will play and who will sit on the bench. In the second model, the party's members are the analog of the corporate 'owners' of the team, able to hire and fire the coaches and players. Because this view recognizes the electoral/governmental role of parties, it is commonly associated with explicit requirements of internal democracy – in particular, the choice of both party officials and party candidates through a process that ultimately is legitimated by a vote of the membership. Moreover, it also tends to be associated with regulations limiting the grounds on which citizens can be denied party membership, both in general (restrictions on the categories eligible to form or be members of parties) and by a particular party (for example, prohibiting discrimination on the basis of gender or ethnicity).[11]

In both of these views, parties are still seen as essentially private entities. In the third view, most clearly exemplified by the United States at the state level, parties are best seen as semi-public entities. While they may be recognized as having some of the rights of independent organizations, they are also implicitly understood to be exercising public functions (e.g., 'Political parties shall participate in the formation of the public will...' [German Basic Law, art. 21])[12] or to be part of the structure of elections rather than merely being participants in them. In this case, parties are likely to be subject to even more detailed regulation – for example, rather than merely being required to be internally democratic, their entire structure may be prescribed in detail.[13] Parties may have no discretion at all concerning their membership.[14,15]

The first of these models is, in effect, the default position. While it may be implicit in regulatory regimes, it requires no explicit party legislation. Parties may, however, be subject to the same regulations (for example, a requirement to have a set of standing orders, or to have its accounts subject to audit) as any private association that is given legal personality

The second model, however, is increasingly prominent both in actual regulatory regimes and in the guidelines of such groups as the European Commission for Democracy Through Law (Venice Commission). First, party regulations generally define parties as associations of citizens.[16]

Laws regarding the official recognition or registration of parties often specify a minimum number of members as a precondition.[17] Moreover, although the requirement of a minimum number of members might be narrowly understood to be no more than a threshold of support required for eligibility to receive public resources, and hence to imply nothing about the internal rights or privileges accruing to party members, in fact, regulations often require that parties be internally democratic – thus institutionalizing the idea that parties are primarily mass membership based, rather than elite based, organizations. The Venice Commission 'Code of Good Practice in the Field of Political Parties' for example asserts that 'a commitment to internal democratic functioning reinforces' the 'good functioning' of democracy at the national level. The article of the German Basic Law cited above goes on 'Their internal organization must conform to democratic principles.'[18] Looking to the third model, although the structure of American national parties is largely unregulated, they are federations of state parties, the internal structure of which is in many cases nearly completely prescribed by law. And those laws, generally dating from the Progressive era, were designed specifically to empower the party base – defined not as party members in the mass party sense, but as those who have chosen to register as partisans as part of the general process of voter registration or as self-professed party supporters or voters.

The specific meaning of internal democracy in these regulations is that important decisions – in particular the selection of party candidates and party officials – be made by vote of the members. A somewhat weaker sense of internal democracy, that these decisions be made by elected representatives of the members is often accepted as adequate, but still seen as inferior.[19]

If the objective is to maximize the opportunities for direct participation in decision-making on the part of the maximum possible number of people, then direct internal democracy is fine. If the objective is to assure that the party is responsive to its members, then internal representative democracy within the party may be no less acceptable than representative democracy at the governmental level – although one might argue that if parties are necessary to structure effective representative democracy at the governmental level, then their functional equivalent, that is organized factions, may be necessary within parties.

If, however, the objective is effective popular choice of government, internal democracy presents a number of problems, discussed by Austin Ranney for the two party American case under the rubric of the responsible party model's 'little civil war about "intraparty democracy"'(1962: 156), but generalisable mutatis mutandis to multiparty systems. On one hand, the idea of internal democracy invites party members to use their votes to express their personal preferences for policies or leaders, rather than to act strategically to choose the candidates or policies that have the greatest chance of success in the general election, or the greatest capacity to negotiate effective interparty agreements[20]. While accurate reflection of the party's constituencies' preferences is desirable at the election stage, once the election is over, the party government model requires flexibility to compromise, but internal democracy threatens those who make compromises with intraparty punishment – as illustrated in the United States by the defeat of 'responsible' politicians by more ideologically 'pure' partisans in primary elections, only to have the 'pure' partisan defeated in the general election.[21]

Moreover, unless internal party democracy results in a system in which a single winner literally takes all, it must be assumed that some party officials, and presumably some party candidates and ultimately some party holders of public office, will represent the internal party minority. Why should they be expected to act cohesively with the representatives of the internal majority – any more than the parliamentary minority is expected to act with, rather than to oppose, the parliamentary majority? But if all of the candidates of a party cannot be expected to act cohesively, how can the electorate, whose choice is naturally limited to those candidates who actually appear on the ballot, make a meaningful collective decision?

Parties as Election Contestants

Particularly in the newer and the (not necessarily the same thing) less self-confident democracies, concern that some party programmes may be subversive of the regime has led to regulation of the allowable content of a party's programme. Violation of these regulations may lead to the disqualification of the party from the ballot, or even to its dissolution and/or the banning of its officials from political activity for a period of years. Least problematic among such regulations would be those that bar the advocacy of the use of violence or other illegal means to achieve the party's objectives. Appeals to or incitement of racial or other group hatred might also be barred, although there is some question as to whether incitement to hatred must also imply incitement to violence before it becomes a valid ground for sanction. Another question concerns the permissibility of advocacy of fundamental constitutional change (abandonment of democracy, secession, etc.) by constitutional means. Related to this, as well as to the question of internal party organization more generally, would be regulations that require a party to have an organizational presence, a significant number of members, or to present candidates within a very large proportion of the national territory, effectively as a back-door way of barring separatist parties – or even parties that seek to represent territorially specific interests without challenging the territorial integrity of the existing state.[22]

A second regulatory area concerning parties as contestants in elections addresses the ability of parties to gain a place on the election ballot, and in turn to gain or retain access to other public resources, privileges or standing that are accorded to parties on the ballot – or indeed to parties tout court. These might relate to the size or support of the party, as indicated by votes received or members elected in a prior election, by petition signatures secured in support of recognition of the party, or by the size of the party's membership.[23] The fundamental questions are the status to be accorded to small parties (parties with unpopular ideologies or simply appealing to a very narrow interest, as well as parties appealing to a highly circumscribed subset of the electorate, such as those living in a particular locality or sharing a minority ethnicity), and the height of the obstacles to be erected against the entry of new parties into the electoral marketplace. The presumption here would be that high barriers to entry will work in the same way as an electoral system with a high threshold of representation (a strong electoral system, in Sartori's terms) to discourage the fragmentation of the party system, as a result either of the entry of new parties or of the splitting of old ones, and encourage the formation of 'big tent' parties.

To the extent that small parties are allowed to enter the electoral contest (and indeed also to the extent that not all 'major' parties are of equivalent strength[24]), a third regulatory question concerns the balance of financial (and other) resources that will be available to them. Two aspects of this question are of particular relevance. The first concerns the permissible sources of resources – particularly money, but also other potentially valuable resources, such as in-kind contributions, the seconding of staff, or the guaranteeing of loans. Potentially restricted sources might include government contractors, all (or some types of) corporations, unions, foreign entities, and possibly citizens living abroad.

The second aspect concerns the levels of resources that parties may deploy in an election, and the amount that third parties[25] may deploy in support or opposition to parties contesting an election. In terms of regulatory philosophy, the major distinction here is between the 'libertarian' ideal of minimizing public regulation and accepting the resulting disparities of resources, and the 'egalitarian' ideal of seeking a level playing field by restricting the activity of third parties, by limiting spending of and contributions to parties, by providing equal time on state (and potentially privately owned but publicly licensed) broadcast media etc. Relating back to ballot access and eligibility for special treatment, implementation of the egalitarian model requires that some threshold of eligibility be established lest parties enter the field merely to benefit from public resources.[26] These may be identified as restrictions on 'frivolous' candidacies, but of course the definition of frivolous remains open to dispute. As well, the rules/model may not be the same for all types of resources (for example, an egalitarian regime for the allocation of broadcast time may coexist with a libertarian regime for party spending – but coupled with restrictions on the sources of the money that parties may spend).

The general thrust of regulation – and particularly of evolving international standards regarding acceptable regulation – has been toward greater freedom of access to the ballot. The Copenhagen Document (sect. 7.5, for example) of the CSCE makes explicit reference to the right of independents to contest elections. Similarly, the ODIHR 2003 summary of 'Existing Commitments for Democratic Elections in OSCE Participating States' emphasizes ease of access to the ballot both for new/minor parties and for independents. A series of Canadian court decisions have ruled barriers to ballot access such as a monetary deposit – and especially a monetary deposit required in a large number of constituencies – not to be justified 'in a free and democratic society.' The major exception to this trend is the United States, in which barriers that often are tantamount to the statutory requirement that there be exactly two parties – and that they be the Democrats and Republicans – are common. Again, the trend is to value the expressive function of political parties, so as to increase the opportunity for citizens 'and to exercise their right to vote in a manner that accurately reflects their preferences' (*Figueroa* para. 88).

The expressive function of elections has also been privileged with regard to regulations concerning the campaign activities of third parties. In contrast to ballot access, the United States, particularly after the recent Supreme Court decision in *Citizens United v. Federal Election Commission* has probably the most libertarian regime, in that so-called independent expenditures[27], by corporations as well as by natural persons, may not be legally restricted. While other countries generally do limit third party expenditures – and indeed the expenditures of candidates and parties on their own behalf – there is a clear trend (often imposed by courts) toward weakening those limits, even while recognizing that the limits may be more restrictive than those applied to candidates themselves. For example, in *Bowman v. The United Kingdom*, the European Court of Human Rights overturned a British third party spending limit of £5 as violating the free speech rights of a third party because the limit was so low as to effectively ban third party spending altogether.[28] In the case of *Harper v. Canada*, the Supreme Court of Canada allowed a much higher limit (CAN$150,000 per general election, no more than CAN$3,000 used to influence the election in a single district) to stand because, while recognizing that the limits infringed on the free speech rights of the applicants, the Court also recognized the danger that unlimited third party spending would allow well-financed interests to drown out their opponents, thus undermining the expressive (free and vigorous debate) egalitarian regime otherwise established by the Elections Canada Act.[29] The complementary danger – that a proliferation of spending by a large number of third parties will result in confusion, with serious arguments drowned out not by a single interest but by a general cacophony – has received less attention, although one Canadian court has recognized that danger with regard to a proliferation of candidates. (*De Jong v. Ontario (Attorney General)* 287 D.L.R. (4th) 90 [2007])

Parties in Government

Once the candidates who have been elected to parliament (or other offices) have been determined, three important questions must be addressed. First, to what extent do regulations allow the parties that then form the government to use the resources of the state for their own ends. Here there are two major categories to consider – each of which may be portrayed in a positive or a negative light, with the problem sometimes described as striking the correct balance, but actually being disagreement as to what constitutes 'abuse of public resources.' One category concerns patronage, that is the introduction of partisan criteria into the allocation of jobs or public contracts. In a negative light, this would appear to represent the conversion of public resources for partisan advantage, and thus to give those currently in power an unfair advantage over their challengers. In a positive light, however, patronage appears as the placing of individuals who will be sympathetic to the policy aims of those in power not just into policy-making positions, but into policy-implementing positions as well, with the aim of making government more effective. The question is where placing those who will be vigorous allies in governing into office becomes primarily a reward for partisan service, and where in turn that becomes a simple bribe.

that effectively became obsolete with the advent of mass suffrage and the associated advent of the mass party, even as they assert the centrality of parties and assume that parties should have most of the structural characteristics of the mass party. In the pre-democratic era from which that view of government is rooted, politics was a gentleman's game. Gentlemen would pursue the national interest which just coincidentally happened to be the interest of their class, the working class not having representation in parliament to tell them otherwise. Gentlemen would be independent, taking orders neither from their parties nor from their constituents; they would use their own judgement.

In the era of the mass party, this ideal was replaced by the idea of party government, which continues to be the fundamental principle both underlying and legitimizing modern parliamentary government (Castles & Wildenmann 1986; Katz 1987). In the last decades, as catch-all parties have become cartel parties, and as all citizens have become 'middle class', there has been a growing distaste for parties and partisanship (for the idea that politics has become a sport for players rather than gentlemen), and a longing for a return to a mythical age in which public spirited gentlemen – and now ladies as well – would pursue the common interest. Bi- (or multi-) partisanship, or simply consensus democracy, are preferred to party conflict and competition. One result has been a marked decline in both party membership and in electoral turnout – trends that have been widely interpreted as indicating a serious problem for democracy. And one response frequently has been legislative action intended to increase popular participation and to reduce partisan conflict – basically, to try to move party politics in the direction of articulation, deliberation and individual expression, at the expense of aggregation and collective decision.

The problem, however, is not just a kind of philosophical inconsistency between the ideals of popular expression and deliberation on the one hand and party government on the other. It is also that the rules enacted and the recommendations made for further reforms have the capacity to be positively pernicious – to undermine, rather than to support, popular government. In particular, while opportunities to 'have one's say' may be appreciated, coordination is required in large scale societies if any voice is to be heard. Reforms to 'democratize' political parties and electoral competition may have the effect of making this coordination difficult or impossible. The most obvious examples concern policies that, in the name of openness of competition or a 'level playing field', lead to such a fragmentation of competition that the legitimacy of the outcome is undermined: the 1993 Polish election of the Sejm, with over 30% of the vote going to parties that could not clear the 5% threshold; the 2002 French presidential election, in which fragmentation led to a second round in which neither of the candidates had received as much as 20% of the vote in the first round – and one (le Pen) could not achieve 20% in the second round either; the 2000 Canadian general election (the last before 2011 to choose a majority government), in which one party won more than 57% of the seats with less than 41% of the vote. Empowering party members can have a similarly pernicious effect – punishing political leaders for the 'crime' of acting responsibly. Ultimately, the question is what balance is to be struck between active participation by the relatively small number of people who choose to be politically engaged, and collective decision by the far broader range of citizens for whom politics is effectively a spectator sport. Or, put another way, the question is whether 'democracy on a large scale is ... the sum of many little democracies', (Sartori 1965: 124) a question to which Sartori's answer is 'no.'

Notes

1 For example, although the 'Code of Good Practice in the Field of Political Parties' adopted by the Venice Commission in 2008 [CDL-AD(2009)021] identifies parties as non-state agencies, it continues (pp. 16): 'Political parties are major actors in any democratic society, hence they enjoy the benefits of the guarantees of [the rule of law, democracy and human rights] by the State, and, accordingly, they must respect and promote these very same principles', and goes on to call for regulation in a number of areas that would be unregulated for most ordinary associations.

2 See Blyth & Katz 2005; Katz 2006 for reasons why one might not accept the principal-agent understanding as empirically justified.

3 Adapting Finer's definition of politics as what happens when 'a given set of persons of some type or other require a common policy; and ... its members advocate, for this common status, policies which are mutually exclusive' (1974: 8), I understand politics to be about reaching a common policy in a way that resolves or contains this kind of conflict, whereas the alternative, a-political, view would suggest that the conflict can be dissolved altogether, or be found to have been illusory in the first place.

4 Note that 'Optimal' in this sentence is stronger than 'Pareto optimal.' For a decision to be optimal in the first sense, it must be the unanimous first choice; for a decision to be Pareto optimal only requires that there be no alternative that is unanimously preferred to it.

5 I use the quotes around 'members' to emphasize that the distinction concerns the essential nature of the party, not simply whether it has formal members, in the sense of people who take out membership cards and pay dues. For example, the traditional nature of the British Conservative Party was clearly as an organization of politicians (e.g., the party leader was chosen by – 'emerged from' – the parliamentary party alone; the party conference made recommendations and requests, not decisions), although the Nation Union of Conservative and Unionist Associations was an organization with formal members.

6 The idea of an exogenously defined interest – that is an outcome that is 'correct' not simply because it is what the people want, but by some standard that is separate from, and superior to, mere preferences – can be illustrated by the choice of abbots and bishops in the early medieval Catholic Church. These were elected, not because election would allow the private preferences of the voters to determine the outcome, but because the votes were understood to be the medium through which the will of God would be expressed. Hence it would be possible for even a nearly unanimous electorate to 'get it wrong', and hence also the requirement of confirmation by an ecclesiastical superior to make a canonically valid election.

7 In this regard, it is significant that the 'egalitarian' in the contrast between egalitarian and libertarian models of election administration seems to emphasize the equality of positions rather than of citizens, for example when it calls for equal spending per candidate, independent of the size of that candidate's support (that is, independent of the number of citizens who support him or her). See Feasby (1999, 2003); Manfredi & Rush (2008).

8 One difficulty with this view is to reconcile the active involvement in real decision-making on the part of citizens with the exercise of independent judgement by MPs. Ideas like deliberative polls may partially bridge this gap by allowing citizens (or at least a sample of them) to participate in parliament-like debates with the purpose not only of educating themselves and whatever other 'ordinary' citizens care to observe, but also MPs and other opinion leaders. See Fishkin 2009.

9 'The candidate of one of the major Parties stands for a connected policy and for a certain body of men who, if a majority can be obtained, will form a Government. This is well understood by the electors. If the Member fails to support the Government or fails to act with the Opposition in their efforts to turn the Government out, he is acting contrary to the expectation of those who have put their trust in him.' British Prime Minister Clement Attlee (1957: 15).

10 While ideally this might be taken to require the approval of an absolute majority of the voters, which might further be taken to require a sufficiently proportional electoral system to assure that only coalitions with majority electoral support also enjoy majorities in parliament, here it can be understood only to require a duly elected majority in parliament, with the electoral system that potentially 'manufactures' the majority accepted as a legitimate counting and/or weighting rule for determining whether a coalition has adequate popular support. In the most obvious example, SMP elections often produce single party parliamentary majorities that were supported by less than a majority of those voting. If one were to insist that strict numerical equality of citizens as isolated and totally autonomous individuals is required, then this would create a serious problem of legitimacy. However, if one alternatively understands citizens to be social beings whose identity is partially defined by their membership in communities, then, as Canadian Chief Justice (then Chief Justice of British Columbia) Beverly McLaughlin put it in *Dixon v. British Columbia (Attorney General)* [59 D.L.R. (4th) 247 [1989]] , 'Factors like geography, community history, community interests and minority representation may need to be taken into account to ensure that our legislative assemblies effectively represent the diversity of our social mosaic. These are but examples of considerations which may justify departure from absolute voter parity in the pursuit of more effective representation; the list is not closed.'

11 For example, Article 11, sec. 4 of the Constitution of Bulgaria, which prohibits parties based on 'ethnic, racial, or religious lines'.

12 Very similar language is used in article 8A of the Treaty of Lisbon with regard to parties at the European level ('4. Political parties at European level contribute to forming European political awareness and to expressing the will of citizens of the Union') and in Article 3 of the Constitution of Hungary ('(2) Political parties shall participate in the development and expression of the popular will'). In a quite opaque section, the Spanish Organic Law on Political Parties says 'although political parties are not constitutional bodies but association-based private entities, they are nonetheless an essential part of the constitutional architecture; they perform functions of primary constitutional relevance'

13 For example, Vermont law requires that the base unit of a political party be the town committee, elected by a town caucus that must be organized in each odd-numbered year, and in which all 'voters of the party residing in town' may participate (17 V.S.A. §§2301-2320). The law specifies that the town committee is to elect five officers (chair, vice chair, secretary, treasurer, assistant treasurer), as well as at least two county committee members (the

number is based on the town's vote for the party's gubernatorial candidate at the last election). The county committees elect their own five officers as well as at least two delegates (one male and the other female) to form, along with the county chairs, the state committee. In the same vein, although much less detailed in its prescription, the Romanian party law specifies that (art. 13: 1) 'The general meeting of the members and the executive body, regardless of the name given in the statute of each party, are compulsory governing forums of the political party and its territorial organizations.' and that the national 'general meeting of the members of the political party or of their representatives' be 'convened at least once every 4 years' (art. 14:1). It also requires that the organization of parties be based on territory, rather than (for example) occupation (art. 4).

14 In Vermont, tests of party loyalty or ideological compatibility for admission to a town caucus are specifically prohibited by law, although the law does, at least, limit each voter to participation in only one party's caucus. Obviously, verification that only the voters of a party participate in its town caucus is impossible in the context of a secret ballot. The Portuguese party law prohibits denial of membership in any party 'due to ancestry, gender, race, language, territory of origin, religion, education, economic situation or social status.' (art. 19)

15 In the United States, partisan registration is generally regarded as the equivalent of party membership, and since it is – at least in those states that use 'closed primaries' – the criterion for admission to participate in the selection of party candidates and officials, it satisfies at least part of the Katz & Mair definition of membership. On the other hand, however, partisan registration entails no obligations to the party, is not subject to party approval, and is generally administered by the state rather than by the party.

16 Note that although laws often define parties as associations of citizens, at least implicitly barring non-citizens from party membership, this in fact appears to violate Article 11 of the European Convention on Human Rights and Article 3 of the (First) Protocol, and would be particularly problematic with regard to EU nationals residing in another EU state – in which they would have the right to vote and to be elected in all but national elections. In the case of Estonia, art. 48 of the Constitution specifically limits party membership to citizens, although sect. 5 of the party law allows EU citizens who are residents of Estonia to be party members.

17 For example, registration requires 1,000 members in Estonia; 2,500 in Bulgaria; declarations of 5,000 voters that they wish the party to be registered in Norway.

18 Similarly, the Portuguese party law requires that 'Political parties shall be governed by the principles of democratic organization and management and of participation by all their members.'

19 '36. Whether directly or indirectly, party leaders must be democratically chosen at any given level (local, regional, national and European). This means that members must be able to vote for their selection....' Venice Commission Code of Good Practice in the Field of Political Parties.

20 Barber (1984) raises what is effectively the same argument against state-level representative democracy with a secret ballot – that it encourages expression of private preference rather than public judgement.

21 An example is the 2008 defeat of moderate Republican Congressman Wayne Gilchrist (MD-1) by hard-right state senator Andy Harris in the Republican primary, only to have Harris lose what had been regarded as a rock-solid Republican district to Democrat Frank Kratovil in the general election. An analogous case from the UK would be the 1976 deselection of Labour MP Reg Prentice by his Newham North East constituency party, essentially for the 'crime' of not being sufficiently left wing. Given the stronger role of party in British electoral choice, and the ability of candidates to switch constituencies, however, this did not cost Labour the seat in the next election. Where Gilchrist nominally remained a Republican, but publicly endorsed Kratovil in the general election, Prentice became a Conservative and was elected for the party at the next election from a different constituency (Daventry).

22 For example, Turkish legal scholars argue that art. 68 of the Constitution, particularly as extended by the Law on political parties, would not only bar secessionist parties, but also parties calling for a more federalized structure of government. (Venice Commission Opinion on the Constitutional and Legal Provisions Relevant to the Prohibition of Political Parties in Turkey – CDL-AD (2009) 006.) Secessionist parties could also be banned in Bulgaria.

23 For example, eligibility for public subsidy is limited in Austria to parties represented in parliament or that have received 1% of the vote; in Portugal to parties with at least one seat or that received 50,000 votes; in Canada to parties that won 2% of the national vote or 5% of the vote in the constituencies in which they had a candidate.

24 For example, the Liberal Democrats versus the Labour and Conservative parties in the UK, the NDP versus to Conservatives or Liberals in Canada (at least until 2011), or the FDP and Greens versus of SPD and CDU in Germany.

25 In this context, the phrase 'third party' is derived from contract law, and refers to individuals or organizations that want to participate in, or influence,

an election campaign without themselves being/having their own candidates. It is, thus, to be distinguished from the use of the phrase in the literature of electoral systems, in which it refers to small parties – particularly those that are not expected to finish first or second in a single-member district.

26 For example, it was claimed that the Canadian Natural Law Party used the advantages of candidacy to advertize its philosophy of transcendental meditation, and its related fee-based programmes, rather than to participate in debate of public issues. On a more restricted level, in the 1986 Fulham (UK) by-election a London wine merchant stood as the candidate of the 'Connoisseur Wine Party', using the election address that his candidacy entitled him to have delivered to every house in his constituency as a cheap (the cost of his lost £500 deposit) way to advertize his business (Rawlings 1988: 182-183).

27 Independent expenditures are those made in support of, or opposition to, candidate (in the US) or party (more generally) without the collaboration of, and not in coordination with, that party or candidate.

28 On the other hand, third party broadcast advertizing is effectively banned in Italy by a provision requiring broadcasters to identify the political party paying for it; the Belgian Law of 4 July 1989 effectively barred third party campaign spending by requiring that it be included in the allowable totals for parties and/or candidates; a 2000 report by the Israeli State Comptroller identified 'extra-party' propaganda as falling into the category of prohibited contributions. See GRECO evaluation of Belgium, http://www.coe.int/t/dghl/monitoring/greco/evaluations/round3/GrecoEval3%282008%298_Belgium_Two_EN.pdf; Legge 22 febbraio 2000, n. 28; Report of the Results of an Audit of the Party Lists for the Election Period of the Fifteenth Knesset and for the Prime Minister (State Comptroller Office, January 2000).

29 This danger is also the basis for the widespread opposition to the US Supreme Court's decision in *Citizens United*.

30 Note that this can stop well short of American congressional ear-marks, which specify a particular project to be put in a particular place by instead specifying a nominally neutral set of criteria – that just 'happen' to concentrate spending or other benefits in areas where the governing parties are strong, or hope to become stronger. In a famous American example, Congress specified that a particular variety of olives were to be purchased for military dining facilities; it was purely 'coincidental' that olives meeting those requirements were only grown in the district of one influential congressman. More generally, however, public works spending can be directed to urban transport or to rural roads, to seaports or to airports, to railways or to highways, each choice favouring one identifiable interest, and potential party clientele, over another.

31 For example, the programme of business of the Italian Chamber of Deputies must be agreed by the conference of presidents of the parliamentary groups (rule 23), but a party must have at least 20 deputies in order to form a group (rule 14) and therefore be included in the conference.

32 Recent examples would include Belinda Stronach's defection from the Canadian Conservatives to the Liberals in 2005, which allowed the Paul Martin minority government to remain in office, US Senator Arlen Specter's 2009 shift from the Republicans to the Democrats, and British Conservative MP Quentin Davies's 2007 shift to Labour. Between 1996 and 2001, 'almost one-fourth of members of the lower house in Italy...switched parties at least once' (Heller and Mershon 2005: 546), but the Italian party system was at that time clearly in a state of flux. Perhaps the most famous case of party switching was Winston Churchill's 1904 move from British Conservative to Liberal parties, only to return to the Conservatives in 1925.

33 Shortly after Stronach switched parties, a private members bill was tabled that would have required a by-election within 35 days of an MP leaving his or her party, but the bill was never voted upon. The Ethics Commissioner of Canada was asked to investigate whether the promise of a senior cabinet post had illegitimately induced her to switch parties; he refused, saying that even if the allegation were true (she did become Minister of Human Resources and Skills Development and Minister responsible for Democratic Renewal), it would not have been illegal.

34 According to Janda (2009), 14% (five [sic]) of older democracies (India, Israel, Portugal, Trinidad & Tobago), 24% of newer democracies, and 33% of semi-democracies have laws against parliamentary party defections.

35 For example, the Portuguese Constitution (Article 160 1.c.) specifies that an MP who joins a party other than the one for which s/he was elected loses his or her mandate; this sanction is not applied, however, if the MP merely becomes an independent. Similarly, Israeli law sanctions party switchers, with the result that those who might otherwise have switched parties remain formally in their old party while coordinating action and voting with their 'new' party. (Rahat 2007: note 25). In contrast, a member of the Thai parliament who is expelled from his/her party only loses his/parliamentary mandate if the member fails to join another party within 60 days.

References

Attlee, Clement (1957) 'Party Discipline is Paramount,' *National and English Review* vol. CXLVIII, no. 887 (January).

Bachrach, Peter (1967) *The Theory of Democratic Elitism: A Critique* (Boston, Little, Brown).

Barber, Benjamin (1984) *Strong Democracy: Participatory Politics for a New Age* (Berkeley: University of California Press).

Biezen, Ingrid van (2008) 'Party Regulation and Constitutionalization: A Comparative Overview,' in Per Nordlund and Ben Reilly (eds) *Political Parties and Democracy in Conflict-Prone Societies* (Tokyo: UN University Press), pp. 25-47.

Blyth, Mark and Richard S. Katz (2005) 'From Catch-all Politics to Cartelisation,' *West European Politics* 28 (January), 33-60.

Castles, Francis G. and Rudolf Wildenmann (eds) (1986) *Visions and Realities of Party Government*, (Berlin: de Gruyter).

Collier, David and Steven Levitsky (1997) 'Democracy with Adjectives: Conceptual Innovation in Comparative Research,' *World Politics* 49(3): 430-451.

Downs, Anthony (1957) *An Economic Theory of Democracy* (New York: Harper and Row).

Feasby, C. (1999) '*Libman v. Quebec (A.G.)* and the Administration of the Process of Democracy under the Charter: The Emerging Egalitarian Model' *McGill Law Journal* 44: 5-39.

Feasby, C. (2003) 'Issue Advocacy and Third Parties in the United Kingdom and Canada' *McGill Law Journal* 48: 11-54.

Finer, Samuel (1974) *Comparative Government* (Harmondsworth: Penguin).

Fishkin, James (2009) *When the People Speak: Deliberative Democracy and Public Consultation* (New York: Oxford University Press).

Heller, William B. and Carol Mershon (2005) 'Party Switching in the Italian Chamber of Deputies, 1996-2001,' *Journal of Politics* 67: 536-559.

Janda, Kenneth (2009) 'Laws Against Party Switching, Defecting, or Floor-Crossing in National Parliaments,' World Congress of the International Political Science Association, Santiago Chile, 12-16 July.

Katz, Richard S. (2006) 'Agenti di chi? Principi, committenti e politica dei partiti,' in Luciano Bardi (ed.) *Partiti e sistemi di partito* (Bologna: Il Mulino), pp. 59-80.

Katz, Richard S. (2003) 'Cartels, Consensus Democracy, and Representation in the European Union' European Consortium for Political Research Joint Sessions of Workshops, Edinburgh, 28 March-2 April.

Katz, Richard. (1997) *Democracy and Elections* (New York: Oxford University Press).

Katz, Richard S. (1987) 'Party Government and Its Alternatives,' in Richard S. Katz (ed.) *Party Governments: European and American Experiences*, (Berlin: de Gruyter).

Katz, Richard S. (1986) 'Party Government: A Rationalistic Conception,' in Francis G. Castles and Rudolf Wildenmann (eds) *Visions and Realities of Party Government*, (Berlin: de Gruyter).

Lijphart, Arend (1999) *Patterns of Democracy* (New Haven: Yale University Press).

Macpherson, C. B. (1966) *The Real World of Democracy* (Oxford: Clarendon Press).

McKeon, Richard (1951) *Democracy in a World of Tensions* (Chicago: University of Chicago Press).

Manfredi, Christopher and Mark Rush (2008) *Judging Democracy* (Peterborough, ON: Broadview Press).

Mayhew, David (1974) *Congress: The Electoral Connection* (New Haven: Yale University Press).

Mill, John Stuart (1962 [1841]) *Considerations on Representative Government* (Chicago: Regnery).

Pitkin, Hanna (1969) *Representation* (New York: Atherton).

Rahat, Gideon (2007) 'Determinants of Party Cohesion: Evidence from the Case of the Israeli Parliament,'*Parliamentary Affairs* 60(2) 279-296.

Ranney, Austin (1962) *The Doctrine of Responsible Party Government* (Urbana: University of Illinois Press).

Rawlings, H. F. (1988) *Law and the Electoral Process* (London: Sweet & Maxwell).

Sandel, Michael (1982) *Liberalism and the Limits of Justice* (New York: Cambridge University Press.

Sartori, Giovanni (1965) *Democratic Theory* (Detroit: Wayne State University Press).

Schattschneider, Elmer E. (1942) *Party Government* (New York: Farrar and Rinehart).

Schumpeter, Joseph A. (1950) *Capitalism, Socialism and Democracy* (New York: Harper).

CHAPTER 2

Dilemmas of Regulating Political Finance, with Special Reference to the Dutch Case

Ruud Koole[1]
Leiden University

Introduction: the costs of democracy

Money is power and the struggle for political power always has a financial aspect as well. The democratic principle, however, asks for specific criteria concerning the sources and the use of money. Pure fraud, for example, donating money to a party or a candidate in exchange for concrete political favours, is allowed nowhere in the world. But apart from that, criteria are rather different, depending – among other things – on the nature of the electoral system, conceptions of the state, the level of the rule of law, and the economic development of a country. It is, for example, difficult to demand a high degree of transparency of the finances of political parties in countries where politicians from opposition parties that receive financial support from foreign sources are not sure that disclosure of their sources will not be used to imprison them or worse, even when that kind of support was not formally forbidden. And, to give another example, in various poor countries a plea for grass roots financing (i.e. political parties and/or candidates receive small donations from many people) may be considered to be naïve, because some parties do not *receive* money from small people, but rather *give* them money or bread or milk during campaign rallies. This may be considered as vote buying, which is seen to be incompatible with campaign practices in well established democracies.

Therefore, when we speak about party finance in this chapter, we limit ourselves to western democracies where the rule of law is well established and free media exist, and that are affluent enough to allow for strict criteria with respect to political finance.

Although the costs of democracy (Heard, 1960) vary among western democracies, most of these democracies have introduced a new source of income for parties and/or candidates: public money. From about the mid-1960s, many countries started to grant state money to political parties (IDEA, 2003; Nassmacher, 2009; Van Biezen, 2010). Increased expenditure, mainly as a consequence of higher campaign costs, was hard to cover by less growing or even decreasing income from membership fees. The state came to the rescue.

West Germany was the first European country to introduce state subsidy of political parties (1967), but in that country a very principled reason was also behind this decision. Memories of the fact that Hitler's NSDAP in the interwar period had received enormous sums of money from some German enterprises convinced many people that a one-sided dependence of parties on donations from corporations should be prevented and donations by a democratically controlled state were to be preferred. The latter took place on a large scale, resulting in very high costs of democracy, also in comparison with the costs in for example the United States, Canada, Austria and the Netherlands (Nassmacher, 1982; Koole 1985; Cordes , 2002). Is is true that comparisons of real financial data between countries are notoriously difficult to make, but the relatively high costs of democracy in Germany (and other countries on the European continent for that matter) are to be explained by the fact that parties spend a lot of money not only on campaigns, but also on their permanent party organizations.

Thus, for a good understanding of political finance one has to distinguish between campaign costs and routine costs, as well as between expenditure by individual candidates and by party organizations. Combined with the specifics of the various electoral systems, these elements allow for great variation in the regimes of political finance between countries.

Variation, however, is not just the reflection of the technical features of political systems. Behind these technicalities, different ideological conceptions of the role of the state in democratic systems may also explain diversity among distinct regimes of political finance. Recently, various pleas have been made to treat political finance as the dependent variable: instead of looking for the consequences of specific forms of state regulation, the emphasis has shifted to the question why state regulation has taken these specific forms. Scarrow (2004) points to the importance of political strategies of political parties for the outcome of debates on political finance reform. Van Biezen (2010, 84) stresses the salience of more philosophical considerations: 'debates over political finance are essentially based on competing conceptions of democracy'. Koss (2010, 205) also emphasizes the need to treat public funding as a dependent variable, and he concludes that 'a consensus of the relevant parties is a necessary condition for the introduction and reform of state funding to political parties'. According to Koss, the consensus is often catalysed by a debate on corruption. The substance of that consensus, however, may vary as well.

This chapter explores the importance of ideological considerations for the variation in political finance regimes. A political agreement between the major political forces on public subsidy of political parties (and, more generally, on the regulation of the political financing of candidates and parties) may reflect either the dominant conception of the role of the state in a society or the compromise made between different conceptions. Lawmakers do not act in an ideological vacuum, and their regulatory work on political finance, be it in reaction to corruption scandals or to profound societal changes, is difficult to isolate from prevailing views on the role of the state. The approach in this chapter, therefore, differs from the analysis of the legal regulation of political parties from the perspective of competing conceptions of democracy (Hopkin, 2004; Katz in this volume), in that it starts from another level of abstraction: general views on the role of the state.

The next section presents two opposite general views on the role of the state which will be used to construct a typology of rationales of political finance by confronting these general views with the recent call for more transparency in the field of political finance. Based on this typology, the following section deals with dilemmas of state funding of political parties that lawmakers in modern democracies are faced with when trying to formulate legal regulations. The dilemmas of state funding are closely related to the dilemmas of the more general question of state regulation of political parties. The latter exist also in countries where public funding is hardly available. Therefore, although it concentrates on dilemmas of public funding of political parties, this section also includes some broader dilemmas of state regulation of parties and candidates where these can help us to understand the problems of state support for parties.

In the final section of this chapter, we will apply this typology and these dilemmas to the case of the new Dutch law on party finance.

A typology of rationales of political finance regulation

In a famous judgment, the Canadian Supreme Court stressed the importance of underlying ideologies for the assessment of political finance regulation. In the case about limits on expenditures by third parties (Harper v. Canada, 2004) the Court concluded:

> "The Court's conception of electoral fairness as reflected in the foregoing principles is consistent with the egalitarian model of elections adopted by Parliament as an essential component of our democratic society. This model is premised on the notion that individuals should have an equal opportunity to participate in the electoral process. Under this model, wealth is the main obstacle to equal participation... Thus, the egalitarian model promotes an electoral process that requires the wealthy to be prevented from controlling the electoral process to the detriment of others with less economic power. The state can equalize participation in the electoral process in two ways... First, the State can provide a voice to those who might otherwise not be heard. The Act does so by reimbursing candidates and political parties and by providing broadcast time to political parties. Second, the State can restrict the voices which dominate the political discourse so that others may be heard as well. In Canada, electoral regulation has focussed on the latter by regulating electoral spending through comprehensive election finance provisions. These provisions seek to create a level playing field for those who wish to engage in the electoral discourse. This, in turn, enables voters to be better informed; no one voice is overwhelmed by another. In contrast, the libertarian model of elections favours an electoral process subject to as few restrictions as possible." (Supreme Court of Canada, 2004, s 62)

The different models of elections in this quotation correspond with broader conceptions of the state. These conceptions may be helpful in analysing the different approaches states take to regulating and financing political parties and candidates. Depending on the conception of the role of the state, the willingness to grant public money to parties will vary. In a *narrow conception*, the state serves only as the institution that is to provide basic goods (like internal and external security) that cannot be brought about without its help. In a *wider conception* the state must also act when goods that could be produced without the help of the state can be distributed more evenly only with its help. The first conception does not leave much room for limits and obligations posed on the citizens (therefore this model is sometimes refered to as the 'libertarian model'), while in the second view these limits and obligations are – up to a certain level – defended ('the egalitarian model'). The adherents to both conceptions will claim that their approach contributes most to a desired society. But while for the first the ideal society is determined by individual freedom, for the second freedom for all is predominant.[2] A long history of political philosophy lies behind these two conceptions (Hopkin, 2004; Feasby, 1999).[3] Their popularity changes over time and varies between different countries, and within countries between different political families. Essentially, it is an ideological debate that also impacts on the debate about public funding of parties and candidates.

In recent times, another theme has come to dominate the discussion on political finance: *transparency*. The nature of this theme is less ideological than the aforementioned views on the role of the state. This may be one of the reasons that the call for more transparency very often transcends or cuts trough ideological divisions.

This call is not limited to countries granting state subsidies to parties and candidates, and is increasingly being heard. In order to increase trust in the political system, democracies are more and more willing to introduce higher standards for the transparency of political finance. Accountability has become the international buzz word for good governance, and a high level of transparency is seen as a precondition, as well as a good thing in itself. The United Nations launched a Transparency & Accountability Initiative (UNTAI) in 2007 and International Transparency has become an influential NGO that critically assesses the level of transparency and corruption in many countries all over the world.

The increased attention given to transparency left its traces in the debate on political finance, although the demand for transparency is not new. The German constitution (basic law, 1949) prescribes that parties must publish information about their income and expenditure, as well as about their financial reserves.[4] Disclosure was the central element of the new Federal Campaign Act (FECA, 1971) in the United States. Donations of more than 200 dollars a year had to be made public. A few years later, the Canadian Elections Expenses Act (1974) set the treshold at 100 Canadian dollars (today: 200 dollars). In western Europe the disclosure treshold varies from 125 euros in Belgium to 10,000 euros in Germany (IDEA, 2012).

Even if one does not want to limit donations above a certain amount of money or to ban gifts from certain types of donor altogether, a high degree of transparency can be defended with the argument that in a democracy it is the voter who decides about the desirability of certain donations. To be able to make an informed decision, the voter needs to have reliable information about the financial resources of parties and candidates. Hence, the plea for as much transparency as possible.

The principle of transparency, however, cannot be easily categorized along the ideological dimension. Of course, transparency needs some action of the state (disclosure needs enforcement), but it can be combined with both a narrower and a wider conception of the state. This leads to a two-dimensional typology of political finance rationales:

	low level of transparency	*high level of transparency*
narrow conception of state	**1. closed libertarian** →	**2. open libertarian**
wider conception of state	**3. closed egalitarian** →	**4. open egalitarian**

Figure 1. Typology of political finance regimes

The dimension of state conceptions relates to the normative, ideological view that the state's role in enhancing fairness in electoral competition should be limited (narrow) or active (wider). The transparency dimension ranges from no transparency at all to full transparency. In recent decades, a general trend towards more transparency has been observed (the arrows in the figure), both in the narrower and the wider state conception. Theoretically, other shifts are possible as well, for example from the closed libertarian model towards the open egalitarian model. Countries without any form of state regulation of political finance may introduce transparency rules and egalitarian regulation at the same time, thus moving from regime 1 to regime 4. Another country may give up its efforts to reach a more egalitarian model of political finance, while introducing more transparency in order to let the voters judge, hence moving from regime 3 to regime 2. Countries can be ordered according to this typology, and a first effort will be made after we have described the most important reasons that are given for the introduction of public subsidies to parties and discussed some of the dilemmas lawmakers face in various western countries when dealing with regulations on state subsidy.

Reasons to introduce state subsidy to political parties

Public financing of political parties (and/or candidates) is now routine practice in many countries. The reasons lawmakers put forward to introduce state subsidy to parties are different, of course. Apart from the rather general reasoning that parties are instrumental in the formation of the political will in a democracy, and therefore deserve to receive money from the state, we will highlight some of the most frequently cited other reasons.

The example of Germany, already mentioned above, shows that events in the past strongly impacted upon the willingness to introduce state subsidies. As early as 1950, the professional organization of German lawyers advocated state subsidy to *fight undesirable influences on political parties*. It explicitly mentioned the important donations by corporations (like Thyssen, IG Farben, AEG and Siemens) to Adolf Hitler's NSDAP (Dragstra, 2008, 404). The idea was that state subsidy would make parties (and/or candidates) less inclined to look for other sources of income, that were considered to be undesirable, although not forbidden.

Fighting corruption is a second argument in favour of public funding (cf Koss, 2010). This is not the same as trying to prevent big donors influencing political decision making. As long as formal rules do not forbid donations from corporations or unions or rich individuals, such gifts do not fall into the category of corruption, except in cases of clear fraud (i.e. gifts in exchange to concrete political favours). The argument that public funds help to fight corruption is the following: parties are in permanent – and often increasing – need of money. Without enough help from the state, parties will be tempted to look for other resources, even if they are illegal, thus perverting the outcome of democratic elections. This kind of reasoning reveals a rather cynical, but in some cases no less realistic, view of the nature of parties: they would be prone to corruption if the financial need were high enough. Although a direct relationship between the level of corruption and the level of state funding is hard to assess (van Biezen, 2010, 70), it would be worth investigating whether this kind of reasoning is used more often in countries where the level of corruption is relatively high. In countries with a low level of corruption, the argument of introducing state subsidy to fight corruption is probably not very convincing. Political culture in these countries is likely to be one of 'rather bankrupt than corrupt'.

A specific problem linked to the problematic relationship between state funding and corruption is what I would call the *corruption paradox*. State funding is always accompanied by regulation, in some countries more than in others. The higher the level of formal regulation, the higher the chances of illegal practices. Rules that do not exist cannot be broken. Of course, various informal or moral rules may exist that can be broken, and corruption defined – by the World Bank – as '*the abuse of public office for private gain*' is not limited to cases in which formal rules are broken (sometimes formal rules can even be considered as tools for abuse of public office for private gains). What is meant here, however, is the idea that attempts to fight corruption by stricter regulation (possibly as a consequence of the introduction of state subsidy) may result in more cases of illegal practices. And illegal practices are generally conceived by the general public as corruption. To give an example: the political life of German chancellor Helmut Kohl was in serious trouble at the end of the 1990s, because he admitted to having received undeclared contributions for his party, but he refused to give the names of the donors. In his own words at the time:

> "These donors trusted me with this sum of money under the condition that they wouldn't be named. They were German citizens who had nothing to do with government decisions or policy in any sector. They wanted to help me. And I don't intend to reveal any names because I gave them my word."(Deutsche Welle, 2010).

Investigations followed, but the names of the donors and the exact amount of money remain unknown. The very refusal to disclose the names of the donors was against the law in Germany. If Kohl had been the prime minister in the Netherlands in the same period, a scandal might have arisen as well, but he could not have been accused of illegal practices, simply because the Dutch rules at the time did not contain an obligation to declare contributions.

A third reason for introducing state subsidy lies in the wish to *promote a level playing field* for all political parties and/or candidates (see also section 2). If resources are distributed unevenly between parties, state money may help to level out these differences. Perfect equality of political competition will never exist, but public money will at least make it possible for poorer parties to have a chance to reach the voters. This idea of fairness is reflected in the abovementioned judgment of the Canadian Supreme Court (Harper v. Canada, 2004), and was also an important reason for introducing public subsidy in the new Central and Eastern European democracies, immediately after the removal of the Iron Curtain. Without help from the state, the rich former Communist parties would have had a quasi-monopoly on the electoral market. Thus, state subsidies were meant to correct market failures (van Biezen and Kopecký, 2007). The same holds for various African countries where opposition parties have little financial power when the incumbent party has a majority position using state resources for its own benefit (Saffu, 2003).

Germany tried to go one step further. *Chancengleichheit* (equality of chances) has always been one of the main principles that guide German regulation of party finances, but in 1984 a very complicated system was introduced to compensate poorer parties for the fact that they would profit less from an increase in the tax deductibility of donations to parties. This system of *Chancenausgleich* (levelling of chances) was abolished again in 1992, because the German Constitutional Court ruled that it had created new inequalities, and hence was at odds with the principle of *Chancengleichheit* (Bundesverfassungsgericht, 1992, 264).

Dilemmas of regulating political finance in Western democracies

Decisions to introduce public subsidies and the accompanying regulation are further complicated by the effects lawmakers foresee or fear. State subsidy may have unwanted consequences, just like the absence of state subsidy. Not all of the possible unwanted consequences are guaranteed to take place. Uncertainty rules. State subsidy will indeed give parties more financial means, but will it – for example – also inevitably lead to the petrification of the party system? Even if this is not the case, legislators may not be sure about that or may have to reckon with possible allegations by political opponents that they intend to prevent new political parties from entering the electoral market. In other words, they are faced with dilemmas and they try to anticipate them. Thus, they are forced to concentrate on the possible effects of the intended legal measures, but in order to find a way out of the dilemmas they may rely on pre-existing ideological views. Here the recent scholarly emphasis on the independent variables (the reasons why specific types of political finance regimes emerge) meets the practical prominence legislators give to the dependent variables (possible effects of legal measures) when deliberating and deciding about political finance.

State Subvention and the Status Quo

In democratic systems, political parties through their representatives in parliament decide about laws, including laws on the state funding of parties.[5] This makes them vulnerable to accusations that they (too) easily decide on tax-payers' money for their own interests. Popular criticism of political parties often includes the alleged self-serving attitude of politicians and parties. Almost everywhere in the world, parties figure high on the lists of institutions that are perceived by the ordinary citizens to be corrupt (Transparency International (2007). Public subsidy for parties easily fits into this rather cynical view, even if state subvention itself is not corruption. Although individual politicians are not necessarily considered to enrich themselves, their parties are sometimes accused of 'legal theft' by using public money to subsidize their own organizations.

Apart from this popular – no to say populist – idea that parties and politicians tend to enrich themselves with tax money coming from 'hardworking citizens', a more general argument against state subsidy is often put forward: the danger of petrification of the party system (f.e. Alexander and Shiratori, eds, 1994; Pinto-Duschinski, 2001). State money may have the effect of preserving the status quo, which is difficult to reconcile with the ideal of equality (between old and new parties). This argument has been further developed in the thesis of the cartel party (Katz and Mair, 1995). The most discriminatory feature of the cartel party is the high dependence on public subsidies. If public funding is allocated in favour of incumbent and larger parties, it may become less easy for new and small parties to be successful in the political arena. Although the term 'cartel' suggest a conscious conspiracy among the larger incumbent parties to serve themselves to the detriment of the outsiders, which is hard to prove (Koole, 1996), the possibility of the suggested petrifying effect (or 'cartellization') cannot be excluded, although it has not been proven as yet. Legislators wishing to avoid accusations of serving only the established parties will have to look for conditions of state subsidy to parties that minimize this alleged effect.

Equality of Chances and the Freedom of Speech

As stated above, *Chancengleigheit* (equality of chances) is an important principle for German political finance. Under other labels (level playing field, fairness, equality), it also exists in other countries. In this respect, state activism by way of public subsidies or regulations about spending and expenditure limits is defended as a way to improve the fairness of political competition and the proper working of an electoral market.

Sometimes the equality of chances for parties is accompanied by the equality of chances for citizens. The introduction of direct subsidies to parties in Germany was the result of this combination. Not very long after tax deductablity of donations to parties had been introduced in 1954, the German Constitutional Court observed conflict with the principle of Chancengleicheit, because parties with rich members would profit more from this opportunity than parties with less wel-to-do people among their members, but also because the equality of citizens was at stake. The tax deductability of donations would give individuals with a higher income a greater say in politics than poorer people. This ruling led to an effort to introduce direct and general state subsidies to parties. Again, the Constitutional Court proved to be an obstacle. According to the Court, general subsidies are at odds with another principle, that of *Staatsfreiheit* (autonomy of parties). But it also ruled that the state is allowed to introduce state subsidy (on the basis of *Chancengleichheit*) to give relief from the specific costs of election campaigns, since those costs are directly related to the free and fair elections that are prescribed in the German constitution. The result was the *Parteiengezetz* (party law) of 1967.

In 1992, in yet another ruling, the Court changed its position and decided that state money was allowed not only to fight the costs of campaigns (*Wahlkampfkostenerstattung*), but also to be used by parties for general purposes, while at the same time the tax deductabilty of donations was abolished (Bundesverfassungsgericht, 1992).

In the United States and Canada, a completely different debate took place around the principle of equality of chances. In the USA the Federal Election Campagn Act (FECA) dealt not only with transparency, but also with the principle of fairness. After the Watergate affair (1972) limits on campaign expenditure were considered to be an adquate instrument to create a more level playing field. But the Supreme Court, in a famous judgment (Buckley v. Valeo - 1976), ruled differently. Limits on expenditure were seen to impose too great restraints on the freedom of speech. Spending money is a form of speech; important limits on it violate the First Amendment and are thus unconstitutional. The Supreme Court considered the idea of 'equality' in this respect 'wholly foreign to the First Amendment' (Persily, 2006).

The debate in Canada centred around the same dilemma, but with a different result. Expenditure limits in order to improve equality of chances also collided with the principle of speech, but in 2004 the Canadian Supreme Court – as we have seen above – accepted a more egalitarian view on political finance. Thus, while in Canada and Germany the principle of equality of chances (for both parties and citizens) leads the debate on political finance, in the USA freedom of speech is paramount.

Transparency and Privacy

The call for more transparency is not uncontested. The main argument against a high degree of openness is the donors' right to privacy. Does one have the right to do good by stealth? When exactly does the public interest in the disclosure of financial sources outweigh the individual's right to privacy? As stated above, in Canada and the United States, the individual right to privacy with respect to donations is limited. In Germany, on the other hand, the threshold above which donations must be disclosed is rather high.

The recent trend towards more transparency is clearly visible in some Scandinavian countries. Traditionally, in Sweden and Norway there was great resistance against the obligation to disclose donations (Van Dijk, 2009, 14-17). The right to privacy was strengthened by yet another argument: the autonomy of parties (see also the next section). The state was to refrain from any interference with the internal affairs of parties; even an obligation to account publicly for the way the very high state subsidies are spent was considered to infringe the organizational freedom of parties. In 2002, after much hesitation, in both countries independent committees of experts were set up. As a result, the transparency of political finance was put high on the political agenda. In Sweden this has not yet resulted in obligations to disclose donations above 20,000 SEK (ca 1,800 Euro) as the Swedish committee suggested; in Norway all donations above 30,000 NOK (approx 3,300 Euro) at the national level, 20,000 NOK (2,200 Euro) at county council level and 10,000 NOK (1,100 euro) at the local level have to be disclosed (Greco, 2009). The Swedish and Norwegian examples show that the transparency argument has gained salience over time, but this does not mean that all arguments against it have disappeared. In Norway, the importance of the autonomy of parties continues to be stressed, there are no conditions for how state subsidy is to be spent by the recipients.

State Regulation and the Freedom of Organization

All the above mentioned dilemmas touch upon the more general question of how compatible state regulation is with the autonomy of political parties. The Swedish and Norwegian hesitation in accepting rules on transparency comes close to the German principle of *Staatsfreiheit* (freedom from the state), which was the main argument for the Constitutional Court initially forbidding the introduction of general subsidies to political parties. In the North American continent, however, the autonomy of political parties does not figure prominently in the debate on political finance. Regulations on political finance are geared more to individual candidates than to party organizations.

Nevertheless, in all countries the state plays a steering role vis-à-vis political party organizations. Each electoral system has a profound impact on how parties organize. The debate, therefore, is not about *whether* the state has the right to influence parties, but about the *quantity* and the *domain* of influence. States need to have regulations on how general elections are organized; this is fairly uncontroversial. Every democracy has an electoral law. The contents of that law and of other regulations concerning candidates and parties, however, is often at the heart of political discussions, because it concerns the distribution of power.

The simple statement that 'free and fair elections' form the core feature of democracies in itself bears the seeds of many political quarrels. Free from the state? But is the state not needed to ensure fair elections? A special *Declaration on criteria for free and fair elections* issued by the Inter Parliamentary Union in 1994 holds that the state should be active on both fields. On the one hand, 'states should take all necessary and appropriate measures to ensure that the principle of the secret ballot is respected, and that voters are able to cast their ballots freely, without fear or intimidation', and on the other hand 'in order that elections shall be fair, states should take the necessary measures to ensure that parties and candidates enjoy reasonable opportunities to present their electoral platform.' (IPU, 1994) What exactly is meant by 'reasonable opportunities'? Is a (financial) level playing field necessary for "reasonable opportunities" to exist? The answer to this question is the quintessence of the debate on political finance.

As said, states always have a certain steering influence on the functioning of political parties, especially through electoral laws. But a consensus exists that this influence ought to be limited to the party *organization* (although of course not unconstrained), and not extended to the party *orientation.* Norway, which has always put great emphasis on the autonomy of parties, has now accepted some regulation relating to transparency, but on the condition that the freedom of orientation remains unchallenged, not only with respect to ideology and policy, but also in terms of control over the goals for which state subsidy is used.

In Germany, the concept of *Staatsfreiheit* remains very important, but its interpretation has changed over time. Before 1992, it mainly addressed the principle that the state should not intervene in the free formation of the political will. In 1992, the Constitutional Court used a broader interpretation. Parties need to be *staatsfern* (at distance from the state) and *bürgernah* (close to the citizens). As a consequence, parties must rely on citizens for a considerable part of their income, and state subsidy to them may not exceed the income of the party from all other sources. The Court's new vision has been interpreted as 'an obligation to ensure the anchoring of parties in society'.[6] Especially in Germany, where parties receive an enormous amount of money from the state, this new interpretation of the concept of *Staatsfreiheit* was not unexpected. Table 1 give an impression of the relatively high level of German (and Austrian) public subsidy.

Table 1: Direct public subsidies to political parties in selected European countries, 2008*

Country	**Total amount of state subsidy (in euros)**	**Number of inhabitants**	**Amount per capita (in euros)**
Germany	477,000,000	82,369,548	5.79
Austria	41,46,233	8,205,533	5.11
Belgium	19,85,560	10,403,951	1.89
France	74,22,853	62,150,775	1.20
Ireland	5,609,962	4,156,119	1.35
The Netherlands	15,446,167	16,645,000	0.93
United Kingdom	2,256,594	60,943,912	0.04

** Including subsidies for election campaigns and for ancillary organizations.*
Source: Lucardie, Voerman and Van Zonneveld (2010), 16. See also: Algemene Rekenkamer (2011), 21.

The information in this section about rules on political finance in various countries allows us tentavively to place those coutries in order according to the typology mentioned in figure 1: the United States in quadrant 2 ('open libertarian' regime); Norway and Sweden in quadrant 3 (closed egalitarian), although Norway has recently moved towards 4 (open egalitarian); Canada and Germany in quadrant 4. Of course, positions within a quadrant can also vary and change over time. A more detailed analysis of the Dutch situation may illustrate this. It will also show that a debate characterized at first sight by pragmatic argument is dominated by rather ideological orientations when inspected more closely.

A new Dutch law on political finance

The new Dutch law on party finance (*Wet Financiering Politieke Partijen* - Wfpp), which replaces the 1999 law on state subsidy to political parties (*Wet subsidiëring politieke partijen* – Wspp), deals with both state subsidies and the transparency of party finances. With the new law the Dutch government also responded to the very critical report of the Group of States against Corruption (GRECO, 2008), part of the Council of Europe, on the Dutch regulation on the transparency of party funding. The 1999 law was considered to be powerless with respect to enforcing the transparency of party finances. It took a rather long time before the new law was introduced into parliament, which in a sense reflects the traditional unwillingness in the Netherlands to regulate the life of political parties.

Dutch parties and constitutional law

In the constitution of The Netherlands, political parties are still not mentioned, notwithstanding the fact that in recent decades a 'hidden process of codification' has taken place (Koole, 1992). As well as the electoral law, all kind of formal stipulations were introduced, resulting in the aforementioned law on state subsidy for political parties (1999), but parties continue not to be mentioned in the Constitution. Several attempts have been made to change this situation. In 1954, for example, an official commission set up by the government concluded in its report that the absence of political parties in the Dutch constitution was an 'anomaly', and therefore 'the image of the Dutch political system in de Constitution is not real'. (*Eindrapport,* 1954, 55). The government, however, did not adopt the idea of repairing this 'anomaly'.

The traditional reluctance to give the state a more than minimal role when dealing with political parties is due to the long term predominance of protestant political ideas current in Dutch politics (including the parties ARP and CHU, which merged into the Christian Democratic Appeal in 1980). The protestant conception of the state (called 'sovereignty in its own circle') was one in which the state was only one among other 'circles' in society, albeit a special one. These circles were to stay aloof from each other as much as possible, thus granting each other as much freedom as possible. Even in 1982, Donner, an influential and eminent lawyer with an ARP background, said in this respect, 'Let us postpone official recognition of political parties as long as possible, because by nature law implicates regulation; and he who regulates also introduces limitations'

(Koole, 1992, 216). Liberals, who in general argue for a low level of state interference in societal matters, sided with this protestant reluctance.

Notwithstanding this predominant attitude, the Dutch parties have become subject to a growing set of legal stipulations. Of course, the electoral law has always had an important impact on the way parties organize themselves. As in other countries, the organizational structure of political parties generally reflects the way elections are organized. The local party chapter deals with elections to the municipal council, the regional party body with the provincial elections, and the national party organs with the national and (since 1979) the direct elections for the European parliament. The proportional electoral system (PR list system) equally has an important impact on how parties prepare for elections. In the electoral law, however, the term 'political party' is not used. Instead, the law mentions 'political groupings' next to individual candidates. By avoiding explicit mention of the term 'political party', the Dutch legislator allows non-party individuals to participate in elections by presenting their own lists of candidates; thus guaranteeing an open electoral system. At the local level, these personals lists are presented regularly, although they constitute a minority of the lists of candidates. At the supra-local level almost all lists of candidates are presented by parties, and not by individuals. One rather recent and well-known exception was the List Pim Fortuyn (LPF) during the national elections of 2002, when Pim Fortuyn was ousted from his party Leefbaar Nederland and immediately afterwards presented his own list for the impending elections.

Apart from the electoral law, other formal regulations impact on Dutch political parties. As early as in 1954 donations to political parties were tax deductible, since parties came to be considered as registered charities or 'institutions for the public good'. The rules on associations in the Civil Law also apply to political parties. Almost all parties are formally associations. That was also the case before 1989 when a change in the Electoral Law stipulated that henceforth parties could use their names or acronyms on the ballots sheets only of they were associations by law. As early as in the 1930s, political parties were allotted free time on the radio; since 1957 this has equally been true for (public) televisison. And from the 1970s state subsidy was given to political parties at the national level only, and destined for specific purposes: research institutes, educational institutes and youth organizations. All parties represented in Parliament were entitled to receive state subsidy, consisting of a fixed amount plus an amount that depended on the number of parliamentary seats. In order to receive these goal-oriented subsidies, special foundations had to be set up.

At the time, direct subsidy to political parties was still a bridge too far, because of the dominant view that the state should remain at a distance from the functioning of parties. Paradoxically, activities that had hitherto been carried out within the framework of the parties themselves were now taken care of by these affiliated foundations. Only money to fight the production costs of radio and television programmes in the free time on the public channels allotted to parties was given directly to parties.

In 1999 the Law on State Subsidy to Political Parties (Wspp) was introduced. The law introduced a basis in formal law for subsidies for research, educational work and youth programmes. The 1999 law introduced some changes. From 1999 onwards the subsidies were given directly to the parties. They continued to exist at the national level only and remained goal-oriented, but the list of goals was broadened somewhat (now also including: the maintenance of contacts with sister parties outside the Netherlands, information to party members, etc). Campaign spending was still explicitly excluded from state subsidy, for two reasons: 1. the risk of continual demands for extra subsidy because campaign spending tends to rise incessantly; 2. the state should stay aloof from the direct struggle for power at elections, and should concentrate on supporting other ways to reinforce the intermediary position of political parties (for example. subsidies for more specific goals). In 2004, however, this reasoning was abandoned, and from then on state subsidy could also be spent on election campaigns. In the same year the total amount of state subsidy to all political parties was raised from 10 million euros to 15 million euros.

From the very start, the 1999 law was critized for its vagueness in terms of transparency and enforcement. Various efforts were made to draft a new law. As stated before, the Greco report of the Council of Europe in 2008 put pressure on this process. In February 2011 the Netherlands Court of Auditors critized the Dutch government for being very slow in implementing the proposals suggested in the Greco report (Algemene Rekenkamer, 2011). Later that year a proposal for the new law on party finance (*Wet Financiering Politieke Partijen* - Wfpp) was submitted to the Dutch parliament. The new law was adopted by the Senate in March 2013.

The new law on party finance (Wfpp)

The new law is a combination of a subsidy law and a transparency law.[7] Especially, with respect to transparency, the new law includes somewhat stricter regulation. The main new elements of the law are: donations from both natural persons and legal entities to political parties, their affiliated organizations and/or individual candidates above 4,500 euro have to be made public; in-kind donations are subject to the same rule; a stronger regime of sanctions is imposed, including administrative fines of up to 25,000 euro; and political parties that enter parliament for the first time may use their state subsidy to pay for campaigns costs incurred before entering parliament. With respect to transparency and enforcement, the new law is more precise compared with the former one. But the Council of Europe will probably remain critical, because no independent enforcement agency is introduced (enforcement will remain the responsibility of the Ministry of Home Affairs, although an 'independent' committee of experts will be set up to advise the minister); no annual limits ('ceilings') for receiving gifts from the same donor are included in the law; and the new law only deals with political parties at the national level, leaving much room for the circumvention of rules via sub-national party branches.[8]

This modest result in terms of legislative progress contrasts with the eulogy on political parties in the explanatory notes to the bill. The reasons for granting public subsidy to political parties are worded as follows:

> 'Political parties are an essential and necessary condition for the functioning of democracy. They form the bridge between political decision-making and the citizens... A well functioning political party adds to a stable democracy. A future without political parties is difficult to imagine. Political parties voice the wishes and opinions of the populace, and – for the benefit of political decision-making – they integrally weigh distinct and often contradictory wishes and interests. They inform and stimulate voters to go to the ballot box in a well informed way, and they take care of the education of party members. The recruitment and selection for political functions is a special responsibility of political parties. The activities of political parties are done in the democratic interest. Because of these reasons the government furnishes subsidy to political parties'.[9]

Notwithstanding this appraisal, the Dutch goverment was faced with dilemmas. More far-reaching proposals like caps on donations, a lower threshold above which donations have to be made public, or the inclusion of sub-national party organs in the law did not reach the bill. The government explicitly refers to a dilemma between the completeness and consistency of the law on the one hand and its feasibility on the other.[10]

The argument of feasibility is often linked to the argument of avoiding too much red tape for parties. This reasoning was also useful to overcome ideological differences between several parties in parliament. For example: while the conservative-liberal VVD warmly agreed with the absence of caps on donations and with the general striving for a low administrative burden for the parties, the social-democrat PvdA wanted an annual cap on donations of 50,000 euro and a prohibition on gifts from abroad. The VVD clearly adhered to a narrow conception of state and the PvdA to a wider one. Common ground was found in the goal of more transparency.

One party, the PVV, clearly objected to the striving for more transparency. The party takes a 'closed libertarian' perspective on party finance and perceives the bill as an 'anti-PVV law', especially drafted to deprive the party of sources of income.[11] The PVV fears losing donors both from abroad (the United States especially) and in the Netherlands if their names are to be disclosed. The earliest proposals to sharpen the 1999 law in terms of transparency, however, were drafted long before the PVV was founded in 2005. And the irony of history is that it was the governmental coalition of the CDA and the VVD, which in a special construction was supported by the PVV, that finally sent the bill to parliament in April 2011. The bill, however, was no part of the governmental deal with the PVV, and therefore the CDA and VVD felt free to seek support from other parties for this proposal. That is why they stressed the importance of transparency (which is acceptable to all parties except the PVV), while at the same time staying as much as possible within the dominant paradigm of reluctance to intervene in party matters, which marries so well the ideological views of the CDA and the VVD. Parties with a wider conception of state were disappointed by the limited scope of the changes made by the law, but supported the adoption of the new law in order to avoid the continued existence of the much criticized 1999 law.

According to the government, the wish to increase the transparency of private financing of political parties was at the basis of the drafting of the new law in order to serve 'the purity of political decision making'.[12] When explicitly asked why this new law did not take into consideration the principle of equality, the minister answered in 2012 that the government had not opted for promoting a level playing field, because it considered transparency 'at this moment' to be sufficient and adequate: transparency makes it possible for a political party to be held accountable and it will possibly have a moderating impact on the size of a donation. Five years after its introduction an evaluation of the new law will take place, which will also go into the question of big donations, and eventually lead to changes in the law.[13] During the final debate in the Senate in February 2013, the new minister positively answered the question whether the principle of equality would be taken explicitly into consideration during this evaluation.[14]

Conclusion

Governments are confronted with dilemmas when introducing rules on party finance. Public subsidy to political parties and the wish for more transparency of political finance have considerably broadened state regulation of political parties. However, the intended goals of state measures are almost always linked to the possibility of unintended consequences of such measures. The resulting dilemmas confront lawmakers and courts with choices between, for example, giving state subsidy to existing parties and avoiding the preservation of the status quo, between transparency and privacy, between equality of chances and the freedom of speech, or between state regulation and the freedom of organization. The particular history of the legal treatment of political parties in a specific country reveals a dominant (ideological) view that impacts on the content of the choices to be made. These choices are to a large extent path-dependent, but developments such as decline in party membership, changing power relations within a country or growing international pressure for more transparency may influence decisions on party finance. Thus, the political finance regime in a specific country may change as well.

In this chapter particular attention was paid to the Dutch case. The Dutch tradition of aversion to state interference with political parties is still visible in the decisions of government and parliament on whether and how to regulate parties. Nevertheless, a gradual codification of Dutch political parties has taken place, although the Dutch constitution still ignores their existence. Also recently this process of codification was visible in the drafting of the new bill on political finance (Wfpp). When positioned in the typology of political finance regimes presented earlier in this chapter, the political finance regime of the Netherlands has consequently changed.

As figure 2 shows, the adoption of the new Dutch law on party finance (NL 2013) indicates that the Netherlands has moved in the direction of a more open regime of party finance, while hardly changing its intermediary position between an egalitarian and a libertarian regime of political finance. Pressure from the Council of Europe (Greco) helped to push the Dutch government in that direction, although the steps taken will probably not fully satisfy the Council.[15] The refusal of the government to consider the

	low level of transparency	*high level of transparency*
narrow conception of state	**1. closed libertarian** **(NL 1999)**	**2. open libertarian**
wider conception of state	**3. closed egalitarian**	**(NL 2013)** **4. open egalitarian**

Figure 2. Typology of political finance regimes: position of the Netherlands

new law not only as a vehicle to promote transparency, but also as an instrument to advance a more level playing field in Dutch political finance corresponds to the abovementioned tradition. But the choices made by Dutch lawmakers with respect to the dilemmas of regulating political finance reveal the ideological centrist position between a narrower and a wider conception of state. State subsidy is given to all parties represented in parliament proportionally to the number of seats they hold, but with a slight advantage for smaller parties due to a fixed basis amount of subsidy. And the allocation of free time on radio and television on the public channels is equal for all parties, irrespective of their size. These measures reflect an egalitarian approach. On the other hand, the new law does not introduce caps on donations, while these donations are at the same time tax-deductable, thus revealing a libertarian perspective. Although the latter corresponds with the traditional reluctance of the Dutch state to interfere with political parties, the former shows that path dependency is not complete. This is equally true for the transparency dimension. The predominance of the philosophy of 'sovereignty within one's own circle' had already declined somewhat with the introduction of state subsidies in the 1970s. The new law takes an important further step: the obligatory disclosure of donations and its enforcement. But again this development stops at a rather centrist position: the disclosure threshold is relatively high (indicating the enduring importance of the argument of privacy), and the new rules do not (yet?) apply to the sub-national level. These results demonstrate the compromisory character of the Dutch political finance regime, which – after all – comes as no surprise in a country long known for its consensus-seeking political system.

Notes

1 Thanks to Ingrid van Biezen and Hans-Martien ten Napel; to the participants in the panel on *Regulating Party Finance* at the IPSA/ECPR Joint Conference, University of Sao Paolo, Brazil, February 16-19, 2011; and to the participants in the symposium on *Political Parties and Public Law: The Netherlands in Comparative Perspective*, Leiden, 25 June 2010, for their valuable comments on earlier drafts of this chapter.

2 Nassmacher (2001, 14) speaks about 'Political Funds between Freedom and Equality'.

3 Feasby (1999), following John Rawls, makes a distinction between 'equality of liberty' and 'absolute liberty': 'equality of liberty may be achieved by limiting the freedoms of the wealthy,' and 'this may be achieved only through State action', but this state interference 'must not impose any undue burdens on the various political groups in society and must affect them all in an equitable manner'. Thanks to Tanja van Dijk for showing me this last reference (Van Dijk, 2009, 22).

4 '*Die Parteien (…) müssen über die Herkunft und Verwendung ihrer Mittel sowie über ihr Vermögen öffentlich Rechenschaft geben*' art 21.1 German Constitution (*Grundgesetz*).

5 Note that state funding must be clearly distinguished from the practice of incumbent parties in some countries of using state money and state functions for their own organization and their own people. Corruption and patronage are illegal, or at least informal, practices that must not be confused with state subsidy based on formally adopted laws.

6 '*Gebot zur Sicherung der Verankerung der Parteien in der Gesellschafft*', Schwartmann, as cited in Dragstra (2008, 354).

7 Wet financiering politieke partijen. *Staatsblad*, 2013, nr 93 (Wet van 7 maart 2013, houdende regels inzake de subsidiëring en het toezicht op de financiën van politieke partijen).

8 Pressure from the Lower House in parliament resulted in the insertion into the law of a stipulation that parties that participate in national, regional and/or local elections must have internal rules on (the transparency of) donations (art. 34). These rules have to be made public, and also apply to the subnational party chapters. However, in December 2013 the minister announced to erase this stipulation, because the administrative burdens for the parties would be too high.

9 *Proceedings of Dutch parliament*, 32752, nr 3 (*Memorie van Toelichting*, 27 April 2011), p1 (my translation – RK).

10 *Proceedings of Dutch parliament*, 32752, nr 7 (*Nota naar aanleiding van het verslag*, 26 oktober 2011).
11 *De Volkskrant* (Dutch newspaper), 27 January, 2012.
12 *Proceedings of Dutch parliament*, 32752, C, p. 2, 13 July 2012.
13 *Ibidem.*
14 *Proceedings of Dutch Parliament*, 32752, nr 18, p. 2 (26 February 2013).
15 *Financiëel Dagblad* (Dutch newspaper), 17 juli 2012: 'Financiering partijen nog niet transparant'.

References

Alexander, Herbert E. and Rei Shiratori (eds.) 1994), *Comparative Political Finance Among the Democracies*. Boulder, Westview Press.

Algemene Rekenkamer (2011), *Financiering Politieke Partijen*. Den Haag, Algemene Rekenkamer. Also to be found in the Proceedings of Dutch Parliament, 32634, no. 2.

Biezen, Ingrid van (2010), 'Campaign and Party Finance', in: Lawrence Leduc, Richard G. Niemi and PippA Norris (eds), *Comparing Democracies 3: Elections and Voting in the 21th Century*, London, Sage, pp. 65-97.

Biezen, Ingrid van, and Petr Kopecký (2007), 'The State and the Parties: Public Funding, Public Regulation and Rent-seeking in Contemporary Democracies,' in: *Party Politics*, vol. 13, no. 2, pp. 235-254.

Bundesverfassungsgericht (1992), *Entscheidingen des Bundesverfassungsgericht*, nr. 85 (9 April).

Cordes, D. (2002) *Die Finanzierung der politischen Parteien Deutschlands, Österreichs und der Niederlande. http://docserver.bis.uni-oldenburg.de/p/dissertation/2002/corfin01/pdf/corfin01.pdf.*

Dijk, Tanja van (2009), *Fundamentele dilemma's in de financiering van politieke partijen: grenzen aan overheidsingrijpen*. Unpublihsed MA thesis, Leiden University.

Dragstra, Laurens (2008), *Enige opmerkingen over partijfinanciering. De regelgeving voor publieke en private financiering van politieke partijen in Nederland en Duitsland nader bekeken en beoordeeld.* PhD-thesis University of Amsterdam.

Eindrapport van de Staatscommissie tot herziening van de Grondwet (1954), The Hague.

IDEA (2003), *Funding of Political Parties and Election Campaigns*, Stockholm.

IDEA (2012), *Political Finance Database*, Stockholm: http://www.idea.int/political-finance/ (consulted July 16, 2012).

Deutsche Welle (2010), 'The scandal that rocked the government of Helmut Kohl', 18 January (http://www.dw-world.de/dw/article/0,,5137950,00.html).

Ewing, K,D. and Samuel Issacharoff (eds) (2006), *Party Funding and Campaign Financing in International Perspective*, Oxford, Hart Publishing.

Feasby, Colin (2006), 'The Supreme Court of Canada's Political Theory and the Constitutionality of the Political Finance Regime', in: Ewing and Issacharoff (eds), pp. 5-38.

Greco (2008), Evaluation Report on the Netherlands on 'Transparency of State Funding' (http://www.coe.int/t/dghl/monitoring/greco/evaluations/round3/GrecoEval3(2007)8_Netherlands_Two_EN.pdf).

Greco (2009), *The Third Evaluation Round on Norway on Transparency of Party Funding.* (http://www.coe.int/t/dghl/monitoring/greco/evaluations/round3/GrecoEval3(2008)6_Norway_Two_EN.pdf).

Gidlund, Gullan and Ruud Koole, 'Political Finance in the North of Europe: The Netherlands and Sweden', in: Karl-Heiz Nassmacher (ed), 2001, 112-130.

Heard, Alexander (1960) *The Costs of Democracy.* Chapel Hill, University of North Carolina Press.

Hopkin, Jonathan (2004), 'The Problem with Party Finance; Theoretical Perspectives on the Funding of Political Parties', *Party Politics,* vol. 10, nr, 6, 627-651.

IPU (1994), Inter Parliamentary Union, *Declaration on criteria for free and fair elections.* (http://www.ipu.org/cnl-e/154-free.htm).

Katz, Richard S. and Peter Mair (1995), Changing Models of Party Organization and Party Democracy: The Emergence of the Cartel Party'. *Party Politics*, 1, pp. 5-28.

Koole, Ruud (1985), 'Partijfinanciën: lessen voor Nederland uit de recente Westduitse praktijk', *Beleid en Maatschappij*, juni, pp. 142-149.

Koole, Ruud (1992), *De opkomst van de moderne kaderpartij: veranderende partijorganisatie in Nederland 1960-1990.* Utrecht, Spectrum.

Koole, Ruud (1996), Cadre, Catch-all or Cartel? A Comment on the Notion of the Cartel Party, in: *Party Politics*, vol. 2, no. 4., pp. 525-534.

Koss, Michael (2010), *The Politics of Party Funding. State Funding to Political Parties and Party Competition in Western Europe.* Oxford, Oxford University Press.

Lucardie, A.P.M., G. Voerman and J.K. van Zonneveld (2010), *Partijfinanciering in Europa; Een vergelijkend onderzoek naar regelingen voor overheidssubsidie en giften voor politieke partijen.* Groningen, Rijksuniversiteit.

Nassmacher, Karl-Heinz (1982) 'Öffentliche Rechenschaft und Parteifinanzierung: Erfahrungen in Deutschland, Kanada und in den Vereinigten Staaten', *Aus*

Politik und Zeitgeschichte, Beilage zur Wochenzeitung Das Parlament, 10 april 1982, pp. 3-18.

Nassmacher, Karl-Heinz (ed) (2001), *Foundations for Democracy; Approaches to Compartaive Political Finance*. Baden-Baden, Nomos.

Nassmacher, Karl-Heinz (2009), *The funding of party competition: political finance in 25 democracies*. Baden-Baden, Nomos.

Persily, Nathaniel (2006), 'The Law of American Party Finance', in: Ewing and Issacharoff (eds, 2006), pp. 213-239.

Pinto-Duschinsky, Michael (2001), *Political Financing in the Commonwealth*. London: Commonwealth Secretariat.

Saffu, Yaw (2003), 'África Anglófona', Manuel Carrillo et al. (eds), *Dinero y Contienda Político-Electoral; Reto de la Democracia*. Mexico, Instituto Federal Electoral, 119-137.

Scarrow, Susan E. (2004), 'Explaining Political Finance Reforms. Competition and Context', *Party Politics*, vol. 10, nr. 6, 653-675.

Scarrow, Susan E. (2007), 'Political Finance in Comparative Perspective', *Annual Review of Political Science*, 10, pp. 193-210.

Supreme Court of Canada (2004), *Harper v. Canada* (http://scc.lexum.umontreal.ca/en/2004/2004scc33/2004scc33.html).

Transparency International (2007), *Report on the Transparency International Global Corrruption Barometer 2007*, Berlin, , p. 8 + tabel 4.2. (http://www.transparency.org/policy_research/surveys_indices/gcb/2007).

CHAPTER 3

Lessons from the Past: Party Regulation in the Netherlands

Remco Nehmelman[1]
Utrecht University

Introduction

Dutch professor on Constitutional Law and former Judge of the Court of Justice of the European Union, A.M. Donner, suggested in a contribution to the annual Dutch constitutional conference in 1982: '*Let us postpone as long as possible the official recognition of the party system (in the Netherlands), because in its nature Law just brings regulation, and he who regulates, restricts.*' The Dutch legislator has taken this statement into account, because hitherto the legislation on Dutch political parties has been very limited. Now and then the question arises whether it is desirable to embed the special constitutional position of these organizations in the Dutch Constitution, but these attempts have also been unsuccessful. Although Dutch public law does not pay much attention to political parties, they are very important in daily political practice in the Netherlands.

The aim of this paper is to give an overview of the different discussions in the past on regulating Dutch political parties. Furthermore the aim of this contribution is to see if lessons can be drawn from the past discussions on regulating political parties. First of all I will give an overview of the development of Dutch political parties. Special attention will be paid to the question how legal doctrine criticized these developments. Secondly an outline of the legal discussion is given. In this section one will notice that occasionally the question arises whether political parties need to have a provision in the Dutch Constitution. Thirdly an inventory is made of the current legal provisions concerning Dutch political parties. Although these legal provisions in Dutch public law are few and far between, there are provisions which are important if one wants to participate in Dutch politics. At the end of this contribution some final remarks and suggestions will be made.

The development of political parties in the Netherlands

The amendment of the Dutch Constitution of 1848 can be seen as one of the most important constitutional reforms in the Netherlands; most of these amendments still apply. One of the most important was probably the introduction of political ministerial responsibility.[2] Before 1848 it was the King who was fully in charge and could not be held responsible in parliament for his actions. After 1848 '*the King could [no longer] do no wrong*', but ministers were held responsible for the actions of the King as well as for their own actions. The power of the Dutch parliament was born. Furthermore in 1866-1868 an important unwritten rule was vested in Dutch constitutional law. When a minister or the Cabinet loses the confidence of Parliament (especially of the Dutch Lower House (Second Chamber), the minister or Cabinet has to resign. Due to these developments the Netherlands became a parliamentary system.

Early steps towards party formation: the new 1848 electoral system
Although both rules (ministerial responsibility and the rule of confidence) can be seen as the most important constitutional rules which developed in the nineteenth century, in the constitutional amendment of 1848 two other changes were introduced into the Constitution which led to the early development of Dutch political parties. In the first place the fundamental right of freedom of association and assembly was guaranteed. This provision was further developed in 1855 in an Act on freedom of association and assembly. In the second place a modification of the Electoral system was achieved. Before 1848 (1815-1848) the 100 members of the Second Chamber of the Dutch States-General were elected by the representatives of the Dutch Provinces. In this period the King appointed the members of the First Chamber. After 1848 the system fundamentally changed. The members of the First Chamber where elected by the representatives of the Dutch Provinces. For the members of the Second Chamber general elections were introduced. Although this sounds very progressive, the right to vote for the members of the Dutch Lower House was granted to only certain groups of male taxpayers. Nevertheless, for the first time in the Kingdom of the Netherlands (since 1814) citizens were allowed to choose their representatives directly. These elections were organized on a majority system. The country was divided into 100 districts. The candidate who had the absolute majority was elected to the Second Chamber. This system of 'general' elections also led to the early development of political parties in the Netherlands. In the first few years after 1848 this development was

limited. The reasons for this can be found in the first place in the fact that the focus of (taxpaying) voters was limited to representatives of their own district (Elzinga 1982, P. 27). Furthermore certain provisions of the Penal Code still applied in the Netherlands, which, for instance, meant that political meetings could be forbidden by the Dutch government. This led in the period prior to 1848 to secret political meetings. The provisions of the Penal Code were no longer fully observed. Besides in 1848 the fundamental right of freedom of association was also introduced in the Netherlands. In the early period after 1848 one can see that certain so-called voting associations came to promote their candidates in the different voting districts. Moreover it was the liberals who bravely decided in 1846 to gather together in the '*Amstelsociëteit*' (Elzinga 1982, p. 24). After the constitutional amendment of 1848 other political movements followed.

Legal constitutional scholars in those days were very critical of these developments. J. de Bosch Kemper (1865, p. 177), a very well-known constitutional scholar, stated in his book '*Handleiding tot de kennis van het Nederlandse Staatsregt en Staatsbestuur*' that the voting associations were in his opinion oligarchies. Only a very few members attended the meetings of these associations, although important decisions, such as who would stand as candidate, were being made during those meetings. Furthermore he stated that the members of the boards of the different voting associations had too much influence on the members of parliament. In his opinion this influence was contrary to the fundamental parliamentary rule that members of parliament should not be bound by a mandate or instructions when voting.[3] These critical views on these voting associations were very widespread (see e.g. Vissering 1864, p. 260; Olivier 1876, p. 45). Despite the critics the voting associations transformed themselves into more solid party organizations. This resulted in the development of the first political party in 1879, the Anti-Revolutionary Party founded by Abraham Kuyper, a member of the Second Chamber and prime minister (1901-1905). In the following years other political movements (socialists, liberals) followed. The critical view of these political organizations decreased a little. Some scholars stated that the rule that members of parliament should not be bound by a mandate or instructions when voting did not conflict with the existence of political parties. J.T. Buys (1883, p. 454), a well-known constitutional scholar and professor (Amsterdam and Leiden), at the end of the nineteenth century stated that voters were seeking sympathizers and therefore political parties fulfilled a valuable role in society. Another famous scholar and professor of Constitutional Law (Vrije Universiteit, Amsterdam) at that time, A.F. de Savornin Lohman (1907, p. 397), demanded that there be a moral bond between voter(s) and representative(s). Nevertheless legal scholars were still suspicious of the new political organizations. Academic communis opinio was that these political organizations should not have too much influence in the relationship between the electorate and its representatives (De Beaufort 1904, p. 184).

The consolidation of Dutch political parties

In 1887 the Dutch Constitution was reformed again, which led to an even more consolidated organization of political parties. More citizens (men) were granted the right to vote. Beside taxpayers, other people who had certain signs of capability and prosperity (for instance PhDs) were also able to vote.[4] The enlargement of the electorate was an important incentive for the formation of political parties.

In 1917 a major constitutional event led to the firm consolidation of political parties. Besides the recognition of the general right to vote for all men and women, a new electoral system was introduced in the Netherlands. The absolute majority (district) system for elections to the Second Chamber was abandoned and exchanged for a system of proportional representation. This system still exists to this day. The system of proportional representation creates a direct relationship between the number of votes cast and the number of seats allocated to the parties in parliament. Under this system of proportional representation groups of voters (political parties) present lists of candidates; these lists are linked to a nationwide list because the total number of votes obtained in the country is of crucial importance and decisive as regards the number of seats in parliament obtained. The country of the Netherlands has therefore since 1917 no longer been divided into electoral districts. The country as a whole can be seen as one district with nationwide electoral lists of candidates and leaders. The system of proportional representation de facto entailed the recognition of political parties in the Netherlands (Elzinga 1982, p. 31). Parties transformed themselves into real oligarchies with centralized organizations. The introduction of proportional representation resulted in the reinforcement and firm consolidation of political parties.

This consolidation also resulted in a new era of criticism from constitutional scholars of the functioning of political parties. In the interbellum period it was mainly A.A.H. Struycken and R. Kranenburg, both professors of Constitutional and Administrative Law in Amsterdam, who dominated this debate. Although both stated that political parties could be seen as a precondition for a parliamentary democracy, both scholars also had strong criticisms of those organizations in the new electoral system. A.A.H. Struycken (1925, p. 21) criticized the emergence of centralization of political parties due to the new electoral system. Party leaders became too dominant in his opinion. R. Kranenburg (1928, p. 115) also feared that strong political parties would harm the common interest, which in his opinion should be dominant in a democracy. Despite this criticism, general opinion of political parties was positive in the period between 1917 and 1928. This changed however in the years to come. During 1928-1945 public opinion of the multi-party system changed in the Netherlands (Elzinga 1982, p.33-38). In this period confidence in democratic organizations, including political parties, decreased due to the economic crises and the emergence of national socialism. The Dutch cultural historian, J. Huizinga (1946, p. 42), expressed severe criticism of political parties, as is illustrated by his observation that "the party system shows daily that it is superfluous and inefficient."

This criticism of the functioning of political parties found broad resonance. Even the prime minister in the 1930s, H. Colijn (1940, p.48) (Anti-Revolutionary Party), was not in favour of the increasing influence of political groups. Others were even more sceptical. They had especially strong feelings against anti-democratic political movements such as the Dutch National Socialistic Movement (*Nationaal Socialistische Beweging*, (NSB)). This Dutch fascist political party was very hostile to other political movements. In its opinion, political parties crippled strong leadership. The NSB never gained much influence in Dutch politics before World War II. After 1936 existing and new political movements challenged the National Socialistic Movement. A famous constitutional scholar in those days, C.W. van der Pot (professor of Constitutional Law, Groningen) (1940, p.205), wrote in the first edition of his leading handbook on Dutch constitutional law that one should not be too critical of the electoral system on proportional representation as introduced in 1917. In his opinion the objections to the functioning of political parties were grossly exaggerated. In particular,the constitutional provision which guarantees that a member of parliament cannot be bound by a mandate or instructions when casting his vote[5] was, in C.W. van der Pot's opinion, very important to protect a Member of Parliament. Although political parties can be very influential in Dutch politics, in the end it is (the conscience of) a Member of Parliament who is decisive in a parliamentary vote.

During the war period (1940-1945) criticisms were made of the system of political parties. After the war a new national unity was to be brought about, without a diverse landscape of political parties. Despite the criticism of the party system, very quickly after the War the old political parties were re-established. This was proven by the fact that the main political movements were still present in Dutch society. Due to the fact that in the first period after 1945 the governments were very stable, political parties were accepted by Dutch society. Although they were accepted, they ought not to be given too many privileges in the opinion of constitutional scholars. A bottom-up approach was therefore much appreciated for those organizations. Political parties should evolve from the population itself. Political parties were seen as the hinge between the electorate and the representatives (Van Raalte 1958, p.5-9). This bottom-up approach in which political parties were seen as civil organizations became the dominant doctrine after 1945. The state should not have too much influence on political parties, let alone regulate those organizations.

Proposals for the regulation of political parties

Since 1848 many attempts have been made to regulate political parties in one way or the other. These attempts can be divided into four questions: first, whether a special provision for political parties in the Dutch constitution is desirable or not; second, whether the organization of political parties should be regulated; third, whether there should be a legal provision to ban political parties; and, finally, whetherf there should be a law which regulated the finances of political parties. Due to the fact that political parties were for long very controversial, all proposals were of a defensive or even repressive nature. The influence of political parties in public decision-making should be restricted. In this section we will discuss the proposals that have been made to regulate certain topics concerning Dutch political parties such as (1) limiting the influence of political parties in nominating candidates; (2) a legal provision on the banning of certain political parties; (3) a provision for political parties in the Dutch Constitution; and finally (4) a (special) Act for political parties.

Early proposals: the nomination of candidates

It was J. de Bosch Kemper (1865, p.178) (Member of the Second Chamber (Liberal) and social scientist) who in 1865 formulated probably the first proposal for a legal provision to restrict the influence of political parties on the nomination of political candidates. In his opinion political parties had too much influence in putting their favourites on the nomination list; he proposed legally to guarantee every voter the right to nominate his own (political) candidate. In 1918 A.A.H. Struycken (1917-1918, p. 401-404) strongly recommended introducing a certain provision in the Electoral Act on political parties concerning their role with regard to the nomination of candidates. In contrast to De Bosch Kemper, in Struycken's opinion this competence of political parties should be legally formulated in the Electoral Act. Others dramatically went even further; he proposed abolishing all general elections (Harthoorn 1929, p. 150). Instead of those elections, each citizen should join (obligatorily) a political party. The general board of the political party should provide for parliamentary candidates who were elected by the members of the political party itself.

In 1926 and 1931 both N.J.C.M. Kappeyne van de Copello (lawyer and public prosecutor Amsterdam) (1926) and N. Kolff (constitutional lawyer) (1931) agreed with A.A.H. Struycken (professor of Constitutional Law Amsterdam) that political parties had too much influence on the nomination of candidates for parliament. From their point of view this influence of political parties was contradictory to the equal right of each Dutch citizen to elect the members of the general representative bodies. Only a small minority of the electorate were members of a political party. Why should only they decide who would be nominated as candidates for a representative body, especially both Chambers of the States-General. To restrict the influence of political parties on the nomination of candidates, Kapeynne van de Copello proposed a system in which each member of a political party could nominate himself; during a general election voters could state their preference by voting for these candidates, which would be presented on an alphabetical list of candidates rather than by party. Kolff was not in favour of the system proposed by Kapeynne van de Copello. He was not convinced that the influence of political parties on this issue would diminish. He promoted a system in which some form of regulation concerning the democratic structure of a political party was introduced. In his opinion it was allowable for the state to intervene if a political party misused the freedom of the organization of political parties due to the fact that these organizations were of public interest. Furthermore Kolff (1931, p. 165-168) was in favour of introducing some form of deposit if a party wanted to participate in general elections. The reason behind this measure was to prevent a fragmented landscape of political parties.

In the 1930s the emphasis of the debate on regulating political parties shifted towards the question how anti-democratic political parties should be prevented from rising or banned from the political process. In his inaugural speech in 1936, Professor Van den Bergh (1936, p. 1-22), professor of Constitutional Law (Amsterdam), paid special attention on this issue. Van den Bergh recognized that a liberal democracy in principle should not impose restrictions on the freedom of political association. Nevertheless he considered the banning of an anti-democratic political party to be justified if such party violated the principles of spiritual freedom and equality in law. In his opinion the High Court in the Netherlands (*Hoge Raad*) should answer the question whether or not a ban on a political party is justified. Furthermore another related question came up in this period; is it possible to end the membership of parliament of a politician who has strong revolutionary opinions? Although in 1934 a special (independent) Commission of the government (State Commission) concluded that such a provision in the Dutch constitution would be desirable, the amendment of Constitution never took place due to the fact that a two-thirds majority was lacking in the Second Chamber (Elzinga 1982, p. 42).

A provision for political parties in the Dutch Constitution?

After World War II the question arose whether a special provision in the Dutch Constitution or a special Act of Parliament should be made in which political parties were regulated. Shortly after 1945, a multitude of questions was raised concerning the need to change the constitutional system. The ideas of Kapeynne van de Copello and Kolff, which have already been discussed, were further elaborated in a report of a Commission on the 'League of the Constitutional State' (*Genootschap van den Rechtsstaat*) (Kappeyne van de Copello 1946). The constitutional problems in the Netherlands in the interbellum period were, in the Commission's opinion, caused by too great a diversity of political parties which were an obstacle to the efficient formation of a government. Furthermore these political parties, in the Commission's view, had too much influence and power in politics as well as in society as a whole. According to the Commission strong political leadership was lacking in the 1918-1940 period. At the end of its report the Commission suggested new radical ideas concerning the regulation of political parties. The Act on associations and assemblies (of 1855) should be amended in such a way that political parties were recognized by law as organizations. Furthermore one-issue parties should be banned, according to the Commission. Also, the statutes and practice of political parties should be periodically reviewed. What should be reviewed in particular was the question whether political parties complied with the Constitution and other Acts of Parliament. If not, a political party could lose its seats in parliament. Besides political parties which had fewer than 50,000 members should not have the right to participate in general elections. Finally a provision was proposed legally to end the situation in which a representative could be held accountable for his (parliamentary) actions towards the political party he belonged to.

Not only were legal scholars engaged in questions concerning the regulation of political parties. Political parties themselves were also participating in this discussion. Anti-revolutionary and Christian-Historical political movements were basically against any form of regulation concerning political organizations. The former Dutch Catholic Party (Katholieke Volkspartij (KVP)) however was convinced about regulating the banning of certain anti-democratic political parties. It also proposed a legal provision guaranteeing the transparency of the proceedings of political parties (J.J. de Jong 1957, p. 40). In 1950 C.H. Rutten (1950, p. 17-25) summarized the ideas of the Dutch Catholics as follows:

> '*Given the very specific and partly public character of political parties and the fact that they can employ constructive as well as destructive activities in terms of our Constitution, legislation on political parties must be considered necessary.*'

The Social Democrats had a different approach towards the discussion on political parties. In their opinion it was not the increasing political influence of political parties that was a reason to regulate those organizations, but the fundamental function of the party system should be the motivation to do so (Van der Goes 1945, p. 62-65). M. Van der Goes Naters, a leading party member of the Dutch Social Democrats, felt that a strong party system was essential for a 'healthy' structure of the State'. In his opinion the disadvantageous side of the functioning of political parties was not a reason to eliminate the party system as a whole. His answer was to give political parties public status in an Act on political parties, in which transparency and supervision would be included. In this Act all kind of provisions would be regulated; supervision by the Civil courts would be noteworthy and for disciplinary measures concerning conflicts with Members of Parliament a special Honorary Court should be established. In 1950 a special Commission of the Scientific Bureau of the Social Democrats (*Wiarda Beckmannstichting*) (1950, p. 674-700) came to the same conclusions, although that Commission above all emphasized that a political party should be obliged to have an internal democratic structure. In the Commission's opinion such an obligation would be the best provision for discouraging political parties with anti-democratic purposes.

These different ideas on the regulation of political parties from legal scholars as well as from political parties themselves led to special attention being given to this topic in the different State Commissions which were constituted in the 1950s. Firstly the State Commission on Constitutional reform (1950 p. 55), so named by its Chairman Van Schaik,[6] proposed in its final report in 1950 to include a special provision on political parties in the Dutch Constitution. More specific this provision was to read that '*In the interest of a pure political will shaping, regulations can be made on political parties in an Act of Parliament.*'

The Commission explained its proposal as follows: Given the very important position which political parties in the Dutch constitutional state have, the Commission saw it as an anomaly that the Constitution took no notice of their existence. The Commission wanted to fill this gap by amending the Constitution in such a way that a new provision was added, in which is stipulated that in a Act of Parliament regulations could be made in the interests of *pure political will shaping.* Furthermore the parliamentary debate on such a provision should lead to formal consideration by the legislator of this issue.

In 1958 however another State Commission on the subject of the Electoral system and the regulation of political parties (1958, p. 21-29) came to a negative conclusion on the question whether special legal provisions on political parties were necessary. A legal provision on banning political parties was considered inappropriate. Furthermore regulations on the transparency of party funding (subsidy) were also not necessary because the Commission had not noticed any form of abuse on this issue. Besides the Commission also did not want to take any legal measures concerning the internal organization structure of political parties. The nomination of candidates for Parliament should not be regulated because political parties, in the eyes of the Commission, did not have a monopoly on nominating candidates. The Commission (State Commission on the subject of the Electoral system and the regulation of political parties 1958, p. 21-29) concluded therefore that introducing legislation relating to political parties was altogether not sufficiently justified.

In 1966 a draft proposal on a new Dutch Constitution was made by several leading constitutional scholars (Ministerie van Binnenlands Zaken 1966). They came to the same conclusion as the State Commission on the Electoral system and the regulation of political parties of 1958. A minority of another State Commission on the (Dutch) Constitution and the Electoral Law (1971) proposed a Constitutional provision on political parties. However the majority of this Commission concluded that such a provision would not be of much help because it could not be achieved and furthermore was not desirable. The (majority of the) Commission had serious objections to a general Act concerning political parties because such an Act could lead to a limitation on the freedom of political association and the risk that the rights of political minorities would not be sufficiently guaranteed (Van den Brink 1959 and Boukema 1968).

During the Parliamentary debate on the Constitutional reform of the Dutch Constitution of 1983, Members of the Social Democrat group (Partij van de Arbeid, the Dutch Labour Party) in particular insisted on guaranteeing the functioning of political parties in the Constitution with the aim of securing free political will (Dutch Parliamentary Documents, Handelingen der Tweede Kamer, 1979-1980, *Kamerstukken*, nr. 14 222, nr. 11, p. 4.). The Minister of Internal relations refused to do so. In his opinion the special nature of public interference with political parties was already sufficiently insured by the adoption of the fundamental right of association and assembly in the (new) Constitution. Therefore a specific Constitutional guarantee for political parties was not necessary, according to the minister (Dutch Parliamentary Documents, Handelingen der Tweede Kamer, 1979-1980, *Kamerstukken*, nr. 14 222, nr. 11, p. 5).

Although since 1983 several important (State) Commissions have written reports on constitutional reform in the Netherlands, no fundamental amendments have been proposed to the regulation on political parties.[7] An exception is the subject of the funding of political parties. Since 1999 a special Act on State funding of political parties has been passed (see below). In 2009 a new State Commission on the Dutch Constitution was set up. Although the former government initially gave the Commission the task of also examining whether a special constitutional provision on political parties is or is not necessary, in the final instructions this question was deleted.

Recently new political parties have arisen in the Netherlands and have won seats in the Second Chamber. After the *Lijst Pim Fortuyn* (LPF), which in the general elections of 2002 won 26 seats in the Second Chamber, in 2010 the *Partij van de Vrijheid* (Party for Freedom - PVV) was the winner during the June elections. The PVV, with Geert Wilders as its leader, in the 2010 elections won 24 seats and in the last elections (2012) 15 seats in the Lower House for the Second Chamber. The structure of this political party can be characterized as non-democratic. The party has only two members; namely Geert Wilders himself and the Foundation

Friends of Geert Wilders. It is not possible to become a member of the PVV. A supporter can only make a donation to it. Although Wilders does not do anything illegal, in the recent discussion one may note criticism of this clever use of a loophole in current Dutch legislation.[8] In my opinion it might be considered to modify the Dutch Civil Code or the Electoral Act such that a political party must allow supporters of the party to become members. While such an amendment infringes the right of freedom of association of the party itself, it would at the same time guarantee individuals the right to become a member of the political party they support. Furthermore a membership organization would enable the creation of an internal system of checks and balances, by which members of the general assembly of the party can hold the leadership accountable.

In conclusion, since 1848 several attempts have been made to regulate political parties in the Netherlands. In the period after World War II the discussion focussed on the question whether these organizations should be regulated in the Dutch Constitution or in a special Act on political parties. None of these attempts have resulted in legislation. Dutch political parties are mainly dominated by civil law and their own statutes.

Existing regulations on political parties

It thus may seem that few, if any, legal provisions for parties exists in the Netherlands. This proposition does however not reflect reality. Although Dutch regulation on political parties may seem scarce, there are Acts of Parliament which impose certain rules and privileges on political parties (Drexhage & Nehmelman 2010). In a (negative) sense article 67, par. 3 of the Dutch Constitution can be seen as an important rule for political parties not to intervene in the mandate of individual members of parliament. This article reads that "*The members shall not be bound by a mandate or instructions when casting their votes.*"

This constitutional provision is indeed very important in constitutional theory; in Dutch political practice one often sees that political parties are still very dominant over individual Members of Parliament (MP). Nevertheless in the end it is the free conscience as guaranteed in art. 67, par 3 Dutch Constitution that will 'protect' the MP.

Besides this Constitutional provision the Dutch Electoral Law also contains certain important provisions in which the term "political groups" is used. If a political party wants to put forward certain candidates for a general election under a certain party name on the electoral list, the Dutch

Electoral Law requires (Article G1 (Dutch) Electoral Act). The party to have organized itself as a full legal association as mentioned in the Civil Code (Article 27, Book 2 Civil Code). All Dutch political parties can be characterized as such. This means that a political party is also bound by a considerable number of legal provisions regarding (fully legal civil) associations. Although a political association can also itself define many rules in party statutes, certain rules in the Civil Code are obligatory. These rules are, for instance, to have an executive board, a general assembly, to set out explicitly the purpose of the association in the statutes etcetera (Article 27, Book 2, Civil Code).

It is important to stress the general provision mentioned in article 20, Book 2, Dutch Civil Code. This article enacts a general provision dissolving and banning a legal entity, including a political association, if its activities conflict with *public order*. By court ruling a political association can be dissolved and be proscribed if it undertakes activities which are contrary to public order. The legislator has left much room for interpretation of the concept of *public order* to the judiciary. So far only one political party has been dissolved and proscribed; in 1997 the Dutch High Court proscribed the *CentrumPartij'86* (CP'86), an extreme nationalistic political party (Hoge Raad 30 September 1997, Ars Aequi 1998, p. 113-119, annotated by Y. Buruma).[9]

Besides the general legal provisions in the Dutch Civil Code, a small number of public provisions have also been made. Firstly the abovementioned Electoral Law has certain articles which especially concern political parties[10] A political party can, as mentioned above, put forward candidates for general elections if the party has organized itself as a full legal association as mentioned in the Civil Code. If a political party does so, other provisions of the Electoral Law become applicable. For instance the Electoral Commission can deny political parties to use certain names or acronyms on their candidate lists. Moreover, it is not necessary to participate in the general elections as a political party; a natural person can do so as well, although this never happens. If one wants to stand for election to the Second Chamber, one has to pay a deposit of € 11,250.00. This amount will be paid back if one obtains 75 per cent of the electoral threshold (usually around 45,000 votes) (Article H12 Electoral Act).

On 1 May 2013 a new Act of Parliament concerning the way political parties are financed came into force (Act on Financing of Political Parties) (Dutch Parliamentary Documents, *Kamerstukken II*, 2010-2011, 32 752, *Stb.* 2013, 93. See also Koole in this volume). Dutch political parties have received substantial amounts of subsidy from the Dutch government since

1999, which was regulated in the Act on Subsidising Political Parties. This Act on state funding for political parties provides rules for the funding only of parties which have seats in parliament. The funds are earmarked to be used for certain aims such as scientific research, organizing a youth section of the political party etcetera. Only article 18 of this old Act is stipulated that amounts of € 4537,80 given to a political party from a legal person had to be be made publically transparent, but know sanction was provided in the Act. The new Act of Parliament (2013) not only regulates the public subsidies political parties may receive, but also includes stronger provisions and sanctions concerning the transparency of party funding. It stipulates, for example, that certain amounts of private money (above € 4,500) must be made transparent to the public. This new Act was passed after the international organization Groups of States against Corruption (GRECO) of the Council of Europe strongly recommended the passing of new legislation on this topic.

Finally the Dutch Media Act has certain clauses guaranteeing the (free) use of public broadcasting. Political parties are given a certain public broadcasting time to promote their political statements (Greco, Third Evaluation Round, Interim Compliance Report on the Netherlands "Transparency of Party Funding" 2013).

Increasing influence of the ECtHR and the Dutch judiciary

Although the Dutch legislator has always been very careful not to intervene severely in the organization of the structure of political parties, in the last decade the increasing influence of the judiciary in questions concerning political parties has been noticeable. Not only has the Dutch judiciary been confronted with difficult questions on the freedom of political association, but the European Court on Human Rights (ECtHR) has also lately increasingly been involved in difficult cases on political freedom as guaranteed in article 11 of the European Convention on Human Rights.[11] It is obvious that the judiciary will become involved in questions concerning political parties if the legislator only regulates certain basic provisions, with vague terms such as *public order*, concerning such organizations. The legislator leaves it to the judges to fill in these vague terms. Nevertheless one has to consider that judicial interpretation can have far-reaching consequences. In the end the judiciary is asked to give an opinion on the concept of democracy. Courts have to formulate their vision of democracy. Is this concept only a formal one in which the will of the majority is decisive and every citizen must have the right to gain political power? In this concept pluralism is of great value. On the other hand a Court may choose a more substantive definition of democracy. Not only is the rule of the majority and the freedom to gain political power then decisive, but other elements of the Constitutional state, for instance equality, are important as well.

Case Law: Refah Partisi and SGP

Two recent cases; one from the ECtHR and one from the High Court of the Netherlands, are illustrative of the increasing influence of the (inter)national judiciary. One of the most important ECtHR cases on this issue is the *Refah Partisi* (Welfare party) case in which the Court had to decide whether article 11 ECHR had been violated by the Turkish State (Refah Partisi (The Welfare party) a.o. v. Turkey, ECtHR, Case No. 41344/98 (Grand Chamber)).[12] The Supreme Court of Turkey had banned the Welfare Party for violating the principle of secularism in the Turkish Constitution. Although the popularity of the Welfare Party was considerable, the ban was upheld by the European Court.

The Dutch judiciary has recently also been confronted with a difficult case concerning the limiting of the political freedom of a political party. It all started in a civil case in which a few Dutch 'pro women' NGOs (*Clara Wichmann a.o.*) requested – in the interests of all Dutch women – that the (State of the) Netherlands take action against the SGP, a small fundamentalist theocratic political party, with two seats in the Second Chamber (Oomen, Guijt & Ploeg 2010). The SGP did not grant passive voting rights to women. Therefore women could not be candidates for the SGP. However the Netherlands was a party to the Convention on the Elimination of All Forms of Discrimination against Women (CEDAW), article 7 of which guaranteed amongst others that *States Parties shall take all appropriate measures to eliminate discrimination against women in the political and public life of the country and, in particular, shall ensure to women, on equal terms with men, the right (a) to vote in all elections and public referenda and to be eligible for election to all publicly elected bodies and … (c) to participate in non-governmental organizations and associations concerned with the public and political life of the country.* After several lower court decisions the SGP lodged an administrative appeal against the withholding of the state subsidy to the Dutch Council of State, which ruled in favour of the political party. In weighing the fundamental rights at stake, the administrative court argued that the right to political participation is of more value in this situation than the violation of the principle of non-discrimination against women. In the same month however the Appeal Division of the Civil Court in The Hague ruled that the Dutch State should take measures against the SGP to end the discrimination. The Court stated that the right to equality had been violated in its essence. The High Court of the Netherlands (*Hoge Raad*) followed this conclusion. It stated that the Dutch State should take effective measures to ensure that the SGP would grant passive voting rights to women as guaranteed in article 4 of the Dutch Constitution. The High Court stated that these measures should infringe as little as possible the fundamental political rights of the SGP (Ten Napel 2011). On 10 July 2012 the European Court of Human Rights (ECHR) declared the complaint of the Dutch political party Staatkundig Gereformeerde Partij against the Netherlands inadmissible (SGP v. the Netherlands, Application, ECtHR 10 July 2012, no. 58369/10). The Court held that it had to refrain from stating any view as to what, if anything, the respondent Government should do to put a stop to the present situation. It indicated that it could not dictate action in a decision on admissibility; it was, in any case, an issue well outside the scope of the present application. The Court concluded that the application was manifestly ill-founded and had to be rejected in accordance with Article 35 §§ 3 (a) and 4 of the Convention. For these reasons, the Court unanimously declared the SGP's application inadmissible (Van den Brink & Hans-Martien ten Napel 2013).

An old idea as guarantee for political parties

The Refah Partisi case and the SGP case have been criticized by many (legal) scholars Ten Napel & Karim Theissen 2009, p. 363-392; Hoge Raad 2010, p. 492-504). Both cases illustrate that in recent years the judiciary has been filling out the concept of democracy in such a way that political parties have to accept that the free shaping of the political will also has its limitations, such as the principle of non-discrimination or the Turkish principle of secularism. Reviewing these cases makes one ask whether the time has come to include a specific Constitutional provision to guarantee the free shaping of the political will of political parties. Such a reform of the Constitution was, as we have seen, proposed as early as in 1950 by the Dutch State Commission Van Schaik. This Constitutional provision would provide for a special guarantee for political parties besides the already existing right to freedom of association. The advantage would be that the State (legislator, administration and judiciary) would have to be even more careful to restrict political parties than it already is. If the State (for instance the judiciary) wants to infringe the free shaping of the political will, it has to make it explicit why in a certain case such an infringement is necessary.

Conclusion

In this contribution I have tried to give a short overview of the past discussions concerning the evolution and regulation of political parties in the Netherlands. As of 2011 legislation on Dutch political parties is (still) very scarce. Scholars as well as politicians have been very cautious about regulating these organizations. Also most State Commissions concluded not to opt for a special provision for political parties in the Dutch Constitution or in a separate Act of Parliament. An exception was State Commissioner Van Schaik who in his final report in 1950 proposed to introduce a special clause in the Constitution in which *the free shaping of the political will* was secured. However the discussion after 1950 on regulating political parties was dominated by the statement as summarized in 1983 by A.M. Donner.

I began this paper with the quotation from Donner in which he stated: '*Let us postpone as long as possible the official recognition of the party system (in the Netherlands), because in its nature Law just brings regulation, and he who regulates, restricts.*' Due to the dominance of A.M. Donner in Dutch constitutional Law in the 1955-1985 period, his statement is still valid. However in my opinion one must place Donner's quotation in the era he lived in. Times have changed, also in the evolution of the system of political parties. Since 2002 new political parties have arisen in the Netherlands, and nowadays a political party, the PVV, with 15 seats (of the 150 seats) in the Second Chamber of the States-General does not have an internal democratic structure. In my opinion, regulating the right of an individual to become a member of the political party he supports should be seriously considered. Even though this is an infringement of the right of association of the political party, the importance of becoming a member of a political party is of such high value that it should prevail over the right of the political party itself. The internal democratic structure of a political party is the best guarantee of a sound system of checks and balance.

Furthermore I have argued for securing the freedom of the political will in the Dutch Constitution as proposed by State Commissioner van Schaik in 1950. Important recent judicial cases have shown that the balance between the freedom of association and contradictory fundamental rights is, in my opinion, not always well considered. A specific constitutional provision in which the individual as well as (political) association has, within certain limits, the fundamental right freely to shape its own political will would ensure that all public authorities, particularly the judiciary, must explicitly come up with a balance between this and other fundamental rights.

Finally, I would no longer postpone the official constitutional recognition of the political party system in the Netherlands. On certain elements special regulation is much needed. Although in its nature Law just brings about regulation, he who regulates not only restricts but also guarantees.

Notes

1 Professor of Public Institutional Law, Utrecht University, the Netherlands.

2 Article 42, section 2 of the Dutch Constitution reads as follows: *The Ministers, and not the King, shall be responsible for acts of government.*

3 This rule still applies in the Dutch Constitution, see article 67, par. 3, Dutch Constitution.

4 This provision was called the 'Caoutchouc-provision' because it was not clear who were defined by it. Caoutchouc is a sort of rubber.

5 Nowadays this rule is guaranteed in article 67, par. 3, Dutch Constitution.

6 Van Schaik was at that time vice-Prime Minister of the Netherlands (he was a member van Dutch Catholic Party (KVP)). *Staatscommissie ter herziening van de grondwet*, 1950.

7 State Commission on the relation electorate and policymaking (Staatscommissie van advies inzake de relatie kiezers-beleidsvorming (State Commission Biesheuvel)), Final report in 1985 and the Special Commission on certain constitutional issues of the Second Chamber of the State-General, Bijzondere Commissie Vraagpunten van de Tweede Kamer (Commissie-Deetman).

8 The critics came from another Member of Parliament of Wilders'own PVV namely Hero Brinkman, http://www.elsevier.nl/web/Nieuws/Politiek/268001/Wilders-Positie-Hero-Brinkman-staat-niet-ter-discussie.htm?rss=true (last seen on 4th September 2014).

9 Dutch High Court, Hoge Raad 30 September 1997, *Ars Aequi* 1998, p. 113-119, annotated by Y. Buruma.

10 The Electoral Law itself does not speak of political parties but political groups, e.g. Chapter G, Dutch Electoral Act.

11 Article 11 – Freedom of assembly and association
   1. *Everyone has the right to freedom of peaceful assembly and to freedom of association with others, including the right to form and to join trade unions for the protection of his interests.*
   2. *No restrictions shall be placed on the exercise of these rights other than such as are prescribed by law and are necessary in a democratic society in the interests of national security or public safety, for the prevention of disorder or crime, for the protection of health or morals or for the protection of the rights and freedoms of others. This article shall not prevent the imposition of lawful restrictions on the exercise of these rights by members of the armed forces, of the police or of the administration of the State.*

12 See also Bale in this volume.

References

Books & Articles

De Beaufort, W.H.F. (1904) Staatkundige partijen, *Staatkundige Opstellen.* Rotterdam: Nevens.

Van den Bergh, G. (1936) *De democratische staat en de niet-democratische partijen.* Amsterdam: De Arbeiderspers.

De Bosch Kemper, J. (1865) *Handleiding tot de kennis van het Nederlandse Staatsregt en Staatsbestuur.* Amsterdam: Müller.

Boukema, P.J. (1968) *Vragen van partijrecht.* Alphen aan den Rijn: Samsom.

Van den Brink, H.J. (1959) Een wettelijke regeling der politieke partijen,? *Socialisme en Democratie.* p. 608-617.

Van den Brink, J. & ten Napel, H.M. (2013) The Dutch Political Reformed Party (SGP) and Passive Female Suffrage: A Comparison of Three High Court Judgments from the Viewpoint of Democratic Theory. *Merkourios*, 29 (77). p. 29-41.

Buys, J.T. (1883) *De Grondwet, toelichting en kritiek, deel. I.* Arnhem: Gouda Quint.

Colijn, H. (1940) *Op de grens van twee werelden.* Amsterdam: Standaard.

Elzinga, D.J. (1982) *De politieke partij en het constitutionele recht.* Nijmegen: Ars Aequi Libri.

Van der Goes Naters, M. (1945) *De leiding van de staat.* Haarlem.

Harthoorn, M.A.G. (1929) Het Recht en zijn handhaving. *Rechtsgeleerd Magazijn*, Aanhangsel, 48th year.

Huizinga, J. (1946) *Nederlands Geestesmerk.* Leiden: Sijthoff.

De Jong, J.J. (1957) *Staat en partij*. Amsterdam: Calvinistische Juristen Vereniging.

Kappeyne van de Copello, N.J.C.M. (1926) *Vertegenwoordigend stelsel*. Haarlem: H.D. Tjeenk Willink & Zoon.

Kappeyne van de Coppello, N.J.C.M. (1946) *Staatkundige Hervormingen*. Rapport uitgebracht aan het Genootschap voor den Rechtsstaat. Haarlem: Tjeenk Willink.

Kolff, N. (1931) *Over den invloed van politieke partijen op den Nederlandsche regeeringsvorm*. Leiden: Vilders.

Kranenburg, R. (1928) *Positief Recht en Rechtsbewustzijn*. Groningen: Noordhoff.

Ministerie van Binnenlandse Zaken (1966) *Proeve van een nieuwe Grondwet*. 's-Gravenhage: Staatsdrukkerij.

Ten Napel, H.M. (2009) The European Court of Human Rights and Political Rights: The need for more guidance. *European Constitutional Law Review*. p. 464-480.

Ten Napel, H.M. & Karim Theissen, F.H. (2009) Taking Pluralism seriously: the US and the EU as Multicultural Democracies. In Labuschagne B.C. (eds.). *Religion, politics and law: philosophical reflections on the sources of normative order in society*. p. 363-392.

Ten Napel, H.M. (2011) Finishing the Work Begun by the French Revolution: A Critical Analysis of the Dutch Supreme Court Judgment on the Political Reformed Party and Passive Female Suffrage. *European Public Law*, 17 (11), p. 61-70.

Olivier, W.C.D (1876) *Van de Staten-Generaal*. 's-Gravenhage: D.A. Thieme.

Oomen, B.M., Guijt, J. & Ploeg, M. (2010) The Bible and the State of the Netherlands: the struggle over orthodox women's political participation and their responses. *Utrecht Law Review*. 6 (2). p. 158-174.

Van der Pot, C.W. (1940) *Handboek van het Nederlandse Staatsrecht*. Zwolle; W.E.J. Tjeenk Willink.

Van Raalte, E. (1958) *Het Nederlandse parlement*. 's-Gravenhage: Staatsdrukkerij en Uitgeverijbedrijf.

Rutten, C.H. (1950) Een wettelijke regeling der politieke partijen. *Katholiek Staatkundig Maandschrift*. p. 17-25.

De Savornin Lohman, A.F. (1907) *Onze Constitutie*. Utrecht: Kemink.

Struycken, A.A.H. (1917-1918) De evenredige vertegenwoordiging, de samenstelling der candidatenlijsten. *Van Onzen Tijd*. no. 34, p. 401-404.

Struycken, A.A.H. (1925) Kiesrecht. Bij de grondwetsherziening van 1917. *Verzamelde Werken, deel. I*. Gouda: Quint.

Vissering, S. (1864) Een dubbelzinnige triomf. *De Gids*.

Reports

Greco & Council of Europe (2013), Third Evaluation Round, Interim Compliance Report on the Netherlands "Transparency of Party Funding"[online] Available from: http://www.coe.int/t/dghl/monitoring/greco/evaluations/round3/GrecoRC3(2013)8_Interim_Netherlands_EN.pdf. [Accessed: 2nd September 2014].

The Netherlands. Commission of the Social-Democrats. (1950) Een statuut voor politieke partijen. *Socialisme en Democratie*. p. 674-700.

The Netherlands. State Commission for amending the Constitution Van Schaik (1950) *Final report of the State Commission for amending the Constitution.*

The Netherlands. State Commission on the subject of the Elector system and the regulation on political Parties Donner/Teulings (1958) *Final report of the State Commission on the subject of the Elector system and the regulation on political Parties.* Den Haag: Staatsdrukkerij- en Uitgeverijbedrijf.

The Netherlands. State Commission on the relation electorate and policymaking Biesheuvel (1985) *Final report of the State Commission on the relation electorate and policymaking.*

Case law

European Court on Human Rights, Refah Partisi (The Welfare party) a.o. v. Turkey. ECtHR, Case No. 41344/98.

European Court on Human Rights, SGP v. the Netherlands, Application, ECtHR 10 July 2012, Case no. 58369/10.

High Court of the Netherlands, Hoge Raad 30 September 1997, Ars Aequi 1998, p. 113-119. Annotated by Y. Buruma.

Hight Court of the Netherlands Hoge Raad 9 april 2010, *Jurisprudentie Bestuursrecht* (Jurisprudence Administrative Law), 17 (7). p. 492-504. Annotated by: R.J.B. Schutgens & J.J. Sillen.

Other

Dutch Parliamentary Documents, Handelingen der Tweede Kamer, 1979-1980, *Kamerstukken*, nr. 14 222, nr. 11, p. 4.

Dutch Parliamentary Documents, Handelingen der Tweede Kamer, 1979-1980, *Kamerstukken,* nr. 14 222, nr. 11, p. 5.

Dutch Parliamentary Documents, Kamerstukken II, 2010-2011, 32 752, *Stb.* 2013, 93.

CHAPTER 4

The Constitutionalization of Political Parties in Post-war Europe[1]

Ingrid van Biezen
Leiden University

Introduction

The constitutions of western liberal democracies have traditionally paid little attention to the role of political parties. In part, this is a consequence of a historical sequence in which the adoption of the constitution in many countries predated the appearance of political parties. In addition, the long-standing absence of political parties from national constitutions can also be seen as a product of particular normative conceptions of democracy, which have long been incompatible with the phenomenon of political parties. These conceptions tended to be premised on the association between democracy and direct rather than indirect forms of political participation and decision-making, and generally perceived political parties as a threat to the – supposedly neutral – common interest (Daalder 2002). Ultimately, it seemed that the phenomenon of the political party remained difficult to reconcile with democratic traditions that are based either on the notion of individual liberty or with those which embrace the existence of something like a general will.

In contemporary democracies, however, political parties have come to be seen as procedurally necessary and democratically desirable institutions, even amid increasing concern that their actual functioning may sometimes undermine the quality of democracy. The relevance of political parties for modern democracy has also become recognized increasingly in constitutional terms. Indeed, the period following World War Two has witnessed an ongoing process of party constitutionalization in European democracies, with the restoration of democracy in Italy and the Federal Republic of Germany, in 1947 and 1949 respectively, providing the most notable examples. This practice of party constitutionalization has since been followed in constitutional revisions in many other polities,[2] to the point where the large majority of European democracies today acknowledge not only the existence of political parties in their constitutions in one form or another but also that political participation, representation, pluralism and competition in many democratic constitutions have come to be defined increasingly, if not almost exclusively, in terms of party. Indeed, especially in many of the more recently established democracies in Southern and Eastern Europe that emerged out of recent waves of democratization, the very establishment of democratic procedures was often identified with the establishment of free competition between parties. Political parties were thus often attributed a pivotal role and privileged constitutional position.

Relatively little is known, however, about the process of party constitutionalization, about the substantive content of the constitutional position of political parties, about the regional or temporal variation between and within countries, or about the normative connotations of the parties' constitutional codification. As Bogdanor (2004: 718) observes, 'it is perhaps because the law has been so late in recognizing political parties that constitutional lawyers and other writers on the constitution have taken insufficient note of the fact that parties are so central to our constitutional arrangements'. This chapter partly addresses that gap in the literature by providing a cross-sectional and longitudinal overview of the patterns of party constitutionalization across Europe and exploring both the empirical and normative dimensions of party constitutionalization. In doing so, its aim is not only to contribute to a better understanding of the ways in which the constitutional codification of political parties varies between countries and over time, but also of the underlying normative conceptions about their role and place within the institutional architecture of the democratic polity.

Constitutionalizing party democracy

This section presents a descriptive overview of the process of party constitutionalization in post-war European democracies. By party constitutionalization we understand the incorporation of (an) explicit reference(s) to political parties, either as direct or indirect subjects, in the national constitution. The process is schematically represented in Figure 1, which depicts the chronology of party constitutionalization in post-war Europe. As can be seen from it, the constitutionalization of political parties was somewhat of a novelty in the immediate post-war period. By the end of the 1940s, only a handful of constitutions (Iceland,

Austria, Italy and Germany) contained references to political parties. In the subsequent two decades, only three more countries followed suit (France, Cyprus and Malta). The strongest impulse in the diffusion of party constitutionalization emerged from the third and fourth waves of democratization in Southern Europe in the mid 1970s and post-communist Central and Eastern Europe in the early 1990s: each of these new democracies enshrined the position of political parties in their new constitutions in the wake of the transition towards democracy. Most recently, Finland and Switzerland (both in 1999) and Luxembourg (in 2008) have amended their constitutions so as explicitly to include special references to the role and functions of political parties.

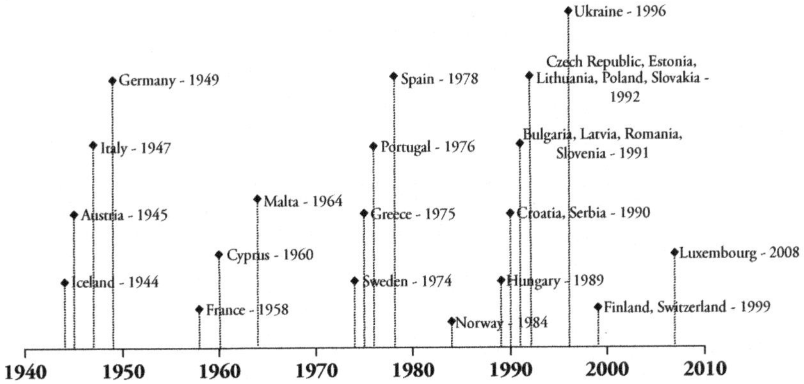

Figure 1. Waves of post-war party constitutionalization

The result of this ongoing process of party constitutionalization is that the large majority of post-war European democracies (28 out of 33) now acknowledge political parties in their constitutions in one form or another. It is in only in four of the longer-established European democracies (Belgium, Denmark, Ireland, and the Netherlands – see also Nehmelman in this volume) that political parties are not mentioned in the national constitution.[3] This codification of parties by national constitutions corresponds with a more general trend, as described by the various contributors to this volume, by which political parties in contemporary democracies are becoming increasingly subject to regulations and laws that govern their behaviour, activities, and organization.

Figure 1 shows that Iceland presents the earliest instance of party constitutionalization in post-war Europe. This occurred in 1944, when the country became formally independent from Danish rule.[4] It provides a good example of the indirect constitutionalization, with article 31 stating that:

> [...] In allocating seats according to the election results, it shall be ensured to the extent possible that each political party having gained a seat in Althingi receive the number of Members of Althingi which is as closely as possible in accordance with the total number of votes it has obtained.[5]

Elections rather than parties are the actual subject of constitutional regulation in this case, as the main purpose of this constitutional provision is to enshrine a principle of proportional representation for national parliamentary elections rather than describing the role of parties within the political system. The reference to political parties in the Icelandic constitution thus appears only incidental and the allusion to their presence seems to take their existence for granted. Nonetheless, albeit couched in implicit terms, the Icelandic constitution presented a constitutional novelty in Europe at the time, being the first to create an unequivocal association between political parties and elections and thus effectively to acknowledge the institutional relevance of parties in the context of a modern representative democracy. We shall call this type of constitutional codification, whereby political parties are acknowledged, implicitly or explicitly, as necessary institutions for modern representative democracy, the constitutionalization of parties as a *functional necessity.*

Similarly, the subsequent case of party constitutionalization, i.e. Austria in 1945, is one in which parties are equally treated primarily as indirect subjects. The Austrian constitution was adopted in the wake of the restoration of democracy following World War Two and effectively reinstated the pre-war 1929 federal constitution (which had first been adopted in 1920 following the collapse of the Austro-Hungarian monarchy after World War One), while at the same time rescinding the Austrofascist constitution of 1934. Despite containing a relatively large number of provisions referring to political parties, the Austrian constitution does little to elaborate on the significance of political parties for the political system or the democratic decision-making process and seems to take their necessary existence more or less for granted (Pelinka 1971: 265). Moreover, the Austrian constitution barely recognizes or acknowledges political parties as institutions in their own right, but usually refers to them in their manifestation as parliamentary groups, or in their electoral capacity (i.e. as *Wahlparteien*). The only reference in the Austrian constitution to political parties per se consists of a negative clause: persons who hold office in a political party cannot be members of the Constitutional Court (art.147.4). The Austrian constitution does illustrate, however, that the constitutionalization of parties is not exclusively a post-war phenomenon, as it incorporates a number of provisions from the earlier pre-war constitution. Moreover, the case of Austria echoes the 1919 constitution of Weimar Germany, in which the reference to political parties involved a requirement for the political neutrality of public officials, stipulating that 'civil servants are servants of the public as a whole, not of a party' (art. 130). As we shall see below, similar constitutional provisions, aimed at safeguarding the neutrality of the institutions of the state from partisan interests, can be found in many contemporary democracies.

The constitutionalization of parties in Iceland and Austria was followed by Italy in 1947 and by the Federal Republic of Germany two years later. The German Basic Law, together with the similar, but less detailed, article on political parties which had previously appeared in the Italian constitution, was one the first cases of what could be called a positive constitutional codification of political parties in post-war Europe, attributing to political parties a constructive role in the democratic system. The Italian and German constitutions thus, as Pelizzo (2004: 130) notes, 'represent a novelty in the history of formal constitutional texts as they explicitly recognize the constitutional role and relevance of political parties in the functioning of democratic polities.' Moreover, and perhaps more importantly, both constitutions establish that the constitutional relevance of political parties is not confined to the role they perform in elections. This stands in sharp contrast to the earlier cases of party constitutionalization in Iceland and Austria, as well as some later examples such as in Sweden, Norway and Finland, where the constitutional relevance of political parties is essentially linked to their electoral functions. The Italian and German constitutions thus recognize that political parties are not only necessary but also desirable institutions in modern democracies. We shall refer to this type of constitutional codification as the constitutionalization of political parties as a *democratic desirability*.

While the Italian constitution stipulates that '[a]ll citizens shall have the right to associate freely in political parties in order to contribute by democratic means to the determination of national policy' (art. 49), it is only in the German Basic Law that political parties, rather than citizens (as in Italy) or elections (Iceland and Austria), become the direct subject of constitutionalization. Article 21 – entitled Political Parties – regulates issues such as the freedom of political parties, their role in the formation of the political will, intra-party democracy, and the duty of parties to account for their assets. Furthermore, the German constitution does not tolerate political parties with purposes or activities antithetical to the democratic constitutional order, a provision which has subsequently provided the foundation for a constitutional ban on the descendants of the Nazi and Communist Parties (Kommers 1997: 217-24). More specifically, article 21 of the Basic Law, as amended in 1984, states:

> (1) The political parties participate in the formation of the political will of the people. They may be freely established. Their internal organization must conform to democratic principles. They must publicly account for their assets and for the sources and use of their funds as well as assets.
> (2) Parties which, by reason of their aims or the behaviour of their adherents, seek to impair or destroy the free democratic basic order or to endanger the existence of the Federal Republic of Germany are unconstitutional. The Federal Constitutional Court decides on the question of unconstitutionality.
> (3) Details are regulated by federal legislation.

Article 21 thus constitutionalizes political parties, and 'formally acknowledges that they have a genuine and legitimate function to perform in modern democratic government.' (Schneider 1957: 527). By assigning a key role to parties in the formation of the political will of the people, the German constitution associates one of the key principles of democracy with the institution of the political party and invests parties with the status of institutions under constitutional law. At a time when political parties had been constitutionally codified in only a handful of European democracies, the German Basic Law represented the most comprehensive set of constitutional rules on political parties (Tsatsos 2002).

The practice of party constitutionalization has since been followed in constitutional revisions in many other countries, with many taking their cue from the German model. This is true in particular of the new (third and fourth wave) democracies, in which parties are usually the direct subject of constitutionalization and which in most cases have constitutionalized political parties as a democratic desirability. In most of the older democracies, parties tend to be constitutionalized as indirect subjects and are usually regarded implicitly as a functional necessity for democratic elections (see Table 1).

Table 1. Constitutional recognition of political parties in post-war Europe

	Parties are a functional necessity	**Parties are democratically desirable**	**Other**
Indirect subject	Iceland (1944), Austria (1945), Cyprus (1960), Malta (1964), Sweden (1974), Norway (1984), Finland (1999)	Italy (1947), *Latvia (1991), Lithuania (1992), Ukraine (1996)*	*Slovenia (1991), Estonia (1992)*
Direct subject	France (1958)	Germany (1949), *Greece (1974), Portugal (1976), Spain (1978), Hungary (1989), Croatia (1990), Serbia (1990), Bulgaria (1991), Romania (1991), Romania (1991), Czech Republic (1992), Slovakia (1992), Poland (1992),* Switzerland (1999), Luxembourg (2008)	

The only older countries to resemble Germany and the newer democracies are Switzerland and Luxembourg, which have recently amended their constitutions so as to incorporate political parties. In the latter, a new article was added to the constitution in 2008, which reads that 'Political parties contribute to the formation of the popular will and the expression of universal suffrage. They express democratic pluralism.' (art. 32bis) (Dumont *et al.* 2008: 1061).[6] This amendment was officially motivated by the perceived need to modernize the constitution in line with the political reality of representative democracy and a desire to underscore the importance of political parties for the healthy functioning of the democratic system.[7] In reality, however, an important part of the need constitutionally to codify their democratic importance seems to have been driven by the desire to provide a more solid legal basis for, and thereby enhance the legitimacy of, the direct state subsidies to political parties (Borz 2011). At the same time, the underlying logic behind the constitutional codification of parties in this case may be the basic principle of *do ut des* (Pacini & Piccio 2012): political parties benefiting from public funding (or other resources such as media access) should become embedded within a regulatory framework so as to provide a legal basis for both their privileges and obligations.

The differences in the nature of party constitutionalization suggest that significant differences exist between new and old democracies. In this light, it is important to observe that the pattern of party constitutionalization as sketched in Figure 1 corresponds closely to the waves which Elster (1995) has identified as waves of constitution-making and which Huntington (1991) has observed for democratization processes (for a more elaborate discussion see van Biezen 2012). On this view, Iceland, Austria, Italy and Germany form part of the first wave of post-war party constitutionalization. A next wave was connected with the break-up of the French and British colonial empires: the establishment of the French Vth Republic in 1958, as well as Cyprus and Malta on acquiring independence in 1960 and 1964 respectively. A further wave of party constitutionalization corresponds to the third wave of democratization in Southern Europe (Greece, Portugal and Spain) in the mid 1970s, while a in a fourth wave the post-communist democracies in Central and Eastern Europe adopted new constitutions after the fall of communism in the late 1980s and early 1990s.

This suggests that moments of institutional restructuring in post-war Europe, including the establishment or the restoration of democracy as well as the (re)establishment of independent nation states, was always accompanied by the incorporation of parties in the newly written constitutions. The constitutional codification of political parties, therefore, is usually a product of a (re)constitutive moment, which often occurs in a context of institutional flux. Conventional amendments, on the other hand, such as the ones we find in Norway, Finland and Luxembourg, constitute a rather unusual mode of party constitutionalization. That political parties, without exception, were incorporated in the very first constitutions adopted by the newly established democratic states is indicative of the ways in which party democracy is understood, be it in normative or empirical terms, by the actors involved in the democratization and constitution-writing processes. It suggests, as Kopecký (1995: 516) has observed in the context of the post-communist democracies, that among the designers of these constitutions a conception of democracy prevailed, whether conscious or unconscious, in which political parties are the core foundation of a democratic polity.

Dimensions of party constitutionalization

Across European democracies, significant variation exists in the intensity as well as the substance of party constitutionalization. The intensity with which constitutions have codified the position of political parties can be measured along two dimensions: the absolute number of constitutional provisions about political parties, which we may call the *magnitude* of party constitutionalization, and the *range* of party constitutionalization, which refers to the scope encompassed by the different constitutional stipulations (van Biezen & Borz 2012). In some countries, the constitution says very little about political parties. Latvia constitutes an example on the extreme end of the spectrum, with the current constitution merely stating that [e]veryone has the right to form and join associations, political parties and other public organizations.' (art. 102). Other examples of low intensity constitutionalization include countries such as Iceland and Luxembourg, cited above, where the constitutions make only a short reference to political parties and the scope is limited to a single feature (elections in Iceland; democratic principles in Luxembourg). At the other extreme, we find countries such as Portugal and Greece, which stand out for high scores on both aspects, with the constitutions containing a high number of provisions on a large number of dimensions, including the rights and freedoms of political parties, their internal organizational structures, access to public resources such as state funding and the broadcasting media, mechanisms of judicial oversight of party activity and behaviour, and so on. In other countries such as Germany, but also Croatia and Serbia, the constitutional regulation of parties encompasses many categories (i.e. a high range) but with a relatively limited amount of detail (i.e. a low magnitude). Finally, in some countries (e.g. Sweden), the constitutions outline the place of parties in a small number of areas (in this case the electoral and parliamentary arena) but in relatively great detail.

Although the range and magnitude of regulation in principle may vary independently of each other (except that the magnitude cannot be lower than the range), in practice there is a strong correlation between the two. In addition, the differences in the intensity of party constitutionalization seem to suggest that the distinction between old and new democracies plays a role, with newer democracies tending towards a higher intensity of constitutionalization than their older counterparts. These differences are corroborated by significance tests: the magnitude of party constitutionalization in the newer democracies, which includes the younger Southern European democracies of Greece, Portugal and

Spain together with the post-1989 democracies in Central and Eastern Europe, is more than twice as high as in the older ones. In addition, the constitutional codification of parties in the new democracies encompasses twice as many areas, with the average range of party constitutionalization more than twice as high as in their older counterparts. The difference between the two groups of countries on both the magnitude and range of constitutionalization is statistically significant at the .05 level. Also significant are the differences between countries with a continuous democratic experience, on the one hand, and those with an unstable (or non-existent) democratic history, on the other. The latter include not only the more recent third and fourth wave democracies in Southern and Eastern Europe, but also the re-established democracies of Austria, Germany and Italy. The constitutions of countries that have experienced a period of non-democratic rule at some point during the twentieth century encompass a range that is more than three times as high compared to the so-called continuous democracies. Equally, the magnitude of party constitutionalization in the former is more than three times as high as in the continuous democracies. The differences between the two groups of countries are also significant at the .05 level on both dimensions (for more details see van Biezen & Borz 2012).

This suggests that a non-democratic experience is a powerful driving force behind the constitutional codification of political parties. Indeed, the constitutions of the more recently established democracies in Southern Europe and Central and Eastern Europe as well as the democracies re-constituted in the immediate aftermath of WWII (i.e. Austria, Italy and Germany) tend to regulate parties significantly more extensively than the older liberal democracies on nearly all domains. The constitutions of the older democracies stand out for privileging the parties in their electoral capacity, which is clearly a consequence of the predominant mode of constitutionalization by which parties are primarily conceived as a functional necessity for the conduct of democratic elections (cf. also Table 1).

The newness of democracy and the democratic history play a role not only with regard to the intensity but also the substance of party constitutionalization. When they refer to political parties, what do constitutions actually say? A content analysis reveals that provisions may range from symbolic and largely unenforceable stipulations about the contribution political parties (ought to) make to the realization of important democratic values and principles, such as popular sovereignty or political participation, for example, to detailed prescriptions about the structure and functioning of the extra-parliamentary party organization, demanding that parties be internally democratic and structured from the bottom op along the lines of the classical mass party. Constitutions may emphasize the democratic rights and freedoms of political parties and their members, such as the freedoms of association, speech and assembly, while at the same time prescribing the activities and behaviour of the parties in the parliamentary, governmental and extra-parliamentary arenas. They may proscribe certain (anti-democratic) forms of behaviour or ideological orientations which are adverse to the democratic constitutional order and may establish a system of judicial monitoring of the parties' behaviour and activities.

For the content analysis of national constitutions we have a adopted an analytical framework of party constitutionalization which is based on four broader domains (cf. Frankenberg 2006): i) democratic principles, outlining the role of political parties in terms of the fundamental values upon which the polity is based, such as participation, popular sovereignty, equality, or pluralism; ii) rights and duties, outlining the parties' relevant democratic liberties, such as the freedoms of association, assembly, and speech, as well as their responsibilities, including their duty to abide by certain rules on permissible forms of party activity and behaviour, or ideological and programmatic identity; iii) the institutional structure of the political system, including constitutional rules that apply to the extra-parliamentary organization, parties in their electoral capacity, parties as parliamentary groups, and the party in public office; and iv) 'meta-rules', establishing the hierarchy within the legal order and outlining the rules of constitutional interpretation and revision, including those which establish external judicial control on the lawfulness and constitutionality of party activity and identity. Each of these can be further divided into several sub-categories, such that we arrive at 11 different categories within four broader domains (for more details see van Biezen & Borz 2012). The relative importance of these elements, as well as the normative importance attached to them, has fluctuated over time and also varies between countries.

A small majority of countries associate political parties with essential democratic principles, such as political participation, pluralism, or popular sovereignty. The first sentence of article 6 of the Spanish constitution, for example, states that 'Political parties are the expression of political pluralism, they contribute to the formation and expression of the will of the people and are an essential instrument for political participation.' With only a few exceptions (e.g. the Luxembourg constitution cited earlier), this type of constitutional codification tends to exist primarily in countries with an authoritarian or totalitarian past. This suggests that a preceding non-democratic experience is a powerful driving force, although not a necessary or sufficient condition, behind the identification of basic democratic values with the presence of political parties. The legacy of the non-democratic past is also manifest, and even more forcefully so, with regard to the identification of political parties with the freedoms of association, assembly, and speech.[8] Indeed, most of the new or re-established democracies insist on a clear separation between political parties and the state by primarily associating parties with basic democratic liberties and underlining the private character of party organization and ideology. The prevalence of this type of provision may in part be a consequence of the growing importance that the constitutional bill of rights has now acquired as the essence of democracy (Bellamy 2007: 6). However, it is also likely that, in post-undemocratic regimes in particular, the constitutional recognition of political parties in terms of fundamental democratic liberties should be understood in light of the desire to identify and strengthen a private sphere that is free from state intervention. Hence, in democracies with an authoritarian or totalitarian past, a legacy of the non-democratic past is reflected in the new constitutions establishing an explicitly private sphere of social life, guaranteed by a judicially enforceable bill of rights (cf. Shapiro & Stone 1994).

Typical of post-communist democracies in particular, the intention to maintain clear boundaries between political parties and the institutions of the state can also be seen from the many provisions which regulate the incompatibility of party membership with certain elected or public offices, such as the judiciary, the law enforcement and security services, and the presidency of the republic. The Slovakian constitution in fact explicitly requires as much, by stipulating that 'political parties and political movements ... shall be separate from the State.' (art. 29.4) By demanding the political neutrality of public officers, such provisions also reflect an attempt to distance the democratic system from the past regime, in which the Communist Parties exercised more or less complete control over the institutions of the state.

Seemingly paradoxically, countries which most strongly emphasize the parties' constitutional freedoms are also the ones which are most likely to constrain party ideology or behaviour, as is revealed by the high incidence of constitutional provisions which aim to regulate permissible types of party activity and behaviour or the parties' programmatic and ideological orientations.[9] It is not uncommon for new and re-established democracies to prohibit political parties that are averse to the fundamental values of the democratic constitutional order. Hence, in an attempt to safeguard the often still fragile new regime from extremist, insurrectionary and separatist parties, these constitutions usually demand that parties respect democratic principles, as well as the national sovereignty and territorial integrity of the state. In doing so, they follow a general pattern whereby post-war constitutions typically reaffirm human rights in general, but also make efforts to restrict these rights in such a way as to make them unavailable to the enemies of constitutional democracy (Friedrich 1951: 18). Banning parties or impeding their activities with a view to the very survival of the democratic system touches upon the question of 'democratic intolerance' (Fox & Nolte 1995): how much tolerance should democratic governments exhibit towards antidemocratic actors in the name of preserving the governments' fundamental democratic character'? (see also Bale in this volume)[10] Political parties appear only qualified bearers of the democratic freedoms of association and speech: they enjoy their rights only to the extent that they themselves are the essential servants of the democratic process' (Issacharoff 2001: 313).

Remarkable in this respect also is the fact that nearly two thirds of the democratic European constitutions contain provisions which regulate the structure and functioning of the extra-parliamentary organization. Many of the newer European democracies in particular appear to follow what Janda (2005) has called a 'prescription model' of party regulation, seeking legally to mould parties to correspond to a certain ideal type and privileging the – arguably outdated – mass party model over other styles of party politics. Various constitutions demand, for example, that the internal structures and organization of political parties are democratic. This requirement was first made explicit in the German Basic Law (art. 21.1) and has since been adopted in a number of other countries, enshrining this condition in the constitution first adopted in the wake of the transition to democracy (as in Spain in 1978) or incorporating it in the process of constitutional revision (Portugal in 1997, Croatia in 2000). The Portuguese constitution is the most explicit and requires that political parties be governed not only by the principles of transparency, democratic organization and management but also by the participation of all of their members (art. 51.5). In other countries, such as Greece, Italy and France or the post-communist democracies of Bulgaria, Lithuania and Poland, the principle of internal party democracy may be considered to be implicitly present in the constitutional requirement that political parties either serve or respect democratic principles or methods. In Italy, for example, although the prevailing interpretation of the 'democratic method' (art. 49) has taken it to refer to the arena of *inter*-party competition, scholars are increasingly willing to consider that the constitution also provides a legitimate basis for the legal regulation of *intra*-party democracy.[11]

By requiring the parties to be internally democratic, these constitutions effectively take the 'democratic intolerance' argument a step further by requiring that the parties themselves must reflect a commitment to democratic principles if together they are to form a democratic polity. In a narrow sense, the doctrine of militant democracy applies to the external activities of anti-democratic parties or their ideological profile. Understood more broadly, however, it may also apply to the internal organization of parties, on the grounds that a lack of internal party democracy signals a lack of commitment to democratic values *tout court*. On this view, efforts to guarantee that parties will not disrupt or destroy democratic government should therefore not be confined to constitutional control over their aims and behaviour but also over the party organization itself. The Israeli lawyer Ygal Mersel (2006) has even argued that a lack of internal democracy should be considered sufficient grounds for banning a party. The perspective advocated by the German Constitutional Court at the time was similar, arguing in its ruling on the constitutionality of the neo-Nazi *Sozialistische Reichspartei* that a logical relationship exists between the concept of a free democratic order and the democratic principles of party organization (Schneider 1957: 536). The rationale for imposing a duty of internal democracy on party organizations centres on a substantive rather than procedural conception of democracy, according to which key democratic values such as representation and participation cannot be realized in the absence of internally democratic parties (Mersel 2006: 96).

Although state intervention in the internal affairs and external activities of parties is often justified with a view to protecting the very survival of the democratic system, it should be noted that it is considered controversial from the perspective of some theories of democracy (see also Katz in this volume). The arguments against are both practical and theoretical. It is not evident, for example, that democracy at the system level requires, or is indeed furthered by, parties that are internally democratic. As Sartori (1965: 124) famously put it, 'democracy on a large scale is not the sum of many little democracies'. In other words, the need for specific democratic values to be realized within the political system as a whole does not necessarily imply that the same values should be realized within each of its constituent parts. Moreover, the outcome of internally democratic procedures is likely to produce policy choices that are closer to the preferences of the party memberships than those of the median voter. Given the continuous decline in party memberships in European democracies (see van Biezen *et al.* 2012), internal democracy is thus less and less likely to represent 'the will of the people'. Furthermore, from a conception of democracy which centres mainly on political competition and the maximization of voter choice, rather than popular participation, there are no compelling reasons to impose internally democratic structures upon the parties as long as the system guarantees, in Hirschman's terms, sufficiently meaningful 'exit' options (e.g. membership exit or electoral defeat). From this perspective, it is difficult to identify the interest of the state in controlling the internal governance of political parties. Such attempts, Issacharoff (2007: 1460) argues, bring 'the force of state authority deep into the heart of all political organizations', and therefore raise serious concerns about the relationship between political parties and the state. More fundamentally, such impositions threaten to compromise the political integrity of the parties and their organizational independence of the state. Political parties can 'play a key role in providing a mechanism for informed popular participation in a democracy precisely because they are organizationally independent of the state.' (Issacharoff 2007: 1461) The danger is that, as the internal life and the external activities of parties become regulated by public law and as party rules become constitutional or administrative rules, the parties themselves become transformed into semi-state agencies or public service entities, with a corresponding weakening of their own internal organizational autonomy (Bartolini & Mair 2001).

An additional consequence of increased state intervention in party politics by legal rules is the enhanced position of the courts, as the primary locus of accountability and adjudication is shifted from the internal organs of the party towards the judiciary. In other words, the constitutionalization of parties, and indeed their regulation more generally, may contribute to the increased judicialization of party politics. The role of the courts in monitoring the constitutionality and lawfulness of party activity and behaviour appears firmly anchored: over 40 per cent of European democracies have constitutionally enshrined a form of judicial oversight over the parties. A more important role for the courts corresponds to a general post-war trend by which the notion that the courts, rather than the legislative or executive authorities, should be the ultimate guardians of the constitution and its values took hold in continental Europe (Friedrich 1951: 20). In the various restored democracies after WII (e.g. Germany and Italy)

Constitutional Courts were established as a mechanism of *ex post* judicial review of legislation, a model which has since been followed by many of the polities established in more recent waves of democratization (Brunner 1992). This makes the courts rather unique among the democratic organs of government today in having been accorded legitimacy by virtue of the fact that they are not political, and therefore presumably neutral servants of the law (Shapiro and Stone Sweet 2002: 3). The judicialization of party politics is reflected in the mechanisms that many of the contemporary – mostly post-authoritarian and post-communist – democracies have established for monitoring party activity and behaviour, by assigning this prerogative, as well as the power to dissolve or ban parties, to the Constitutional Court.

One of the (unintended) consequences of the judicialization of party politics is that it externalizes the channels of political accountability by transferring the primary locus of accountability from the party leadership to the courts. It may thereby create a greater distance from the ordinary party membership in the process, which may constitute an additional challenge for parties in an era in which they are already faced with criticisms of their representativeness and responsibility. In addition, the judicialization of party politics raises concerns on an normative level which are similar to those emerging from the diffusion of constitutional review and an active judiciary more generally: these processes arguably undermine fundamental principles of democracy by effectively transferring powers from representative to non-representative institutions (cf. Shapiro 2003: 64-73). Although the courts may sometimes act as a powerful constraint on the possible undemocratic or anti-competitive behaviour of political parties, the legal regulation of parties evokes anxieties not only about the state centralization and control of political participation and public life, but also about the democratic legitimacy of transferring the ultimate decision-making authority on their behaviour and organization from the responsible organs of the party to a non-elected body of judges (Avnon 1995: 285).

Models of party democracy

When we further explore the various dimensions of party constitutionalization and focus in particular on they ways in which they are associated with one another, our qualitative and quantitative content analysis of the national constitutions suggests that three distinct models of party constitutionalization can be distinguished. Each of these corresponds to a particular conception of party democracy (for details see van Biezen & Borz 2012). The first model (the Party in Public Office) comprises the various categories of constitutionalization that are related to the manifestations of parties in their capacity as electoral agents, parliamentary groups or governmental actors. This model is illustrative of a more instrumental view of political parties and can be found principally in longer-established and continuous liberal democracies such as those of Iceland, Finland, Norway, and Sweden. As we have seen (e.g. Table 1), in these countries parties tend to be an indirect subject of constitutionalization. The constitutional importance of the parties is derived primarily from their role in the electoral process, as well as their manifestation as parliamentary groups or their governmental capacity. According to this model of constitutionalization parties are not necessarily recognized or acknowledged as institutions or organizations in their own right. Nevertheless, by creating an association between political parties and the electoral, parliamentary and governmental domains, this mode of party constitutionalization effectively signals that political parties are a functional necessity for the conduct of democratic elections, and the formation and operation of parliaments and governments. It thus reflects the inextricable and unequivocal connection that exists between political parties and some of the democratic structures fundamental to modern representative democracy, and the reality of party government

In contrast, in the second model (Defending Democracy), parties are seen essentially as permanent extra-parliamentary organizations rather than primarily as electoral, parliamentary or governmental institutions. Here, the constitutionalization of political parties serves primarily to safeguard the continued existence of democracy. We find this model in most of the newly established or re-established democracies. As the bulk of European democracies have witnessed some form of democratic rupture in the past, it should come as no surprise that this is the dominant mode of party constitutionalization in Europe. The German Basic Law perhaps embodies the best-known example, but the model also applies to all of the post-communist democracies. In an attempt to defend the new democratic regime from insurrectionary and separatist parties, these constitutions demand that parties respect democratic principles, as well as the national sovereignty and territorial integrity of the state. As a legacy of their non-democratic past, these countries are keen to underscore the constitutional freedoms of the parties. At the same time, however, they tend rigorously to curtail the conduct of political parties, requiring that their activities, behaviour, ideologies and internal organizational structures are not adverse to the fundamental democratic principles. From this perspective, the state emerges as the guardian of democracy, with corresponding prerogatives to intrude upon the parties' associational freedoms and their behavioural autonomy. The courts play a special role in ensuring their lawfulness and constitutionality.

A third mode of constitutionalization (Parties as Public Utilities) conceives of political parties as a special type of public good. On this view, political parties are the crucial mechanisms for the realization of democratic values and principles, such as participation, representation, and the expression of the popular will. This explicit association between political parties and the realization of substantive democratic values implies an especially close relationship between parties and the state, as these values 'reside in a realm beyond the disposition of the individual and call for their authoritative enforcement from above – usually by the state' (Frankenberg 2006: 456). In order for parties to perform their unique democratic services effectively, therefore, they are to be supported by the state, which is reflected in the constitutionally enshrined availability of public resources, as in Portugal for example, which constitutes one of the best illustrations of this model. The conception of party democracy signalled by this model of party constitutionalization is one in which parties are quasi-official agencies of the state because of the critical functions they perform in a modern democracy, and in which the democratic importance of political parties justifies that they are being supported by public means as well as their privileged status in public law and the constitution. This model of party constitutionalization reflects a notion of parties as public utilities (cf. van Biezen 2004) and a conception of party democracy in which the state assumes a proactive role in supporting parties financially as indispensable institutions for the healthy functioning of democracy.

Conclusion

This chapter has analysed the patterns of party constitutionalization, demonstrating that a clear tendency exists for modern democracies to accord formal constitutional status to political parties. While the constitutions of western liberal democracies have historically paid little attention to the role of political parties and the constitutionalization of political parties constituted somewhat of a novelty in the immediate post-war period, in contemporary European democracies, both old and new, political parties are increasingly accorded formal constitutional status. Today there are only a handful of European democracies that do not acknowledge the role of political parties in their constitution. The European pattern thus trails regions elsewhere in the world, in particular in Latin America, where the phenomenon of party constitutionalization is both older and more pervasive (Zovatto 2006; van Biezen & Kopecký 2007). Because constitutions define the set of supreme rules of the game, the constitutional codification of political parties implies that the constitution acquires prominence in political practice as the explicit legal foundation and point of reference for the judicial adjudication of issues about the operation of political parties. This may involve questions about the admissibility of certain forms of party behaviour or the compatibility of certain ideologies with the fundamental principles of democracy and the constitutional order. This is evidenced, for example, by the increasingly prominent role of Constitutional Courts in the outlawing of anti-democratic or insurrectionist parties. It can also be seen from the rulings by Constitutional Courts such as the German *Bundesverfassungsgericht* on the constitutionality of certain forms of party financing. The constitutionalization of political parties, as indeed party legislation more generally, thus makes an important contribution to the judicialization of party politics.

Constitutions reflect the particular historical and political contexts within which they are designed. We have seen that the constitutionalization of political parties is in large part associated with waves of democratization, as newly established or reconstituted democracies, without exception, have constitutionally codified the position of political parties. Furthermore, a clear and significant correlation exists between the nature and intensity of party constitutionalization, on the one hand, and the newness and historical experience with democracy, on the other. New and re-established democracies are not only more likely than older ones constitutionally to acknowledge the relevance of political parties, they also tend towards more regulation in a larger number of areas, and thus towards more state intervention in party politics.

The increased intensity of party constitutionalization in post-war European democracies underscores that political parties are considered to be an important political and social reality, which are seen to make an essential contribution to the functioning of democracy. The predominant conception of modern democracy today is thus one that is unquestionably couched in terms of party. However, in most of the older democracies the mode of party constitutionalization tends to be indirect, emphasizing the parties' roles as contestants for, or holders of, public office. Here, the constitutional importance of the parties is derived primarily from their functional necessity for the conduct of democratic elections, and the formation and operation of parliaments and governments. In the majority of the newly created or re-established democracies, on the other hand, parties have acquired a more permanent constitutional relevance also outside periods of elections. One of the most significant developments in this regard was the constitutional establishment of political parties as the constituent foundations of democracy following the re-establishment of democracy in the aftermath of WWII in Italy and, most notably, Germany. More generally, the mode of constitutionalization in most countries with a non-democratic history tends to be geared towards defending the new democratic order. As a consequence, they underscore the fundamental freedoms that political parties enjoy while at the same time adopting strict views on the permissible forms of parties' behaviour, ideology and organization, and establish a large degree of external oversight of party activity by the courts. A third model of party constitutionalization reflects a notion of parties as public utilities. On this view, political parties are essential vehicles for the realization of democratic values and principles. Accordingly, the state assumes a proactive role in supporting them as indispensable institutions for the healthy functioning of democracy.

The constitutional codification of political parties has strengthened both their material and their ideational position within the political system. As one of the important consequences of their incorporation in national constitutions, alongside the development of extensive legal frameworks of party regulation, the institutional relevance of political parties has now been firmly anchored within the overall architecture of most modern democratic systems. Their constitutionally enshrined position implies not only that, in comparison to other organizations, parties are bound by tighter restrictions but also that they have been endowed with special privileges. The parties' constitutional relevance not only justifies state support, but also effectively gives them an official status as part of the state: by being given constitutional status, political parties are granted explicit recognition to the institutional importance of democracy (Avnon 1995: 298).

Indeed, according to the German constitutional lawyer and former Constitutional Court Justice, Gerhard Leibholz, the constitutional codification of political parties signalled a revolutionary change, from both an empirical and a normative point of view, which ultimately reflects a fundamental transformation of the nature of democracy itself, from representative liberal democracy to a party state (*Parteienstaat*), which is built on parties as the central institutional mechanisms of political integration. As early as in the late 1950s, Leibholz (1958: 78-93) argued that the constitutionalization of political parties effectively legitimizes the existence of party democracy and transforms political parties from societal organizations into institutions that form part of the official fabric of the democratic state. In the same vein, the German Constitutional Court has affirmed that political parties are more than mere socio-political organizations; they are also the integral and necessary units of the constitutional order. This clearly resonates with a more recent argument advanced by Katz and Mair (1995; 2009) that recent processes of party organizational transformation and adaptation reflect a movement of political parties towards the state and their concomitant embedding within the institutional structures of the state. In this sense, the constitutionalization of parties appears to parallel a more general trend by which the relationship between the parties and the state increases in strength, while the links between parties and civil society become progressively weaker.

The increased incidence of party constitutionalization in modern democracies attests not only to changed historical contexts and different empirical realities but also to changes in ideas and normative beliefs about parties and democracy. It has consolidated both the empirical reality of modern party government and the normative belief that parties are indispensible for democracy. Unlike in earlier epochs, political parties today have become fixed as permanent and often privileged structures of political representation in representative democracies. Furthermore, the existence of political parties is no longer necessarily seen as incompatible with predominant conceptions of democracy. Instead, modern constitutions point to a more or less general acceptance of political parties as the necessary foundations of democratic politics. Finally, it suggests that not only have conceptions of democracy changed but also those of the parties themselves, in that parties are no longer primarily private associations (albeit ones which fulfil important public functions) but to an important extent also public institutions or even semi-state agencies (Katz & Mair 2009), or at least organizations whose public role has become so important that it warrants their formal codification as permanent features of the institutional architecture of representative democracy. It remains to be seen if, and to what extent, the judicialization of party politics further exacerbates the already pronounced tension between the parties' enhanced position as public institutions and their weakening capacity as societal agents of democratic representation.

Notes

1 This chapter is an updated version and merger of several parts of two earlier pieces (van Biezen 2012; van Biezen & Borz 2012).

2 Including the European Union. The Lisbon Treaty places political parties prominently in Part II (Provisions on Democratic Principles), stipulating that 'Political parties at European contribute to forming European political awareness and to expressing the will of citizens of the Union.' (art. 8 A.4)

3 The UK does not have a written constitution codified in a single document and has therefore been excluded from this analysis.

4 Iceland is included in our analysis of *post*-war European constitutions because it forms part of the second wave of democratization and because, together with Austria, Italy and Germany, it can be seen to belong to the first wave of party constitutionalization (see van Biezen 2012).

5 Unless otherwise indicated, all translations are from Gisbert H. Flanz (ed.) (2004), *Constitutions of the Countries of the World.* New York: Oceana Publications.

6 Art. 137 of the Swiss constitution similarly reads: 'The political parties shall contribute to the forming of the opinion and the will of the People.'

7 For more details see: 'Proposition de Revision portant creation d'un article 32bis nouveau de la Constitution', outlining the official positions of the Government, the Council of State and the Committee for Constitutional Reform, on www.chd.lu/archives/ArchivesPortlet, Chambre des Députés, 22 February 2007; 31 August 2007; 13 November 2007; 29 November 2007.

8 E.g. Croatia: 'The formation of political parties is free' (art. 6.1).

9 E.g. Serbia: 'Activities of political parties aiming at forced overthrow of constitutional system, violation of guaranteed human or minority rights, inciting racial, national or religious hatred, shall be prohibited (art. 5).

10 Another often-used term in this context, coined by Loewenstein (1937) is 'militant democracy' (from the German *streitbare Demokratie*). The principle is constitutionally enshrined in the German Basic Law.

11 The question whether art. 49 it should not also be understood to apply to the internal organizational functioning of parties has in fact long dominated the debates among constitutional lawyers. It is with a view to the implementation of this interpretation of the Italian constitution that a number of law proposals aimed to establish minimal requirements for intra-party democracy are currently under examination with the Commission of Constitutional Affairs of the Chamber of Deputies (Piccio and Pacini 2012).

References

Avnon, Dan (1995). 'Parties Laws in Democratic Systems of Government', *Journal of Legislative Studies* 1/2: 283-300.

Bartolini, Stefano and Peter Mair (2001). 'Challenges to Contemporary Political Parties', in Larry Diamond and Richard Gunther (eds.), *Political Parties and Democracy.* Baltimore: Johns Hopkins University Press, pp. 327-43.

Bellamy, Richard (2007). *Political Constitutionalism: A Republican Defence of the Constitutionality of Democracy.* Cambridge: Cambridge University Press.

Biezen, Ingrid van (2004). 'Political Parties as Public Utilities', *Party Politics* 10/6: 701-22.

Biezen, Ingrid van (2012). 'Constitutionalizing Party Democracy: The Constitutive Codification of Political Parties in Post-war Europe', *British Journal of Political Science* 42/1: 187-212.

Biezen, Ingrid van, and Petr Kopecký (2007). 'The State and the Parties: Public Funding, Public Regulation and Rent-seeking in Contemporary Democracies', *Party Politics* 13/2: 235-254.

Biezen, Ingrid van, and Gabriela Borz (2012). 'Models of Party Democracy: Patterns of Party Regulation in Post-War European Constitutions', *European Political Science Review* 4/3: 327-359.

Biezen, Ingrid van, Peter Mair and Thomas Poguntke (2011). Going, going, … gone? The decline of party membership in contemporary Europe', *European Journal of Political Research* 51/1: 24-56.

Bogdanor, Vernon (2004). 'The Constitution and the Party System in the Twentieth Century', *Parliamentary Affairs* 57/4: 717-733.

Borz, Gabriela (2011). 'Contemporary versus Modern Constitutionalism: Political Parties in the Constitution of Luxembourg', Working Paper Series on the Legal Regulation of Political Parties, no. 9. Available at http://www.partylaw.leidenuniv.nl/uploads/wp0911.pdf.

Brunner, Georg (1992). 'Development of a Constitutional Judiciary in Eastern Europe', *Review of Central and East European Law* 18/6: 535-553.

Daalder, Hans (2002). 'Parties: Denied, Dismissed or Redundant? A Critique', in Richard Gunther, José Ramón Montero and Juan J. Linz (eds.), *Political Parties: Old Concepts and New Challenges.* Oxford: Oxford University Press, pp. 39-57.

Dumont, Patrick, Raphaël Kies and Philippe Poirier (2008), 'Luxembourg', *European Journal of Political Research*, 47/7-8:1060-70.

Elster, Jon (1995). 'Forces and Mechanisms in the Constitution-Making Process', *Duke Law Journal* 45/2: 364-96.

Flanz, Gisbert H. (ed.). *Constitutions of the Countries of the World.* New York: Oceana Publications, 2004.

Fox, Gregory H. and Georg Nolte, 'Intolerant Democracies', *Harvard International Law Journal* 36/1 (1995), 1-70.

Frankenberg, Günter (2006). 'Comparing Constitutions: Ideas, Ideals, and Ideology – Toward a Layered Narrative', *International Journal of Constitutional Law* 4/3: 439-459.

Friedrich, Carl J. (1951). 'The Political Theory of the New Democratic Constitutions', in Arnold Zurcher, ed., *Constitutions and Constitutional Trends since World War II.* New York: New York University Press, pp. 13-35.

Huntington, Samuel P. (1991). *The Third Wave: Democratization in the Late Twentieth Century.* Norman: University of Oklahoma Press.

Issacharoff, Samuel (2001). 'Private Parties with Public Purposes: Political Parties, Associational Freedoms, and Partisan Competition', *Columbia Law Review* 101/2: 274-313.

Samuel Issacharoff (2007). 'Fragile Democracies', *Harvard Law Review* 120: 1405-67.

Janda, Kenneth (2005). 'Adopting Party Law', working paper series on *Political Parties and Democracy in Theoretical and Practical Perspectives.* Washington DC: National Democratic Institute for International Affairs.

Katz, Richard S. and Peter Mair, 'Changing Models of Party Organization and Party Democracy: the Emergence of the Cartel Party', *Party Politics* 1/1 (1995), pp. 5-28.

Katz, Richard S. and Peter Mair, 'The Cartel Party Thesis: A Restatement', *Perspectives on Politics* 7/4 (2009), 753-66.

Kopecký, Petr (1995). 'Developing Party Organizations in East-Central Europe: what Type of Party is likely to emerge?', *Party Politics* 1/4: 515-34.

Kommers, Donald P. (1997). *The Constitutional Jurisprudence of the Federal Republic of Germany.* Durham: Duke University Press, 1997, 2nd ed.

Leibholz, Gerhard (1958). *Strukturprobleme der Modernen Demokratie.* Karlsruhe: Müller.

Loewenstein, Karl (1937). 'Militant Democracy and Fundamental Rights I', *American Political Science Review* 31/3: 417-432.

Mersel, Yigal (2006). 'The Dissolution of Political Parties: The Problem of Internal Democracy', *International Journal of Constitutional Law* 4/1: 84-113.

Pelinka, Anton (1971). 'Parteien und Verbande', in Anton Pelinka and Manfried Welan (eds.), *Demokratie und Verfassung in Österreich.* Vienna: Europa Verlag, pp. 265-327.

Pelizzo, Riccardo (2004). 'From Principle to Practice: Constitutional Principles and the Transformation of Party Finance in Germany and Italy', *Comparative European Politics* 2/2: 123-41.

Pacini, Maria Chiara and Piccio, Daniela Romée (2012). 'Party Regulation in Italy and its effects', Working Paper Series on the Legal Regulation of Political Parties, No. 26. Available at: www.partylaw.leidenuniv.nl/uploads/wp2612.pdf.

Sartori, Giovanni (1965). *Democratic Theory.* New York: Praeger.

Schneider, Carl J. (1957). Political Parties and the German Basic Law of 1949', *Western Political Quarterly* 10/3: 527-40.

Shapiro, Ian (2003). *The State of Democratic Theory.* Princeton: Princeton University Press.

Shapiro, Martin and Alec Stone (1994). 'The New Constitutional Politics of Europe', *Comparative Political Studies* 26/4: 397-420.

Shapiro, Martin and Alec Stone Sweet (2002). *On Law, Politics, and Judicialization.* Oxford: Oxford University Press.

Tsatsos, Dimitris Th. (2002) (ed.). *30 Jahre Parteiengesetz in Deutschland: Die Parteiinstitutionen im Internationalen Vergleich.* Baden-Baden: Nomos.

Zovatto, Daniel (ed.) (2006). *Regulación jurídica de los partidos políticos en América Latina.* Mexico City: UNSM/International IDEA.

CHAPTER 5

Party Laws in Comparative Perspective

Fernando Casal Bértoa
University of Nottingham
Daniela R. Piccio
Leiden University
Ekaterina R. Rashkova[*]
University of Innsbruck

Introduction

Political parties have become increasingly subject to legislation in recent years. The liberal principle of non-intervention in political parties' internal matters that prevailed across the European continent from the very emergence of political parties as organizations seems no longer to be the dominant paradigm. The several guidelines adopted by the European Commission for Democracy Through Law ('Venice Commission') and directed to state actors, although not mandatory, offer a clear indication of the degree to which greater intervention in political parties' affairs is currently being sought. According to the 'guidelines on political party regulation' issued in October 2010, "basic tenets of a democratic society, as well as recognized human rights, allow for the development of some common principles applicable to any legal system for the regulation of political parties".[1]

Not only has the regulation of political parties in Europe increased overall, but Europe is witnessing a proliferation of specific Laws on Political Parties or Party Laws. Yet, despite increasing state regulation of the life and statute of the political party, relatively little comparative attention has been given to the development of this phenomenon. As Janda observes, "there are not many systematic cross-national surveys of party law" (Janda, 2005, 6 and 2006b). Indeed, except for some references to the regulation of the establishment of political parties, works studying political parties and the dynamics of party systems say little about the most obvious and direct manner through which the life and existence of a political party is regulated by legislation. Müller and Sieberer (2006, 435) accurately note that party law has been the domain of academic lawyers, and "political scientists, while interested in the substance of party regulation in some selected fields, in particular with regard to election and party finance, have not devoted much attention to party law as such".

We argue that the proliferation of Party Laws across Europe (i) is an important phenomenon *per se*; (ii) has important normative implications concerning the position that political parties have acquired in modern representative democracies; and also (iii) has the potential to affect the organizational development of political parties and party systems. First, it is the role of political parties as main vehicles of democracy (Schattschneider 1942) and their centrality with respect to political representation (Sartori 1976) that, alone, warrants a study of the rules governing party establishment and party life. Additionally, Party Laws contain regulations on a variety of aspects of party organization, varying from their definition, composition, structure, programme and activities to specific rules about party finance and external control over their activities. The proliferation of such rules has been observed in the light of the increasing intervention of the state in internal party matters, which undermines the fundamental nature of political parties as voluntary organizations, transforming them into 'public utilities' (van Biezen 2004). Another reason justifying the interest in the study of party regulation in the Party Law is that often rules specified in, but not limited to, the Party Law affect the format and functioning of party systems; so, for instance, they determine whether or not we see few or many new political entrants (van Biezen and Rashkova 2012) and affect the nature of the competition and competitors (see chapter 9 in this volume on ethnic parties). Finally, as we will discuss in this chapter, there are differences and similarities in the regulation of parties both among states and across time. Thus, by tracing the variation in the constraints and benefits that parties are subjected to, we offer a useful departure base for studies interested in the examination of the causes and consequences of legal regulation, or their effects on party competition, electoral developments, and policy enactment.

This chapter provides an overview of party regulation in the Party Laws of post-war European democracies. Building on previous work studying the constitutional regulation of political parties, a rich and original dataset of party laws has been collected under the *Re-conceptualizing Party Democracy* project.[2] The chapter explores the temporal pattern of promulgation of Party Laws, their main regulatory focus, and shows how regulation through Party Laws differs over time and across countries. In doing so, it presents an overview of the content of party laws, offering a quantitative overview of the range and magnitude of party regulation, thus depicting trends in changes of regulation over time, insights to what aspects of the life of political parties are regulated most heavily and most often, as well as providing an analysis of whether there are significant differences in the evolution of regulation between different groups of countries. The final section of the chapter supplements the quantitative examination of party regulation with a qualitative case study on the party law of Spain. Drawing on Karvonen's seminal study (2007), the Spanish Party Law is analysed, emphasizing three distinct categories believed to have a substantive effect on the life of a party. These are party bans, registration and membership requirements, as well as judicial, legal or administrative sanctions. There, and notwithstanding the special concern of the Spanish legislator with terrorism, we find, as in most European countries, a rather open system of party registration; a prototype of what a party statute should contain which, as in most democracies, tends to be minimal; and, last but not least, both governmental (preventive) and judicial (successive) control of political parties. The chapter concludes with a summary of the data presented and a discussion of potential research directions for the future.

The proliferation of Party Laws across Europe

Before we describe the temporal pattern of regulation of political parties through Party Laws across Europe it is essential to provide a definition of Party Law. Indeed, as Janda remarked, "the term 'party law' is nebulous" (Janda 2006b, 2).[3] Scholars have defined 'party law' as "the total body of law that affects political parties" (Müller and Sieberer 2006, 436), therefore indicating by this term *all* state rules governing, or having an effect on, political parties as organizations. Indeed, state regulation of political parties may originate in different bodies of law, such as Electoral Laws, Campaign Laws, Political Finance Laws, Party Laws, as well as in Media Laws, Laws on Civil Association, national Constitutions, administrative rulings, legislative statutes, and (constitutional) court decisions (see Janda 2005 and 2006b; van Biezen and Borz, 2012).

As the core focus of this research is on the legal regulation specifically directed at political parties as organizations, in this chapter we define Party Laws (PLs) as those laws which make a textual reference to political parties in their title (e.g. Law on Political Parties, Party Law). Laws that are not limited in this regard – such as laws on political associations more generally, electoral laws, or laws on party finance – are not considered in this analysis, even though, as described above, they may also apply to political parties. Hence, legal documents which refer to, but are not exclusively devoted to, political parties are not included in our definition.

Of the thirty-three countries included in the *Re-conceptualizing Party Democracy* project, consisting of the independent and democratic European states in the post-war period (1944-2010), twenty have adopted a Party Law: Austria, Bulgaria, Croatia, Czech Republic, Estonia, Finland, Germany, Hungary, Latvia, Lithuania, Norway, Poland, Portugal, Romania, Serbia, Slovakia, Slovenia, Spain, Ukraine, and the United Kingdom.[4] Figure 1 provides an overview of the establishment of the regulation of political parties through Party Laws in European democracies, listing for each country the year in which Party Laws were first approved.[5]

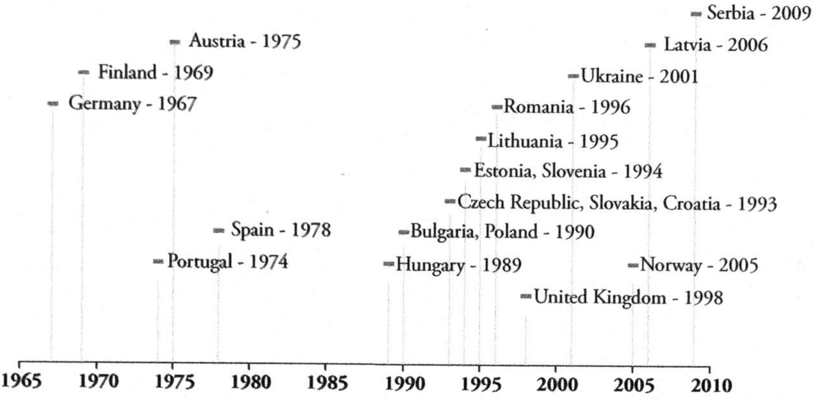

Figure 1. The Adoption of Party Laws in Post-War Europe

Figure 1 shows how the process of party regulation through Party Laws started with the establishment of the German Party Law in 1967. However, although Germany has been considered "the heartland of Party Law" (Müller and Sieberer, 2005, 435), it is important to note here that the so-called *Deutsch Parteiengesetz* was not the first, either in the world or even in Europe (Karvonen, 2007, 451-453). That honour belongs, respectively, to the Venezuelan *Ley de Partidos Políticos, Reuniones Públicas and Manifestaciones* (1964) and the *Siyasî Partiler Kanunu* passed by the Turkish Grand National Assembly in June 1965.[6] Still, it was only after the promulgation of the German Law on Political Parties on 24 July

1967 that this type of legislation began to proliferate on the continent. In other words, it was not the Venezuelan or the Turkish Party Law but the German Act which, bearer of the most comprehensive and detailed regulation, became a model to follow for many national laws on political parties, particularly in the newly created European democracies (Müller and Sieberer, 2006, 438; Kasapovic, 2001, 7).

As others have observed in relation to the "party constitutionalization" phenomenon (van Biezen and Borz, 2012; see also van Biezen in this volume), in the process of Party Law promulgation it is possible to distinguish three different phases. In this context, Germany, Finland, and also Austria – three countries which democratized during the first half of the XXth century – were part of the first wave of party regulation. Even if the latter two differ from the first one in length as well as in the detail of regulation of the parties' internal organizational structure,[7] all of them respond to the necessity of regulating the public finance of political parties, granted at the same time (e.g. Austria and Finland) or just a couple of years before the establishment of the Party Law (1959 in the case of Germany) (Piccio, 2012).

A second wave of party law-making coincides with the beginning of Huntington's 'Third Wave', clustering together both Portugal and Spain. Unlike in the previous 'wave of party regulation', these laws have a different political background. Here the main aim was not so much the regulation of public funding of political parties, which was introduced at a later stage,[8] but the necessity to control the creation and activity of the parties which started to proliferate in the new democratic environment. Indeed, as we will underline in the next sections of this chapter, in both Portugal and Spain the bulk of provisions contained in these first laws deal with the regulation of political parties as organizations *per se*.

The third wave of post-war party regulation is strictly connected to the fall of communism in Eastern Europe in the early 90s. In this sense, it exactly coincides with what some have named the "Fourth Wave of democratization" (McFaul, 2002). Indeed, the interconnection between these two waves is so straightforward that no East-European democracy has remained unaffected by such regulatory process since the passing of the first Party Law in Hungary in 1989. Moreover, in most cases the laws regulating political parties were introduced in the years immediately following the democratic transition.[9] In any case, and with very few exceptions, all these laws, modelled on the German Party Law, have brought together in a single legal document each of the goals examined above: namely, the regulation of both party funding and party organization. As shown later in Table 1, East-European countries have been more inclined to regulate political parties than earlier democratizers. One reason for this may be the lack of confidence of the legislator in the process of democratic consolidation. All in all, the Party Laws adopted in Europe after 1989 have all been enacted in East-European countries, with the sole exceptions of the United Kingdom and Norway. Unlike those enacted in Eastern Europe, the UK and Norwegian Party Laws do not include provisions on party organization, but they were rather designed to provide a regulatory system for party registration (UK), and for the regulation of party finance (Norway).[10]

The content of Party Laws

In the last section we outlined the evolution in the establishment of Party Laws across Europe. But what are Party Laws about, and which specific aspects of party organization do they regulate? Previous research has underlined that Party Laws serve a number of basic purposes: to determine what is entitled to be recognized as a political party; to regulate the forms of activity in which political parties may engage; and to regulate the forms of internal organization and political behaviour that are acceptable for political parties (Katz 2004, 2-3). Karvonen included the establishment of sanctions as a further analytical dimension of party regulation (Karvonen 2007).

In order to make sense of the vast scope of rules which lie in the Party Laws, we used the analytical framework first developed in *The Constitutional Regulation of Political Parties in Post-War Europe* project (see van Biezen and Borz, 2012). As with the analysis of Constitutions, the content of Party Laws is examined with respect to twelve main domains of party regulation: (1) democratic principles; (2) rights and freedoms; (3) extra-parliamentary party; (4) electoral party; (5) parliamentary party; (6) governmental party; (7) activity and behaviour; (8) identity and programme; (9) party finance; (10) media access; (11) external oversight; and (12) secondary legislation.

Democratic principles and *rights and freedoms* include references which define political parties in terms of key democratic principles and values, or which associate parties with fundamental democratic rights and liberties. For example, a discussion of principles such as competition and equality or mention of democratic values like pluralism, participation, popular will, and representation is coded in those two categories. The Party Law of Lithuania, for instance, stipulates that "political parties shall … assist in shaping and expressing the interests and political will of the citizens of the Republic of Lithuania" (Law on Political Parties and Organizations, art. 1) and they shall "enjoy the right to freely disseminate information in written, verbal, or any other way in their activities" (*Ibidem*, art. 18.1). The organization of parties is subdivided into four categories, each dealing with regulations of the party in its specific role – the party outside, the party in the electoral arena, the party in parliament, and the party in government. The *extra-parliamentary* category includes provisions regulating the internal operational structure of political parties. Among these are regulations devoted to the internal democracy of political parties, which refer to the election of party bodies, their accountability, the resolution of party conflict and procedures for nomination to public office, to name but a few.[11] The German Party Law, for example, stipulates that "Party members and delegates in the party bodies shall have equal voting rights" (The Law on Political Parties, art. 10.2). Reflecting the fact that most states have party law provisions about party membership, one of the main components of the extra-parliamentary party category denotes rules on the compatibility of party membership with membership or activity of other elected offices, the civil service, the judiciary, trade unions, or other public office. The extra-parliamentary party category further includes references to the organizational structure and the legal status and registration requirements of political parties. Electoral rules, campaign activity and rules on fielding candidates are part of the second subcategory in the organizational structure of parties entitled the *electoral party*. This category generally reflects references to the party in competition. The behaviour of parties in parliament in reference to regional and local legislature, the participation in parliamentary committees, staffing, and policy formation are subjects in the *parliamentary party* category. Here, all legal references to the conduct of the party in parliament are coded. Lastly, we have a category dealing with the *governmental party* which includes references on how national, regional and local executive are to be composed.

In the *activity and identity* category, the coding scheme registers provisions aimed at restricting or prohibiting certain forms of behaviour or certain ideological foundations of political parties. Many laws contain conditions regarding respect for human rights, the prohibition of the use of violence, the spreading of hatred or the use of undemocratic methods by political parties. The Spanish Party Law offers an example of the last as it prohibits political parties whose actions "univocally show a track record of breakdown of democracy and offence against the constitutional values" (Law on Political Parties, Preamble). Some states go as far as to prohibit the formation of political parties on ethnic, nationalistic or religious grounds. Indeed, the only country within our dataset to ban parties on ethnic grounds is Bulgaria (for more details, see chapter 8). In some cases, while parties are not banned for identity reasons, stringent rules exist that forbid political parties accepting donations from religious institutions, humanitarian or similar organizations. For instance, while the Bulgarian Party Law stipulates that "political parties shall not receive funds from anonymous donations, legal persons, religious institutions and foreign governments" (2009, Article 24), Slovenia not only does not allow parties to be funded by "state and local community authorities, entities governed by public law, humanitarian organizations, religious communities..." (2007, Art. 25) but it also imposes "a fine of €4150 to €20850 ... upon entities governed by public law, humanitarian organizations, religious communities ... if they finance a party" (2007, Art. 29). Such stipulations are in the *party finance* category. Due to the large number of financial matters pertaining to political parties, the category of party finance is subdivided into five further sub-categories. These are *direct public funding*, *indirect public funding*, *private funding*, *regulation of expenditures*, and *reporting and disclosure*. Naturally, the first two include rules about the amount, allocation and use of public funding, while the last three focus on limits, transparency, and use of private funding, as well as on rules of disclosure of funding and expenditure overall. A large part of the lawfulness of party activity is to be monitored by external institutions, such as a supervising authority or a system of sanctions. Provisions relating to the type of monitoring and how parties are to be monitored are in the *external oversight* category. An example of a clause falling in this category is the stipulation in the Polish Party Law that "[e]xamination of cases for ascertainment of non-compliance of the purposes and activities of political parties with the Constitution shall fall within the competence of the Constitutional Tribunal" (Act on Political Parties, Art. 42). Lastly, regulations pertaining to further legislation applying to political parties and provisions about the use of media by political parties are in the *secondary legislation* and the *media access* categories, respectively. The latter consists mostly of allocation and restriction mechanisms for the use of public and private media during electoral and non-electoral periods.

Data analysis

In order to quantify the extent to which different laws regulate specific domains, each Party Law was coded and analysed for references to the twelve dimensions of party regulation described above. How is regulation distributed along those categories? To give a preliminary answer to this question, table 1 presents a comparative overview of the *magnitude* of regulation of political parties that exists in Party Laws.

The top row lists the categories across which the coding of regulation is done. Table 1 includes the twenty European democracies which have adopted a Party Law. Each cell represents the amount of regulation a country enacts in a specific category in relation to the regulation in its entire party law (in percent), while in parenthesis we show the 'raw count' of regulation depicting the number of instances on which a country's law mentions the category in question. So for example, 24.1 per cent of the Czech Republic's party law is devoted to the regulation of the *extra-parliamentary* category, with 39 unique counts of mentions of the internal procedures, membership organization or the organizational structure of the party (all in the overarching extra-parliamentary category). In total, when we add all raw counts presented in the parenthesis horizontally, the magnitude of regulation in the Czech party law amounts to 162. This means that 162 unique mentions of characteristics included under our twelve broad categories were found within the law. To put the figure in comparative perspective, the magnitude of the United Kingdom's party law adds up to a mere 69 mentions. Finland ranks even lower with a magnitude of 50, while Germany, the country where party regulation originated, reportedly exhibits the highest number of regulation instances adding up to 304 altogether.

To ease the comparison between countries, the category in which a country regulates most heavily is shown in bold. We see that Austria and Bulgaria, for example, regulate most heavily in the *party finance* category, while Croatia, Estonia, and Germany, among others, put their regulatory efforts into the *extra-parliamentary* category. The UK, Poland and Estonia, on the other hand, spend half or nearly half of their regulatory attempts in controlling the *external oversight* of parties. Another observation that comes out of the data presented in the table is that the *extra-parliamentary* category is regulated most heavily in the largest number of cases. We see that 10 states devote most of the regulation in their party law to this category. Interestingly, 8 of the 10 states which regulate the *extra-parliamentary party* most heavily are post-communist democracies. Considering that the *extra-parliamentary* category contains regulation about registration rules and requirements which guide the establishment, existence, and competition of political parties, this is not surprising, as we know that a lot of rules attempting to combat the often high party system fractionalization in those countries have been introduced in recent years. For example, the number of citizens who are required to register a political party, which is in the *extra-parliamentary party* category, varies greatly among countries. According to art. 7 (1990) and art. 10 (2009) of the Bulgarian Party Law, "a political party shall be established at a constituent assembly by the agreement of at least 50 citizens with voting rights." In Croatia, the requirement is 100 adults (art. 6, 1999), while in Estonia "a political party shall be registered if it has at least 1,000 members (art. 6, 1994)."

The second most heavily regulated category, according to the data in table 1, is the *external oversight* category – it is the most regulated category in seven countries from our sample. What stands out is the observation that the *external oversight* category is regulated more than *party finance*. The latter is the most regulated category in only four countries – Austria, Bulgaria, Hungary, and Norway. This makes sense when we look at the type of regulations which go into the *external oversight* category. It consists of regulations relating to the external monitoring of the lawfulness of party activity, party organization, party finance, as well as penalties and sanctions against prohibited matters. In the Austrian law for instance, we find a clause asking political parties to "keep strict accounting of the use of the subsidies in accordance with their designation .... In addition, each political party receiving subsidies ... reports publicly the type of its income and expenses" (art. 4, 1975; 2003). Estonia, one of the few countries which take political parties off the registry if they fail to win representation in two consecutive elections, forbids political parties from registring under the name of extant or deleted parties in the party registry (art. 9, 2010).

The great amount of regulation of this category is hardly surprising, given the efforts of the European Union to increase the transparency of political parties in an attempt better to combat corruption. Related to this is the adoption of special Party Finance Laws in many European states, where matters of control, transparency, and accountability of the financing of parties are dealt with directly. Finally, we see that the two least regulated categories are those dealing with the *parliamentary party* and the *government party*. In fact, Latvia, Estonia and Romania are the only states which devote some attention to these categories in their party laws. One explanation for the lack of regulation in those two categories is that rules applying to parliamentary groups and to the party in government are specified elsewhere (for example in the rules of parliamentary procedure, the electoral law, or the Constitution) and thus are not part of the Party Law per se.

Another point of comparison of regulation among countries is the *range of regulation*. Although not reported directly in the table shown here, one can tell the *range* by looking at how many of the twelve broad categories a country regulates. To continue the example of the Czech Republic, we see that according to our coding the Czech party law has a range of 8. This is a relatively high range in comparison to the UK and Norway which have a range of only 5. The highest range achieved by any given country in our sample is that of Portugal. Portugal regulates in all but two categories.[12]

Overall, what our data show is that party regulation has seen a significant increase in the last decade. Among the 16 European states which have more than one PL thus far, only four states – Croatia, Lithuania, Slovenia, and Ukraine – have seen a decrease in the amount of regulation from their first to their current law (data on the first Party Laws not shown). The rest of Europe, led by Poland's rise from a magnitude of 34 in its first party law to a magnitude of 225 in its current law, reports noticeable increases in the amount of regulation.

As discussed earlier, this chapter analyses laws whose titles include a textual reference to political parties. The figures on the regulation of the domains presented above should therefore be understood as exhaustive with respect to Party Laws and not with respect to party regulation more broadly. Hence, the figures on the regulation of the Party Finance category presented in Table 1 do not rule out the fact that there may be other legislative acts regulating party finance. This is for instance the case for Romania, Spain and the UK, whose magnitude scores on the regulation of party finance in their Party Laws are equal to zero, but where the regulation of party finance is included in specific Party Finance Laws.[13]

Variation across countries and over time

So far we have looked at the percentage of regulation each country devotes to the twelve dimensions outlined in the coding scheme. While several patterns stand out, as the previous section contends, there may be patterns which remain unaccounted for.

A first overview of party regulation change is shown in Figure 2 (see below), which ranks the 16 European democracies with more than one Party Law in terms of how much party regulation has changed from the first to the last/current party law. Apart from the pronounced cross-

Table 1. Dimensions of party regulation by country (%)*

Country / Category	Democratic principles	Rights & freedoms	Extra-parliament party	Electoral party	Parliament party	Government party	Activity & behaviour	Identity & programme	Media access	Party finance	External oversight	Secondary legislation
Austria	2.2 (2)	2.2 (2)	4.4 (4)	0.0 (0)	0.0 (0)	0.0 (0)	0.0 (0)	0.0 (0)	2.2 (2)	**47.8 (43)**	34.4 (31)	6.7 (6)
Bulgaria	1.2 (3)	0.4 (1)	20.9 (53)	0.0 (0)	0.0 (0)	0.0 (0)	2.0 (5)	0.0 (0)	0.0 (0)	**36.0 (91)**	29.6 (75)	9.9 (25)
Croatia	0.9 (1)	0.9 (1)	**39.4 (43)**	0.0 (0)	0.0 (0)	0.0 (0)	2.8 (3)	0.0 (0)	0.0 (0)	17.4 (19)	33.9 (37)	4.6 (5)
Czech Republic	0.6 (1)	1.2 (2)	24.1 (39)	0.0 (0)	0.0 (0)	0.0 (0)	2.5 (4)	0.6 (1)	0.0 (0)	27.8 (45)	**37.0 (60)**	6.2 (10)
Estonia	1.0 (1)	1.0 (1)	**35.7 (35)**	2.0 (2)	0.0 (0)	2.0 (2)	5.1 (5)	0.0 (0)	0.0 (0)	22.4 (22)	21.4 (21)	9.2 (9)
Finland	0.0 (0)	0.0 (0)	22.0 (11)	0.0 (0)	0.0 (0)	0.0 (0)	2.0 (1)	0.0 (0)	0.0 (0)	24.0 (12)	**44.0 (22)**	8.0 (4)
Germany	2.0 (6)	0.0 (0)	**37.8 (115)**	1.0 (3)	0.0 (0)	0.0 (0)	0.0 (0)	0.3 (1)	0.0 (0)	36.2 (110)	20.1 (61)	2.6 (8)
Hungary	3.7 (3)	1.2 (1)	12.2 (10)	0.0 (0)	0.0 (0)	0.0 (0)	0.0 (0)	0.0 (0)	0.0 (0)	**46.3 (38)**	28.0 (23)	8.5 (7)
Lithuania	4.9 (4)	6.1 (5)	**47.6 (39)**	0.0 (0)	0.0 (0)	0.0 (0)	7.3 (6)	7.3 (6)	3.7 (3)	2.4 (2)	11.0 (9)	9.8 (8)
Latvia	0.5 (1)	0.0 (0)	**52.9 (99)**	1.6 (3)	1.1 (2)	0.0 (0)	1.6 (3)	2.7 (5)	0.0 (0)	4.3 (8)	28.9 (54)	6.4 (12)
Norway	0.0 (0)	0.0 (0)	17.4 (16)	1.1 (1)	0.0 (0)	0.0 (0)	0.0 (0)	0.0 (0)	0.0 (0)	**38.0 (35)**	**38.0 (35)**	5.4 (5)
Poland	0.4 (1)	0.4 (1)	16.4 (37)	0.0 (0)	0.0 (0)	0.0 (0)	1.8 (4)	1.8 (4)	0.9 (2)	24.4 (55)	**45.3 (102)**	8.4 (19)
Portugal	5.0 (5)	3.0 (3)	**52.5 (53)**	2.0 (2)	0.0 (0)	0.0 (0)	5.0 (5)	4.0 (4)	2.0 (2)	2.0 (2)	18.8 (19)	5.9 (6)
Romania	2.2 (4)	0.0 (0)	**53.3 (96)**	1.7 (3)	0.0 (0)	0.6 (1)	4.4 (8)	2.2 (4)	0.0 (0)	0.0 (0)	31.1 (56)	4.4 (8)
Serbia	1.4 (2)	0.7 (1)	**52.4 (75)**	0.0 (0)	0.0 (0)	0.0 (0)	5.6 (8)	0.0 (0)	0.0 (0)	1.4 (2)	34.3 (49)	4.2 (6)
Slovakia	0.0 (0)	0.5 (1)	29.0 (61)	0.0 (0)	0.0 (0)	0.0 (0)	0.5 (1)	0.5 (1)	0.0 (0)	27.6 (58)	**37.6 (79)**	4.3 (9)
Slovenia	0.7 (1)	0.0 (0)	**34.0 (50)**	0.7 (1)	0.0 (0)	0.0 (0)	1.4 (2)	0.0 (0)	0.0 (0)	29.3 (43)	32.0 (47)	2.0 (3)
Spain	2.3 (3)	2.3 (3)	31.3 (40)	0.8 (1)	0.0 (0)	0.0 (0)	12.5 (16)	5.5 (7)	0.0 (0)	0.0 (0)	**38.3 (49)**	7.0 (9)
Ukraine	1.6 (2)	2.4 (3)	**35.7 (45)**	0.0 (0)	0.0 (0)	0.0 (0)	11.9 (15)	6.3 (8)	2.4 (3)	6.3 (8)	24.6 (31)	8.7 (11)
United Kingdom	0.0 (0)	0.0 (0)	23.2 (16)	4.3 (3)	0.0 (0)	0.0 (0)	0.0 (0)	0.0 (0)	2.9 (2)	0.0 (0)	**58.0 (40)**	11.6 (8)
Total *(magnitude)*	***40***	***25***	***937***	***19***	***2***	***3***	***86***	***41***	***14***	***593***	***900***	***178***
Mean *(magnitude)*	***2***	***1.3***	***46.9***	***1.0***	***0.1***	***0.2***	***4.3***	***2.1***	***0.7***	***29.7***	***45***	***8.9***
N	**16**	**13**	**20**	**9**	**1**	**2**	**15**	**10**	**6**	**17**	**20**	**20**

**Current party laws (as of 2010). Raw count in parentheses. N = number of countries regulating a given category (Total N = 20).*

national variation shown by these summary data, two smaller points of immediate interest can be noted. First of all, and most obviously, party regulation has increased in most European countries over time. The only exceptions to this general rule are four post-communist democracies: namely, Ukraine, Croatia, Slovenia and Lithuania. Secondly, while all Western European cases, as expected, have experienced an increase in the magnitude of party regulation, the fact that Poland and Bulgaria come highest in the ranking is surprising, to say the least. Although the fact that their first party laws, passed at the very beginning of the transition process (i.e. 1990), had a minimal and provisional character – their main aim was to allow for the celebration of free and fair elections – may explain a great deal.

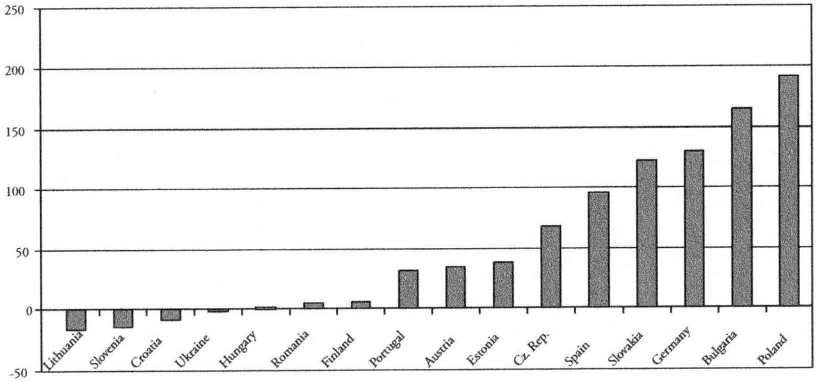

Figure 2. Magnitude change
Note: Only countries with more than one Party Law are included (N=16).

Because the figure above is so crude, we need to undertake an examination of the differences in regulation in a more systematic manner. For that purpose, we use an analysis of variance (ANOVA). In particular, we look for significant differences in the overall level of regulation, as well as within the specific categories, testing for differences between the means of regulation in three groups of countries. The first group, East/West democracy, depicts the relevance of post-communism. The second, New/Old democracy, divides states in terms of the newness of democracy. The third group, Continuous/Discontinuos democracy, reflects countries' democratic experience. The last group tests whether there are significant differences in the amount of regulation between the first and the current party laws. Indeed, with the exception of Latvia, Norway, Serbia and the UK, all countries have adopted changes to their party laws, and thus we consider and track the development between their first and most current version of the law. The results are summarized in table 2.

The analysis shows that for the continuous and discontinuous democracies the difference in regulation is statistically significant in all but four categories. Highest statistical significance is found in the difference of regulation in the *democratic principles*, *extra-parliamentary*, *party activity & identity*, and *secondary legislation* categories. The categories which do not appear to have statistically significant means are *electoral* and *parliamentary party*, *media access* and *party finance*. In fact, these categories do not show statistical significance in any of the four groups compared. Going back to Table 1 we see that the *electoral* and *parliamentary party* and *media access* categories are scarcely regulated anywhere, while the *party finance* category is regulated in all but three states. The differences in the *party activity & identity* categories are also highly statistically significant between the new and old democracies. This group further exhibits significant differences in regulating the *rights & freedoms* category – something quite intuitive, given that new democracies want to establish democratic political competition and thus refer to a party's rights more often.

Another category which exhibits statistically significant difference in the level of regulation in three separate sets of groups – East/West, New/Old, Continuous/Discontinuous – is the *government party* category. While it has the lowest level of statistical significance (single star), this shows that countries provide different amounts of rules for national and local government, but the differences do not seem to change as the category fails to reach statistical significance when the first and current party laws are examined. What changes in a statistically meaningful manner is the regulation of the *extra-parliamentary party*, the *external oversight* and the *secondary legislation* categories. Those categories, as the discussion at the beginning of the chapter states, contain rules about internal party matters, external control of parties and their activities and additional legislation. Therefore, the increase in regulation in them is consistent with the growing discontent with some political actions and the international struggle for more control and higher transparency of party matters. The growing regulation is also portrayed in the statistically significant result for *total magnitude* comparing the first and current party laws. What this signifies is that the total amount of regulation now is significantly different from what it once was. Interestingly, the *total range* of regulation between the first and the current party laws has not changed. This suggests that while the amount of regulation has increased substantially, it has done so in the categories which have already been regulated. Some may interpret this, if regulation is taken to be something restrictive, as strengthening the regulatory regime by deepening the control rather than widening its scope.

Within the growing body of regulation, we identify that internal party matters, provisions restricting their activity or identity, as well as rules keeping them in check are among those which are regulated in most different ways. These overlap with the dimensions of party regulation found in Karvonen's (2007) comparative analysis of party laws, the most comprehensive survey of party law to date. In particular, he deems that, when trying to examine the way political parties have been regulated in a specific country, there are three main aspects or "thematic dimensions"

Table 2: ANOVA tests of significant differences in party regulation

Category	East / West Europe	New / old democracy	Continuous / discontinuous democracy	First / last Party Law
Democratic principles	0.46 (0.65)	-0.33 (0.75)	3.52 (0.00)***	-0.88 (0.39)
Rights & freedoms	-0.73 (0.47)	-2.92 (0.00)***	2.03 (0.07)*	0.14 (0.89)
Extra-parliament party	-1.01 (0.33)	-0.63 (0.55)	6.47 (0.00)***	1.73 (0.09)*
Electoral party	0.73 (0.47)	0.88 (0.40)	0.43 (0.68)	0.47 (0.64)
Parliament party	0.00 (1.00)	0.37 (0.72)	1.36 (0.18)	0.32 (0.75)
Government party	-1.74 (0.09)*	-1.72 (0.09)*	1.72 (0.09)*	0.15 (0.88)
Activity & behaviour	-1.59 (0.13)	-5.39 (0.00)***	5.13 (0.00)***	0.58 (0.56)
Identity & programme	-1.57 (0.13)	-4.14 (0.00)***	4.95 (0.00)***	0.28 (0.78)
Media access	-0.85 (0.40)	-0.73 (0.47)	0.25 (0.81)	-0.27 (0.79)
Party finance	-0.10 (0.92)	0.91 (0.39)	0.70 (0.50)	1.29 (0.21)
External oversight	-1.70 (0.09)*	-0.84 (0.41)	1.86 (0.08)*	3.26 (0.00)***
Secondary legislation	-1.95 (0.06)*	-1.63 (0.12)	3.02 (0.00)***	1.89 (0.07)*
Total range	-2.12 (0.04)**	-2.81 (0.02)**	4.66 (0.00)***	-0.73 (0.47)
Total magnitude	-1.21 (0.24)	-0.42 (0.69)	4.52 (0.00)***	2.54 (0.02)**
N of observations	***24/12***	***28/8***	***6/30***	***16/20***

Note: Two-sample t-test with unequal variances. T-statistic reported, p-value in parentheses;
p<0.1, p<0.05, p***<0.01. ^Only countries with PLs included (N=20).*

that need to be taken into consideration: namely, (1) provisions aimed at restricting certain types of party activity or prohibiting certain ideological elements [*restrictions*]; (2) provisions pertaining to parties as organizations or legal subjects [e.g. internal *organization*, democratic procedures, membership or registration]; and (3) provisions [regulating] the right of the state to punish parties by legal means [*sanctions*] (2007, 443-444).

Borrowing this framework, the next section turns to take a deeper look at one country's party law – that of Spain – which we find to be paradigmatic in the sense that, while being among the countries with the highest level of regulation, it still approaches the average magnitude, touching on each of the abovementioned dimensions in a rather proportional manner.[14]

The Spanish Party Law

As a result of the necessity properly to develop art. 6 of the Spanish Constitution which requires parties, more generally, to "respect the Constitution and the Law" while also asking of them, more particularly, democratic "internal structure and functioning", the Organic Law 6/2002 on Political Parties came to replace the previous regulation (i.e. Law 54/1978). Existing legislation had been strongly criticized for being both pre-constitutional, heir to its most immediate legislative precedent (i.e. the semi-democratic Royal Decree-Law 12/1977) and, most importantly, for being very brief (Casal Bértoa *et al.*, 2012).

Echoing, therefore, the abovementioned constitutional mandate, and in consonance with the majority of Europe's current party laws, the Organic Law 6/2002 requires political parties to organize and function with respect for the country's Constitution and, in particular, to operate in a humanitarian, peaceful and democratic way (art. 9.1). In this context, the current regulation allows for the formation of ethnic, religious (banned in Bulgaria), nationalist (not allowed in Serbia) or "pro-independence" parties (e.g. banned in a certain number of countries such as Croatia, Estonia, Portugal, Romania, Serbia and Ukraine),

The need for a general ("external": i.e. in terms of practices, not principles) adhesion to democracy informs the totality of the 2002 party law, whose main aim – as reflected in the Statement of Motives, the longest by far among all European party laws – is to guarantee the *democratic functioning of the political system.* Interestingly enough, however, such necessity is not so much derived from the existence of ideological forces threatening with the imposition of a non-democratic political system, as is the case in most of the post-communist political systems (and indeed elsewhere);[15] but from the presence of the Basque terrorist movement ETA, whose murdered victims exceed 800. Although some scholars (for concrete examples see Casal Bértoa *et al.*, 2012, 10), together with Basque nationalist forces, have wanted to see an attempt by the legislator to ban certain political parties in Spain, the truth is that the Organic Law 6/2002, as clearly stated in its Statement of Motives as well as declared by both the Spanish Supreme and Constitutional Courts (STS 12.III.2003; STC 49/2003), simply aims to prevent anti-democratic partisan activities, and politically informed terrorism in particular,[16] rather than to control parties' ideological orientation (Karvonen, 2007, 445; Vidal Prado, 2009, 252-255). A clear example of the latter is that both the Communist (PCE) and the Falangist (FN) party, whose main goal is to establish a more-or-less authoritarian system of government, are considered to be legal. In this context, Spain's party regulation seems to converge with that of the rest of European democracies which, with the exception of Germany and, to a lesser extent, Portugal and Italy,[17] adopt a more "procedural" rather than "material" (i.e. "militant") concept of democracy (see Thiel, 2009). As both the Constitutional and Supreme Courts have put it, adopting the position of the scholarly majority,[18] in our legal order

> there is no space for a model in which positive adhesion to the regulations and, above all to the Constitution is imposed, which goes beyond respect (STC 48/2003) [On the contrary,] in our constitutional system there is room for all ideas and all political projects even ..., unlike in other codes, for those ideas which are contrary to the constitutional system, seeking to substitute or derogate or advocate formulas for territorial organization other than those chosen in the constitution (STS 27.III.2003),

provided that they do it by democratic means.[19]

It is within this context that article 9.3 contains detailed provisions intended to describe the conducts for which a party is considered "systematically [to] violate the fundamental rights and freedoms" (art. 9.2a), "encourage, support or legitimate violence" (art. 9.2b) or "supplement and politically support" (art. 9.2c) the use of terrorism: namely,

> a) giving express or tacit political support to terrorism ...; b) creating a culture of confrontation linked to the actions of terrorists ...; c) including regularly in its directing bodies and on its electoral lists persons who have been convicted for terrorist crimes and who have not publicly renounced terrorist methods and aims ...; d) using in an official way symbols, slogans, or other representational elements that are normally identified with a terrorist organization; e) conceding to a terrorist organization ... the same rights and prerogatives that electoral law concedes to parties; f) collaborating habitually with groups that act systematically in accordance with terrorist ... organizations; g) giving institutional support ... to any of the groups mentioned in the preceding paragraph; h) promoting, giving cover to, or participating in activities ... rewarding, giving cover to, paying homage to, or honoring violent or terrorist actions ...; and i) giving cover to actions that socially intimidate, coerce, or disrupt public order and that are linked to terrorism or violence (Turano, 2003:733-734)

Furthermore, the fruit of the Spanish legislator's extraordinary concern with such "anti-democratic" activities is the inclusion of a special provision banning all those parties seeking "to continue or succeed the activity of another political party declared illegal and dissolved" (art. 5.6), which, although particularly aimed at avoiding the re-creation of ETA's political arm,[20] does not avoid its application to both present and future parties, when necessary (STC 48/2003).

As far as the regulation of political parties as *organizations* is concerned, and like in the majority of the European Party Laws, the Organic Law 6/2002 requires their registration in order to acquire legal personality. In clear contrast to other European counterparts, however, the Spanish law is to be considered, together with Austria's, the most liberal in this respect, as it does not require the declared support of a minimum numbers of citizens[21] which, in other cases, ranges from the merely symbolic 50, 100 or 200 (in Bulgaria, Croatia or Slovenia, respectively) to the more demanding 10,000 (in Serbia, Slovakia or Ukraine) or 25,000 (in Romania). Notwithstanding its suspension or dissolution for the reasons we will examine later on, such registration will have indefinite validity (art. 4). In other words, and contrary to what can be observed in other countries, Spanish political parties may continue to exist without agreeing to participate in elections (e.g. Norway, Portugal, Romania, Slovenia, Ukraine) and/or achieving certain electoral results (e.g. Finland, Serbia or Romania), or without having a minimum number of members (e.g.

Bulgaria, Latvia, Lithuania, Romania and Serbia).[22] Given the above-cited liberal inspiration, the Spanish Law does not require the payment of any registration fee,[23] but just the notarization of the so-called *formation agreement* which must include, together with the (personal) identification of the promoters[24] and/or members of the provisional management bodies, the articles of association (i.e. statutes) as well as the address and ("original") name of the party to be formed (art. 3.1). In common with most of the regulations on the subject, the Spanish law does not contain any specific prerequisites in terms of organic composition (an exception was made for the General Assembly – see below), deliberative rules, necessary quorums and/or majorities, duration of mandates, members' (equal) rights and duties,[25] creation/dissolution of party structures, etc.; but it leaves its regulation, implicitly or explicitly, to the statutes of each particular party. Finally, and as in most West European democracies, only judicially incapacitated individuals or those who, having full capacity to act, have not attained 18 years of age are not entitled to be members of a party (art. 8.1).[26]

In clear consonance with the already stressed "democratic concern" of the Spanish legislator, the 2002 Law on Political Parties establishes the urgent need for partisan organizations′ internal "structure and operation" to adhere to democratic principles (art. 7.1). One of the main practical consequences of this is the obligatory use of free and secret voting when filling the party's management positions. Another example of the above-cited concern is the legal embodiment of the principle of accountability, according to which party leaders are subject to the democratic control of the members (art. 7.5).[27] A final reflection of what has been exposed is the consecration of the subsidiary principle of "*simple majority* of those present or represented" (italics are ours) in the adoption of all types of agreements by the party's highest governing body, that is, the General Assembly of all the party members – or their representatives (art. 7.2 and 7.4).

Interestingly enough, but as with many other European countries, the Spanish Law on Political Parties refrains from including any regulatory stipulations either on the finance of these organizations or on the compatibility between membership of a political party and the exercise of certain professions (e.g. judiciary, law enforcement, civil service, etc.) or the membership of other types of organizations (e.g. trade unions, national broadcasting companies, public or semi-public enterprises or even other political parties). These two issues (i.e. party finance and membership compatibilities) are certainly left to separate pieces of legislation (i.e. Organic Law 8/2007 on the Funding of Political Parties, Organic Law

6/1985 on the Judiciary, Organic Law 9/2011 on the Rights and Duties of the Members of the Armed Forces, etc.).[28]

As with most European democracies, the Spanish party law puts the management of the Register of Political Parties in the hands of a governmental institution (the Ministry of the Interior, in this case), which is in charge of examining the fulfillment by the party of the above-cited registration requirements and, finally, deciding about its inclusion in the Register as a mean of acknowledging its legal personality (arts. 3-6).[29] In the same vein, it also leaves the decision on the suspension of party activities or its dissolution to the judiciary: namely, a criminal court, in the case of illegal association, and a Special Chamber of the Supreme Court[30] in the event of democratic breakdowns, in terms of either internal operation or external activity (art. 10). After being dissolved as illegal, the party will be struck from the Register, its activities prohibited and its property liquidated (Casal Bértoa *et al.*, 2012).

Another major sanction included in the Spanish law is the provisional suspension of the party's activities as a precautionary measure in the event of criminal or dissolution proceedings (art. 10.3). Other types of punishments such as electoral disqualification, loss of parliamentary seats or annulment of electoral results are not comprised within the Spanish juridical ordination, in clear consonance with what happens in the rest of the European states. Interestingly enough, the Spanish law does not envisage the imposition of administrative fines or the reduction/suspension of state funds, two popular (pecuniary) sanctions in most European states. The reason for such omission is, however, straightforward: unlike most of the other European party laws, the Spanish act does not contain any rules on the funding of political parties, leaving its regulation (art. 13) to a special law mentioned in the preamble (i.e. Organic Law 3/1987 of 2 July).[31]

Conclusion

This chapter has offered a longitudinal and comparative analysis of the Party Laws of post-war European democracies collected under the European Research Council project *Re-conceptualizing Party Democracy.* We have seen that the time of the adoption of the first Party Law varies from 1967 for Germany, which is the pioneer in the regulation of political parties, to 2009 for Serbia. The chapter introduced the coding scheme used to code the laws and provided an overview of the extent of party regulation in twelve distinct categories.

Thus, for example, using our database and the analysis provided here, one can see how the regulation of *party finance* or *media access* in Party Laws, to take just two arbitrary categories, varies among the different European states. We find that rules about party finance are most extensive in Bulgaria, while countries such as Romania, Spain and the United Kingdom do not regulate this category at all as they have adopted special Party Finance Laws.

Another interesting finding is that the two most heavily regulated categories are those which deal with registration and establishment rules (*extra-parliamentary party*) and with outside monitoring of the lawfulness of party activity, as well as penalties and sanctions for prohibited matters (*external oversight*). Furthermore, in an analysis of variance these two categories appear to be statistically significant in two categories of groups – continuous/discontinuous democracies and first and current party laws. The second group comparison shows especially the fact that the amount of regulation in these categories differs significantly between laws. This is also reflected in the significant coefficient for the variation in total magnitude between the first and current laws.

The finding that party organization and party matters are among the most regulated characteristics pertaining to political parties was further investigated with a case study of the Spanish Party Law. Following Karvonen's (2007) 'thematic dimensions', the law was examined with particular attention to the restrictions, organization, and sanctions references. In consonance with most European laws, the Spanish act requires political parties to adhere to democratic principles, respect human rights (refraining from using violence) and comply with the constitutional and legal order. Influenced by a rather liberal spirit, the Spanish law does not provide for specific requirements in terms of party formation or maintenance, also leaving the regulation of parties' internal organization to their particular statutes. As in the majority of laws in our dataset, party legislation in Spain assigns the control of party creation and dissolution (Spain's major legal sanction) to governmental and judicial institutions. In sum, notwithstanding its particular concern with partisan terrorist organizations, the Spanish Law on Political parties (influenced, in turn, by Germany's legislation) constitutes a paradigm of European party regulation.

Overall, this chapter has observed how the extent of party regulation through Party Laws in Europe has significantly been increasing over time.

This pattern seems to reveal an interesting transformation in the very conception of political parties: from political parties conceived as private associations, being exempted from specific regulatory constraints, to parties as 'public utilities', becoming legitimate objects of state regulation (van Biezen, 2004). Hence, while little comparative attention has been paid to this phenomenon, we contend that the process of party regulation through Party Laws has interesting implications in terms of the place of political parties in modern democracies. Moreover, the results that this chapter has revealed point to interesting possibilities for future research on the effect of the regulatory frameworks on the organizational development of individual political parties as well as on the development of different party systems across the European continent.

Acknowledgments

We would like to thank Evangelos Kyzirakos for his research assistance.

Appendix: Contemporary Party Laws in Europe[32]

Countries	Year of Promulgation	Party Law	Year of latest amendment
Austria	1975	404. Federal Law of 2nd July 1975 on the assignments, financing and the pre-election campaign of political parties (Law on Parties). Entered into force 24.07.1975	2008
Bulgaria	1990	Political Parties Act State Gazette No. 29/10.04.1990	2009
Croatia	1993	Political Parties Act Promulgated on the 30th of July 1993	1999
Czech Republic	2006	Act No. 342/2006 Coll. amending Act No. 424 of October 2, 1991 on Associating in Political Parties and political movements and successive amendments	n/a

Countries	Year of Promulgation	Party Law	Year of latest amendment
Estonia	1994	Political Parties Act Adopted May 11th 1994 (RTI 1994 , 40,654) Entered into force June 16th 1994 (RTI 1994, 40, 654)	2010
Finland	1969	Act on Political Parties (Law 10/1969) Promulgated: 10 January 1969	1992
Germany	1967	Law on Political Parties Promulgated: 24th July 1967	2004
Hungary	1989	Act XXXIII of 1989 on the Operation and Financial Management of Political Parties	2003
Latvia	2006	Law on Political Parties (7th July 2006)	n/a
Lithuania	1990	Law on Political Parties and Political Organizations	2004
Norway	2005	Act 2005-06-17 no. 102: Act on certain aspects relating to the political parties or The Political Parties Act (Entry into force 2006-01-01, 2005-07-01)	n/a
Poland	1997	Act of 27 June 1997 on Political Parties	2010
Portugal	2003	Law governing Political Parties, Organizational Law no. 2/2003 of 22 August 2003	2008
Romania	2003	Law no. 14/2003 on political parties (17/01/2003)	n/a
Serbia	2009	Law on Political parties (12/05/2009)	n/a
Slovakia	2005	Act No.85 as of February 4, 2005 on political parties and political movements	n/a
Slovenia	1994	Political Parties Act (Law 62 of 1994) Promulgated: 07/10/1994	2007
Spain	2002	Law on Political Parties (12756 Organic Law 6/2002)	n/a

Countries	Year of Promulgation	Party Law	Year of latest amendment
Ukraine	2001	Law on Political Parties Promulgated: 5/04/2001	2010
United Kingdom[33]	1998	The Registration of Political Parties Act (199 c48) Promulgated: 19/11/1998	n/a

Notes

* Author names are listed in alphabetical order.

1 'Guidelines on political party regulation', by OSCE/ODIHR and Venice Commission, 25 October 2010 (Study no. 595/2010), p. 6.

2 *Re-conceptualizing Party Democracy* is a project directed by Prof. Ingrid van Biezen and funded by the European Research Council (ERC). More information can be found at www.partylaw.leidenuniv.nl.

3 Elsewhere Janda argued: "[t]he term 'party law' has different meanings to different people, even among party scholars" (Janda, 2005, 3).

4 A list with the legal reference to the laws included in our sample is presented in Appendix.

5 More recently (i.e. March 2011), Cyprus promulgated a "Law on Political Parties", even if it mainly contains political funding regulations. For this reason, but also due to its recent adoption, we do not include it in the analysis.

6 It should be noted, however, that the Turkish Party Law was passed on the basis of art. 57 of the 1961 Constitution which, in turn, was "inspired by art. 21 of the [1949] Constitution of the Federal German Republic" (Dodd, 1969, 130).

7 Both the Austrian and Finish laws are characterized by their lower degree of regulation as compared to the German Law on Political Parties, in particular as far as the internal organization of political parties is concerned.

8 State subsidies funding the activity of political parties were introduced in Portugal only in 1977 and eight years later in Spain. Moreover, both countries shared a legalistic culture where party funding is regulated in a different piece of legislation.

9 In this particular aspect, the only exceptions are Latvia and, to a lesser extent, Serbia, where Party Laws were, respectively, approved only twelve and nine years after the beginning of democracy.

10 The same applies to the recently established Party Law of Cyprus, whose main regulatory focus is upon party finance regulation (see ft. 5).

11 For a comparative analysis of the legal regulation of internal party democracy in Europe see van Biezen and Piccio, 2013.

12 For an in-depth diachronic (content) analysis of the Portuguese case see Casal Bértoa (forthcoming).

13 For the case of Romania, Spain, and the UK, party finance is regulated, respectively, in the Law on the Financing of Political Parties and Election Campaigns, in the Organic Law on the Funding of Political Parties, and in the Political Parties and Election Act. Other countries included in our sample that adopted a Party Finance Law, specifying party finance regulations in detail, are Croatia, Finland, Hungary, Latvia, Norway, Slovakia, Serbia, and Portugal (Piccio, 2012).

14 Data available from the authors.

15 See fn. 18.

16 Out of 12 European party laws banning the use of violence by political parties, a reference to terrorist activities or organizations can be found only in the Spanish 2002 "Organic Law". This, however, does not preclude the general character, in both formal and material terms, of the latter (STC 48/2003).

17 While in Germany political parties are generally banned on ideological grounds (e.g. both the Neo-Nazi and the Communist Party were banned by the Constitutional Court as early as 1952 and 1956, respectively); in both Portugal and Italy, only the "fascist" parties are prohibited.

18 According to the position set up De Otto y Pardo already in 1985 [don't understand], which considered that allowing for the possibility of modifying the Constitution as a whole (art. 168), the constitutional legislator clearly opposed any ideological control on parties (see also Aragón Reyes, 1990; Blanco Valdés, 1990; Rodríguez-Zapata, 2003). More recently, some scholars – a minority – have pointed "towards the possibility of configuring the requirement of respect of the constitution as the requirement for a certain degree of adhesion to its basic principles which goes beyond merely formal compliance" (Santamaría Pastor, 2001:100; see also Montilla Martos, 2004; Tajadura Tejada, 2004).

19 The Spanish case law differs here from the European Court of Human Rights (ECHR), which, in both the *Refah Partisi v. Turkey* (13/02/2003) and *Herri Batasuna & Batasuna v. Spain* (30/06/2009) cases, has adopted a "militant" concept of democracy (Biezen and Molenaar, 2012).

20 From the day of the entry into force of the Law on Political Parties (i.e. 29 June 2002) until the moment of writing this article, the Spanish Supreme

Court has banned up to 14 political formations (or the candidatures connected with them) linked with the above-cited terrorist group: namely, Batasuna, EH and Herri Batasuna (STS 27.III.2003), AuB (STS 3.V.2003), HZ (STS 21.V.2004), AG (STS 26.III.2005), ASB (ATS 22.V.2007), AS (STS 5.V.2007), ANV (22.IX.2008), EHAK (22.IX.2008), Askatasuna (ATS 8.III.2009), D3M (STS 8.II.2009), Sortu (ATS 23.III.2011) and Bildu (STS 1.V.2011). Interestingly enough, the Constitutional Court revoked the illegalization of the last for considering that the resolution of the Supreme Court had violated its right to political participation, guaranteed in art. 23 of the Spanish Supreme Act (STC 62/2011).

21 The absence of such requirement is common also to the British, German, Hungarian and Estonian Laws. However, while in the first three a minimum of electoral activity is required, in the last parties must have at least 1,000 members.

22 The minimum number of members a party must have in order not be dissolved ranges from the symbolic 200 in Latvia to the more "discriminative" 25,000 in Romania, with no fewers than 700 people for each of the 18 state counties, plus Bucharest.

23 Out of the 20 European Party Laws here analysed, only four (i.e. Finland, Latvia, Slovakia and Ukraine) require the payment of an administrative fee.

24 It should be noted here that it is impossible, except in cases of rehabilitation, for individuals with a criminal record (either for illegal association or certain serious crimes) to found political parties. This responds, once again, to the legislator's particular concern with Herri Batasuna's heirs.

25 In any case, members are guaranteed the following rights (art. 8.3): of participation, of suffrage (both active and passive), of information (e.g. of decisions, activities, financial situation, etc.) and of complaint (against illegal or anti-statutory agreements). In consideration for this, members are obliged to share the aims of the party, co-operating in their achievement, pay the fees/contributions duly imposed and accept/comply with the agreements legally adopted (art. 8.4).

26 In clear contrast, most post-communist countries (as well as Portugal) require party members also to be citizens.

27 Surprisingly enough, only two other countries recognize this principle in their Party Laws: namely, Germany and Lithuania.

28 Other countries leaving the regulation of party finance to a specific law are Lithuania, Latvia, Portugal, Romania, Serbia and the UK. On the other hand, only the Bulgarian, Estonian, Serbian and Ukrainian Party Laws contain specific provisions in terms of party membership incompatibilities.

29 Only three countries leave the Party Register in the hands of a judicial, rather than governmental, authority: namely, Poland (Warsaw's District Court), Portugal (Constitutional Court) and Romania (Bucharest Tribunal).

30 Other countries, following the German model, prefer to legitimate the Constitutional Court only (e.g. Croatia, Poland, Portugal, Romania, Serbia or Slovenia). Within the Spanish scholarship, Fernández Segado (2004:200) and Tajadura (2004), among others, have called for a similar solution.

31 This is also the reason why, contrary to most of the European party laws (up to 14), the Spanish law does not provide for the operation of an external/independent "monitoring" authority, even if it is mentioned (in passing) in both the preamble and the (final) article 13.

32 Laws on-line available at www.partylaw.leidenuniv.nl.

33 Although the UK in 2000 enacted the Political Parties, Elections and Referendum Act (PPERA), we included the 1998 Registration of Political Parties Act in our sample. Indeed, the 2000 UK PPERA, and its subsequent amendment (the 2009 Political Parties and Elections Act) are both exceptionally long documents (totalling 260 and 93 pages respectively) which deal almost exclusively with aspects relatingd to the financing of political parties rather than their operations and activities. In order therefore not to bias the results of the content analysis of Party Laws in the direction of party finance, we deal with the 2000 and 2009 UK Acts as Party Finance Laws rather than Party Laws.

References

Biezen, I. van (2012). 'Constitutionalizing Party Democracy: The Constitutive Codification of Political Parties in Post-war Europe', *British Journal of Political Science*, v. 42, n. 1, pp. 187-212.

Biezen, I. van (2004). 'Political Parties as Public Utilities', *Party Politics*, vol. 10, no. 6, pp. 701-722.

Biezen, I. van and Borz, G. (2012). 'Models of party democracy: patterns of party regulation in postwar European constitutions', *European Political Science Review*, Vol 4, Issue 3, pp. 327359.

Biezen, I. van and Molenaar, F. (2012). 'The Europeanization of Party Politics? Competing Regulatory Paradigms at the Supra-National Level', *West European Politics*, v. 35, n. 2, pp. 632-656.

Biezen, I. van and D. R. Piccio (2013). "Shaping Intra-Party Democracy: On the Legal Regulation of Internal Party Organizations". In: R. S. Katz and

W. Cross (eds.) The Challenges of Intra-Party Democracy. Oxford: Oxford University Press, pp. 27-48.

Biezen, I. van and Rashkova, E.R. (2012). 'Deterring New Party Entry? The Impact of State Regulation on the Permeability of Party Systems', *Party Politics*, First View Online.

Blanco Valdés, R. (1990). *Los Partidos Políticos*. Madrid: Tecnos.

Casal Bértoa, F., Rodríguez Teruel, J., Barberá Aresté, O. and Barrio López, A. (2012). 'Uneasiness with the *Status Quo*: Party Regulation and Party Finance in post-Francoist Spain (1976-2011)', *Working Paper Series on the Legal Regulation of Political Parties*, n. 25.

Casal Bértoa, F. (forthcoming). 'Plus ça change: Portuguese Party Regulation Over-Time (1974-2012)', *Working Paper Series on the Legal Regulation of Political Parties.*

Dodd, C. H. (1969). *Politics and Government in Turkey*. Manchester: The University Press.

Fernández Segado, F. (2004). 'Algunas Reflexiones sobre la Ley Orgánica 6/2002, de Partidos Políticos, al Hilo de su Interpretación por el Tribunal Constitucional', *FORO. Revista de Ciencias Jurídicas y Sociales (Nueva Época)*, n. 0, pp. 179-225.

Karvonen, L. (2007). 'Legislation on Political Parties: A Global Comparison', *Party Politics*, 13/4, pp. 437-55.

Katz, R. S. (2004). 'Democracy and the Legal Regulation of Political Parties,' paper prepared for the USAID conference on 'Changes in Political Parties: United States Agency for International Development'. Washington, D.C., October 1, 2004.

Janda, K. (2005). 'Adopting Party Law', working paper series on Political Parties and Democracy in Theoretical and Practical Perspectives. Washington DC: National Democratic Institute for International Affairs_____ (2006b) 'How Nations Govern Political Parties', paper prepared for the 20th World Congress of the International Political Science Association, Fukuoka, Japan, 9-13 July 2006.

Kasapovic, M. (2001). 'Nominating Procedures in Democratic Polities', *Politička misao*, Vol. XXXVIII, No. 5, pp. 3–17.

McFaul, M. (2002). 'The Fourth Wave of Democracy and Dictatorship Noncooperative Transitions in the Postcommunist World', *World Politics*, 54.2, pp. 212-244.

Montilla Martos, J. A. (2004). 'Algunos Cambios en la Concepción de Partidos. Comentario a la STC 48/2003, sobre la Ley Orgánica 6/2002', *Teoría y Realidad Constitucional*, n. 12-13, pp. 559-585.

Müller, W.C. and U. Sieberer (2006). 'Party Law', in Richard S. Katz and William Crotty (eds.), *Handbook of Party Politics*. London: Sage.
Neuendorf, K. A. (2002). *The Content Analysis Guidebook*. Thousand Oaks, CA: Sage Publications.
De Otto y Pardo, I. (1985). *Defensa de la Constitución y Partidos Políticos*. Madrid: Centro de Estudios Constitucionales.
Piccio, D. R. (2012). 'Party Regulation in Europe: A Comparative Overview', *Working Paper Series on the legal regulation of political parties*, n. 18.
Rodríguez-Zapata, J. (2003). 'Partidos Políticos y Democracia Combativa', *Revista Valenciana d'Estudis Autonomics*, n. 39-40, pp. 122-135.
Santamaría Pastor, J.A. (2001). 'Comentario al artículo 6 de la Constitución', in Fernando Garrido Falla (ed.) *Comentarios a la Constitución*. Madrid: Civitas.
Sartori, G. (1976). *Parties and Party Systems: a Framework of Analysis*. Cambridge: Cambridge University Press.
Schattschneider, E.E. (1942). *Party Government*. New York: Farrar and Rinehart, Inc.
Tajadura Tejada, J. (2004). *Partidos Políticos y Constitución*. Madrid: Civitas.
Thiel, M. (ed.) (2009). *The 'Militant Democracy' Principle in Modern Democracies*. UK: Ashgate.
Turano, L. (2003). 'Banning Political Parties as a Response to Basque Terrorism', *International Journal of Constitutional Law*, v. 1, pp. 730-740.
Vidal Prado, C. (2009). 'Spain', in Markus Thiel (ed.) *The 'Militant Democracy' Principle in Modern Democracies*. UK: Ashgate.

CHAPTER 6

Explaining Legislative Conflict over the Adoption of Political Financing Law in the European Union

Wojciech Gagatek
University of Warsaw

In 2003 the European Union passed its first-ever regulation on the recognition and financing of extra-parliamentary EU political parties (in this law formally defined as 'political parties at European level', and known also as the so-called Europarties).[1] By enacting such a law, the (non-state) EU joined the majority of democratic states which provide political parties with public subsidies (Austin and Tjernstrom, 2003, van Biezen and Kopecky 2007). However, the fact remains that political parties at EU level are not central actors in the EU political system. Prior to the adoption of this regulation, they were often described as very loose organizations lacking both resources for political action and real influence (Hix and Lord 1997). Given this, it is then even more important to question why the EU decided to introduce public subsidies for such parties, and, as will be shown in this paper, why some MSs and some national political parties strongly opposed this step.

The central research problem of this paper is to analyse why the topic of regulating EU political parties in law has become so controversial and I will attempt to identify possible sources for this controversy. I will argue that the conflict would result from the tension, first, between various national traditions and specific legislative solutions relating to parties' legal status and their financing and, second, between different views on the present and future of political integration in the EU. By studying this problem, not only do we learn about EU legislative politics and the Europarties, but we also contribute to the vast literature on party law and especially on party financing, since the results of this paper provide

1 This paper was submitted in July 2012.

us with an additional source of knowledge on the models, traditions and habits of regulating political parties at the national level.

This article will be organized in three parts. First, after a review of the literature, it will propose an organizing perspective leading to the identification of the sources and dimensions of the conflict over the adoption of party law in the EU. In the second part, it will present the legislative procedures that led to the adoption of a law that was finally entitled *Regulation 2004/2003 on the regulations governing political parties at European level and the rules regarding their funding*, hereinafter referred to as the Regulation (Regulation (EC) No. 2004/2003). In the final part, the findings of this research will be discussed by analysing the role of and divisions in the European Commission and, subsequently, in the European Parliament (EP). It will also discuss the amendments to the regulation carried out in 2007 and 2011. Finally, it must be noted that this paper is not devoted to an analysis of Regulation 2004/2003 as finally adopted (see Johansson & Raunio 2005), although its content will become clear through the investigation of the legislative works preceding its adoption. In researching this topic, I have analysed the materials coming from the EP (debates, reports, roll-call votes), the internal documents of the Council of the European Union, personal communications and press releases. Additionally, various datasets that provide detailed comparisons between national rules of political financing have been used (e.g. IDEA International dataset Austin and Tjernstrom, 2003, Council of Europe 2004, Party Law in Modern Europe database).

An organizing perspective

The key issue with which we must start is to identify an organizing perspective that will help to answer the main research questions of this paper. The first thing to note is that the subject of party financing is a part of comparative politics and, more precisely, of the party financing literature. However, given that the EU is a unique case both because its institutional environment differs sharply from that of the national states and, second, because EU parties are in very many aspects different from national political parties, we also need to search for analytical insights in the EU studies. These two bodies of literature will be briefly discussed below, and subsequently an organizing perspective for this paper will be presented.

Insights from comparative politics

Given that this paper seeks to analyse the dimensions of political conflict in relation to the adoption of party regulation in the European Union, the first question that must be addressed concerns the extent to which we can identify a dominant trend in relation to regulating political parties in law. From an empirical point of view, there seem to be three clearly visible and obvious trends (van Biezen and Kopecky 2007; Lehmann 2003). First, the constitution in the majority of democratic states includes some rules on political parties. Second, it has become quite commonplace to finance political parties from public funds. Third, particular attention is paid to the rules on transparency in party funding. Scholars announce the overall convergence of funding patterns (Nassmacher 2009). However, among those countries that provide political parties with public subsidies, the variety of national provisions is quite large (see Appendix B for illustration), ranging from the rules on donations to the very principle of how large the state subsidies should be. Furthermore, legal provisions on political parties relate not only to party funding, but generally to all possible measures regulating parties in law: their status as legal persons, their activities, their internal organization and procedures, the rights of members, and many others. Overall, the extent or, to put it differently, the intensity of legal regulation (concerning, for example, the extent to which law regulates internal party organization) is often different. Conceptually, this variety is constrained by means of the models of regulating political parties, primarily based on the cross-national differences in political and legal cultures. The key explanatory factor is the vision of a political party and its role within society. Here countries differ, and this results in the differences in national laws regulating political parties. This variety can be reduced to two models: the prescription and the permission model (for a review see Janda 2005). The first imposes very little on parties, assuming that how they organize, what their programme is should be left to the parties and their members. The prescription model, on the other hand, imposes on parties many more rules stipulated in a more detailed way, especially regarding their internal organization, for example, the selection of candidates or the rights of the members.

Insights from EU studies

To simplify the matter in question, in most cases party law in national states is adopted by parties themselves while acting in parliament, subject to review by the Constitutional Court (Janda 2005). However, in the EU we need to approach this problem in the special, very complex circumstances of EU legislative politics (Hix 2005, Peterson et al. 2008). The most important factor to note is that there are many more political actors to analyse: MSs, the European Commission and the European Parliament. However, contrary to the situation in national political systems, Europarties do not have much control over the final law that governs them, because the link between extra- and parliamentary parties at EU level in any sense is not comparable to that in national party politics (Hix and Lord 1997). In other words, party law is not adopted by the (Euro)parties themselves.

Moving now to the patterns of political conflict in the EU (for a review see Steenbergen & Marks 2004), for many years the standard explanation was based on the so-called sovereignty-integration dimension, in which the opposition or acceptance of further political integration was a key source of political conflict. In the 1990s, some other aspects were added to this first dimension, in particular, the left-right conflict. From comparative politics literature we know that it is the size of the party, rather than its ideological profile, that explains the conflict over the adoption of political financing rules (Scarrow 2004). On the other hand, from the literature on EU political parties we learn that the whole idea of EU political parties and their strengthening means a step towards further political integration. For this reason, it seems that the sovereignty-integration dimension will be a key explanatory factor of the patterns of political conflict over the adoption of political financing law in the EU.

When we now try to think about the mechanism of this conflict, the first precondition for it is that political actors will indeed have different preferences. Based on the comparative politics literature reviewed above, it is clear that MSs differ between themselves in how they regulate (if they do) parties in law. However, the fact that they differ is not sufficient. At the same time MSs and other political actors at the EU level would need to transfer their national preferences to the discussion on party financing at the EU level.

This example touches a more general question whether political actors use their own national experiences in formulating proposals for legislative solutions at the EU level. From a theoretical point of view, an affirmative answer to such question is quite obvious in the historical and sociological versions of new institutionalism. These two bodies of literature make a direct claim concerning preference formation (see Hall & Taylor 1996; Peters 1999). Without going into details, the question the sociological institutionalists focus on is about the sources from which institutional creators took their ideas to create a new institution. The hypothesis states that they 'borrow' those ideas from the existing world of institutional templates and models, a mechanism that is called institutional borrowing. Its equivalent is also present in the theory of constitutionalism as constitutional borrowing, in which states 'borrow' constitutional and legislative solutions from one another (Osiatynski 2003). And if this borrowing mechanism indeed takes place at the EU level too, which party tradition (or some combinations of traditions) prevails?

However, going more deeply into the problem would require asking whether the differences exist not only between the MSs, but also within them. Some prominent scholars argue that domestic conflict may be a key to explaining why some governments support and other oppose integration (Moravcsik 1998). In our case, we must pose a question regarding the extent to which the distinct national traditions and models on party regulation are shared by political forces in a given MS. In this paper, this can be tested by analysing whether the political parties and individual politicians from the same country will have similar ideas relating to the mode of financing of EU political parties and the specific legislative solutions.

Integrating insight from comparative politics and EU studies

The analysis so far allows us to identify two major dimensions of conflict in the process of regulating parties in law at the EU level. The first relates to the wider problem of the future of political integration in Europe. The very idea of strengthening Europarties has always been associated with the advancement of political integration in the direction of a 'federal Europe'. Needless to say, adopting a system of public financing of the Europarties will make them stronger. That is why the views in favour of EU integration are expected to be linked to the very aim and nature of party regulation and so a conflict on the European integration scale (sovereignty-integration) is very likely. For example, Eurosceptics are expected to be against any form of legal recognition and public financing of EU political parties, because that will mean for them a step towards a federal Europe. In other words, it is not possible to detach the discussion on the nature of party regulation in the EU from the very character, goals and activities of Europarties. Hence the first hypothesis: *the conflict over the strengthening of Europarties through the adoption of the party financing regulation will be based on views toward the present and future of European integration.*

On the other hand, the fact that the subject matter of this conflict is the regulation of political parties in law suggests a second dimension around the prescriptive and permissive models of regulating political parties or, in the most detailed account, between specific legislative solutions. For this to be possible, we must assume that these different national traditions will be transferred to the EU level, thus becoming a source of political conflict. For example, given the variety of national legislative solutions concerning the regulation of donations, we would expect that this aspect of political financing will be aired in the discussions on party financing at the EU level, possibly becoming a source of political conflict. Hence the second hypothesis: *the proposals concerning the legal regulation of political parties at EU level will have their source in and will be borrowed from national experiences (the borrowing hypothesis).*

The problem with these hypotheses is that they (and two dimensions of political conflict linked to them) may be intertwined. However, it seems that we may expect that the first dimension will be more visible as far as the goal of the whole party regulation is concerned (whether to regulate parties in law in the first place), whereas the second will be more important with regard to specific legislative solutions, e.g. donations, reporting, transparency, etc.

Introducing the process of adoption of the political financing regulation at the EU level

Following their creation in the 1970s, Europarties were neither recognized by law nor subsidized directly by the then European Economic Community. Their practical functioning was based on the material, personal and financial contributions of either their political groups in the EP or their member parties. In the early 1990s, the three largest Europarties joined forces to lobby for their formal legal recognition, and the process leading to the adoption of laws governing European political parties started. It is useful to note that it can be divided into two distinct periods.

In the first period (after the Maastricht and up to the Nice intergovernmental conference, 1990-2001), the matter on the agenda was whether to constitutionalize European political parties. In practical terms, the question was whether to insert a reference to the European political parties in the basic EU constitutional document (Treaty establishing European Communities, hereafter TEC), and, if yes, what wording to use. This story seems to be rather well described in the existing studies (Johansson & Raunio 2005, Day & Shaw 2005). After intense lobbying by the Europarties and the European Parliament, and with the support of some heads of MSs, the Maastricht intergovernmental conference

(1990-91) took a decision to insert a special Treaty article devoted to Europarties (art. 138a, later renumbered as art. 191, and now art. 10 (4) of the Treaty on the European Union). In this reference, the Treaty attributes an important role to Europarties in "forming a European awareness and expressing the political will of the citizens of the Union". However, the vague formulation of this article came to be understood only as a symbolic reference, rather than a legal basis for further, more specific laws (Bieber 1999). Since that time, even though various amendments to this unclear wording have been proposed, the very idea and concept of European political parties divided the MSs, and for a long time they could not reach agreement on whether and how to proceed (see below for details). However, the key incentive came from the Special Report of the European Court of Auditors (2000), which considered the then existing practice of financing Europarties from the EP political groups' budgets to be inadmissible, since the funds allocated to political groups could not be used to finance any extra-parliamentary activities. This stimulus led to the amendment of the above-mentioned art. 191 of the Treaty so that the Council, acting through the co-decision procedure with the Parliament as co-legislator, was obliged to lay down the regulations governing political parties at European level, and in particular the rules regarding their funding.

In order to satisfy the concerns of some MSs, however, declaration no. 11, a constitutive element of the Treaty of Nice of 2001, stated, *inter alia,* that

> The provisions of Article 191 do not imply any transfer of powers to the European Community and do not affect the application of the relevant national constitutional rules. The funding for political parties at European level provided out of the budget of the European Communities may not be used to fund, either directly or indirectly, political parties at national level.

This declaration and its content explain the main lines of divisions: a threat of a further transfer of political powers to the European Union and the risk of Europarties' interference in national politics.

Once the decision to constitutionalize Europarties was finally taken, the debate moved to some specific concerns over the financing regulation, and the second period began. In this period, the divisions between MSs had less to do with their approaches towards European integration in general – in this context whether to constitutionalize Europarties – but more to do with how to do it: in other words, how to construct a special act devoted to their legal status, financing and potentially their other activities. This is the precise topic of the next paragraph.

The legislative work on the status and financing of European political parties

The conflict that arose with reference to the subsequent legislative proposals had mainly to do with three areas. First, it is often argued that the criteria relating to the allocation system are primarily responsible for the eventual benefits to the existing parties (Pierre et al. 2000). Likewise, at the EU level the first major source of conflict concerned the fixing of the minimum number of MSs a Europarty operates in so that it qualifies to receive EU funding. In other words, in order to be recognized and registered as a Europarty, should it have members (national political parties) from two, five or even more EU Member states? In this paper I will refer to this condition as the representativeness criterion. The second area of conflict related to the question of party sponsorship and donations and, more precisely, what type of donations should be banned. Finally, there was a major difference regarding the extent to which a European law should prescribe party organization and impose on parties the need to respect EU democratic principles and fundamental rights. It does not mean, however, that all the specific legislative solutions were contested. For example, from the beginning agreement was reached that special attention should be given to the transparency of party financing and that there must be a balance between the financing of the Europarties by the EU and their own resources.

Early legislative proposals

The first concrete proposals regarding how the future European party law should be designed saw the light of day as early as in 1996, when the EP adopted the Report on the constitutional status of the European political parties (European Parliament 1996). This report, drafted by a PES Group Member Dimitris Tsatsos, and warmly received by large Europarties, set the agenda and remained a point of reference for all subsequent proposals (see below). The first condition for recognition was that a Europarty had to unite national political parties from at least 1/3 of the MSs and be active at EU level, that is, participate in European elections and create or join a political group in the EP, among other tasks.

The report further formulated three conditions relating to party organization. The first of them imposed a formal obligation to adopt and make available statutes and a party programme. The second was to ensure that the party "be more, in terms of goals and organization, than a mere electioneering organization or an organization that merely supports a political group and parliamentary work". The third required a party to be organized "in a way that is likely to reflect the political will of citizens of the Union" based on a democratic internal mode of work, since "the internal structure of European political parties must comply with their constitutional mission".

Prior to the Nice Treaty (2001), due to the lack of a clear legal basis the Commission was reluctant to initiate procedures proposed by the Tsatsos report, and only after the report of the Court of Auditors quoted above, did the Commission present its draft regulation (European Parliament 2001b). As Commissioner Schreyer explained during a debate in the EP

> When defining European parties we wanted to leave room for manoeuvre and make it possible for the concept to evolve. At the same time, however, we wanted to put in place minimum democratic standards and minimum requirements for European representativeness and guarantee a maximum degree of transparency in respect of financing. On the definition of European parties, allow me to say quite clearly that European parties in no way have to toe a particular European political line, but the values of democracy, the rule of law and respect for fundamental rights must be respected (European Parliament 2001b).

Overall, the Commission's 2001 proposal was more modest in setting the conditions than was the Tsatsos report. Furthermore, the project was less comprehensive, and the Commission refrained from touching such matters as mandatory disclosure of all revenue (e.g. members' contributions or donations) or the possibility of the Europarties acquiring legal personality. Most importantly, however, in practice it continued the representativeness criterion proposed by the Tsatos report, based on two alternative ways of applying for funding. A Europarty had to be represented by either MEPs in the EP, and/or members of the national or regional parliaments, in all cases coming from at least five MSs; or a Europarty or its member parties had to have received at least five per cent of the votes cast in the last EP election in at least five MSs. Neither the Tsatsos report nor the Commission's 2001 draft project devoted any attention to the question of banned donations, although the Commission's project stated that the control and supervision of expenses were to be carried out by means of an independent audit, which would present its findings to the EP and to the European Court of Auditors.

Responding to the Commission's project in May 2001, the EP, in the report drafted by a German EPP Member Ursula Schleicher, tabled some amendments aimed at securing greater transparency of Europarty's finances, especially, banning anonymous donations and those from public sector companies (European Parliament 2001c). It also wanted to rule out the possibility of creating Europarties that would be only a cover for obtaining funding, but not active in practice. It therefore proposed that apart from the statute, the political programme was also to be registered, and that funding was granted only to "established alliances of political parties". Overall, the early proposals reflected or oscillated around the prescription model.

The debate in the Council

Although the Commission agreed to the vast majority of the Parliament's amendments, the Council could not reach agreement. It seems that there was a clash of different national visions of how to regulate political parties. In general, Denmark, the UK and Sweden expressed general scrutiny reservations towards the entire proposal. In this way, they proposed deleting the condition that a Europarty shall respect fundamental democratic principles and EU fundamental rights, which most other countries opposed (Council of the European Union 2001a).

Regarding the threshold for financing (1/3, at that time five EU MSs), most EU countries considered it too rigorous and the Belgian EU presidency proposed lowering it to 1/4. However, the UK, Sweden and Austria demanded it be lowered even further, to just two MSs. At that time, pressed by coalition partners from the Freedom Party of Austria (FPÖ), the Austrian delegation to the Council wanted to ensure that smaller party families would not be excluded from the possibility of registering a Europarty because of such high representativeness criteria (Day & Shaw 2005). The most radical position was presented by the Danes who wanted to resign completely from any representative criteria, requiring only that a Europarty has "established or intend to establish or join a political group in the European Parliament" (see below) (Council of the European Union 2001a). Finally, concerning donations and party sponsorship, the Belgian EU presidency proposed the prohibition of donations over a certain threshold (to be decided) from any legal or natural person. However, the MSs were divided both relating to the principle of this proposal and on the level of any threshold (Council of the European Union 2001c). The most visible conflict arose between France and Germany. In this way, when the Germans wanted to increase the amount of admissible party donations, the French were proposing to limit them or make the procedure more rigorous (Council of the European Union 2001b). How can it be accounted for? The French tradition of regulating political parties largely differs from the German one. One could multiply the differences, but from various datasets (see Appendix B) it becomes clear that in France, contrary to Germany, there is a ceiling on contributions to political parties, a ban on corporate donation, a ban on donations from government contractors and a ban on trade union donations, among others. In short, in France the matter of party sponsorship is treated much more strictly. In this way, France wanted to apply a similar model also in the case of the European legislation, which led to the conflict with a concurrent German model.

Taken together, these three dimensions of conflict led to a failure of the draft regulation. On the one hand, Denmark, the UK and Sweden were not ready to compromise, but on the other hand, the Europarties and their allies did not want to adopt the law at any price. In a letter to the Council dated 26 October 2001 they objected to lowering the representative criterion below 1/3, which they found to be an absolute minimum assuring that only truly transnational Europarties received funding (European Political Parties 2001).

The future discussion was strongly influenced by the fact that the amendments to the Treaty on the European Communities made by the Nice Treaty (which came in force on 1 February 2003) gave the opportunity of applying a different legal basis for the adoption of secondary laws governing Europarties, providing for the co-decision procedure, with the Council deciding by Qualified Majority Voting rather than unanimously, as was the case before.

The Commission's 2003 proposal

In a new attempt, the Commission drew conclusions from the failure of the previous draft, and this time proposed much more pragmatic solutions

(European Commission 2003a). The aim was to adopt a regulation devoted only to Europarties' financing and to lay down a minimum of rules acceptable to all MSs devised in response to reservations expressed during previous discussions in the Council. Most importantly, the very definition of the term 'European political party' was extended. In the newest version, not only would it be an "alliance of political parties" (as in all previous drafts) but also "political party", that is, "an association of citizens pursuing political objectives, and either recognised by or established in accordance with, the legal order of at least one Member State". To register its statute, such a European political party would have to be present in at least three MSs. On behalf of the Commission, Commissioner Loyola de Palacio explained that

> Our basic proposal has sought to avoid political requirements that are too restrictive for European political parties for two main reasons: firstly, we want an open and plural system in which all shades of opinion can be represented in the European debate; secondly, if things were done otherwise, the debate in Council and in Parliament would be drawn out unnecessarily, perhaps even beyond the 2004 European elections (European Parliament 2003a).

In the Council, again the major line of conflict concerned the numerical conditions necessary to register a Europarty. In the first compromise text, the previous condition of 1/3 of the MSs was revived. However, the Italian delegation opposed this in writing, demanding that the threshold of three MSs envisaged at the end of the 2001 negotiations be reintroduced. In response, the next compromise proposal was to set this condition at at least 1/5 of the MSs, and in the end 1/4 (Council of the European Union 2003c).

During its part session on 19 June 2003, the EP gave its opinion at first reading and adopted a set of amendments which corresponded to those agreed by the Council (see below). Subsequently, on 5 September 2003, the Council accepted all of the EP's amendments and adopted the Regulation, with Italy, Denmark and Austria voting against, due to the disagreement described above. The votes of these countries (17 together) were not sufficient to block the adoption of this Regulation (they would have needed at least 25 votes). In order to have a comparative view of how conflictive this process was, the key point is to observe that between 1994 and 1998 79 per cent of decisions in the Council were taken by unanimous vote, and that three or more MSs voted against a proposal in only 2 per cent of cases (Mattila 2004). Between 1998 and 2004, in the General Affairs Councils, Denmark, Italy and Austria voted against only once, precisely in the case of Regulation 2004/2003. It therefore proves that the entire matter of regulating political parties led to fierce conflict and the inability to find a compromise between all the MSs.

A very important point to make is why the UK withdrew its previous opposition to this Regulation. Officially, the United Kingdom made its agreement on further statutes on political parties conditional on following the declaration attached to the Treaty of Nice, namely that Europarties will not interfere in national politics (MacShane 2003). Looking however from the informal point of view, we should remember that at that time the Party of European Socialists (PES) was led by Robin Cook, former UK Foreign Minister. According to two senior politicians in the PES (interviews: 2007), Robin Cook asked his successor in office, Jack Straw, to do him a personal favour so that the UK supported this regulation and Straw did so. This is quite an interesting example of Europarties' lobbying of governments.

An interesting case concerns Italy. In 2001, under the left wing government of Giuliano Amato, it did not officially voice any reservations concerning the representativeness criterion. However, Italy did so in 2003, with a new government of the centre-right with Berlusconi's *Forza Italia* as the largest single party, but with two further coalition partners, the National Alliance and the Northern League, holding rather reserved attitudes towards European political integration and not being present in transnational party activities. Day and Shaw (2003) believe that their opposition was behind Italy's proposals to limit as far as possible the numerical conditions for the recognition of Europarties. Finally, the case of Denmark can be explained by her traditionally very reserved stance towards the tightening of EU political integration, but also bearing in mind that in Denmark practically speaking there is no party law, and only parliamentary parties receive funding (Council of Europe 2004). The notion of political party in Denmark strongly emphasizes its participatory character and its private nature. Such comments are very commonly voiced by all Danish MEPs who participated in the debates (see below), and from the reports of the debates in the Council it became clear that they also stood behind the attitude of the Danish government on this matter. In most situations, it acted against any detailed regulation concerning parties' legal personality, against the need to safeguard EU democratic principles and fundamental rights, as well as, contrary to the text of the proposals, arguing for the need to share the subsidies between Europarties on a more proportional basis, rather than take into account mostly the number of MEPs as the pro-rata basis for the division of funds. Their vision of Europarties strongly emphasized that they should be associations of citizens, rather than federations of political parties, that they should not be limited in their right to set up their political programme or internal organization, and, finally, that the criterion of transnational representatives should be totally removed (Council of the European Union 2001a, 2001c, 2003a, 2003b). Most of the Danish amendments were rejected; therefore, the Danish delegation finally voted against this Regulation.

The role of the European Commission

While the European Commission is perceived as a non-partisan representative of the European interest, this does not mean that it is left out of political, partisan influence. Its role is particularly important given that it has the sole right of legislative initiative, and the way it formulates legislative proposals clearly places it on one or the other side of the political spectrum.

As shown before, the Commission during the debates in the EP always exhibited a rather positive approach towards the introduction of EU subsidies for Europarties, though this does not mean that it always fully supported the Parliament's view. For example, some politicians of Europarties (EPP and PES senior officials, interviews: 2006) complained that the Commission could have pressed further and proposed to prepare a fully-fledged statute of European political parties. They mean that such statute should regulate not only the questions of party financing, but all other aspects of their legal status (e.g. legal personality). However, many times the Commission representatives (as Loyola de Palacio quoted above) argued that their aim was to offer flexibility to allow different concepts, definitions and status for European political parties in each MS, and at the same time to ensure no oligarchy or prevention of new parties entering the system.

Although normally the Commission tries to exhibit a united stance, this time internal divisions between the commissioners came to light. Two British commissioners, Chris Patten and Neil Kinnock, were reported as standing against the proposals since the college of commissioners did not agree to their demands to lower the representativeness criteria (Fletcher 2001). The British Conservative party strongly opposed the proposal for public financing of European political parties, both as a matter of principle (that any party should not be financed from public funds), but also in opposition to a scheme perceived as privileging pro-European parties, what they called 'fund for federalism' (Baldwin 2001). Most importantly, however, the British Tories, contrary to two other major British parties, at the time were not members of any European political party, so the representativeness criteria would exclude them from any funding. The newspapers noted that sources close to Chris Patten said he did not believe that the Commission's intention was to exclude the Tories for political reasons, but objected because it might look that way. Neil Kinnock objected for "reasons of democracy and political common sense" (Fletcher 2001). Overall, the former Secretary General of the Party of European Socialists, Anthony Beumer (interview: 2007), believes that the two British Commissioners, and especially Neil Kinnock, questioned this proposal based on their national tradition where the parties traditionally are not publicly funded.

The debates in the European Parliament

The European Parliament (and concretely its four biggest political groups) always stood as the staunch supporter of the strengthening of Europarties that it associated with the idea of the tightening of EU political integration. Full support for the idea has always been expressed by the Group of the European People's Party (EPP) without the British Conservatives however, the PES Group (now S&D Group), the majority of the Group of the European Liberal, Democrats and Reformers (ELDR, now ALDE), and the majority of the Group of the Greens (Greens/EFA). The opponents were mainly found in the Confederal Group of the European United Left – Nordic Green Left (GUE/NGL), the Group of Europe of Democracy and Diversity (EDD, now Europe of Freedom and Democracy), the Union for Europe of the Nations Group (UEN, now transformed into European Conservatives and Reformists Group) and the majority of Independent Members (NI) (European Parliament, 1996, 2000a, 2003a). It is clear then that the supporters always had a large majority, and in the voting on the adoption of the Regulation 345 MEPs voted in favour, with 102 against and 34 abstaining. The left-right divide was not predictive of voting patterns, and the MEPs' vote choice was based on their support of or opposition to further EU political integration (Ringe 2010).

The outcome of this vote is not surprising. Indeed, the commonplace argument advanced in the literature on the voting patterns in the EP is to claim that MEPs of the PES (now S&D), the EPP and the ELDR (now ALDE) have indistinguishable attitudes in favour of tightening political integration against the small groups such as the EDD (Thomassen et al.

2004). However, the crucial point here is that an important part of their pro-European attitudes is precisely the idea of European political parties. One of the reasons why the three largest political families created their EU-level party federations in mid-70s was their belief that the existence of Europarties will push political integration forward. From this point of view, support for the Regulation strengthening Europarties was not just a matter of dispute between the pro-European and anti-European parties, but also between the oldest and largest Europarties (strongly pro-European) and those MEPs who were critical of the idea of Europarties precisely due to their Euroscepticism. So while our first hypothesis is confirmed, it cannot be explained without making a point relating to the size of the parties. I will return to this issue in the last section of this paper.

However, was this debate only a matter of dispute between the advocates of European integration and their opponents or did it also concern the general attitude towards party financing? In the light of above analysis, we know that the question of donations and their limits was one of the most divisive issues. From an analysis carried out by Ringe we learn that MEPs from MSs that specify ceilings on party donations were slightly more likely to support the Regulation, as it contains the provisions stipulating such ceiling (Ringe 2010). This finding would thus be one of the arguments in favour of the borrowing hypothesis. Moving to the qualitative analysis concerning the type of arguments used, individual MEPs many times referred to their national experiences. For example, a Danish MEP from the ELDR protested against the adoption of the Regulation due to his total opposition to the whole idea of financing political parties from "citizens' purses" – in Denmark, as explained, the law does not regulate the matter of financing political parties, and only political groups in the parliament are subsidized. Many MEPs, especially the regionalists from Greens/EFA and the communists from GUE/NGL criticized the general idea of a political party as a transmission belt between the citizens and the state, in a sense referring to the end-of-the-parties thesis. As noted above, based on their national experience the British Conservatives disapprove of the idea of public financing of political parties in general, and of public financing of European political parties accordingly. It could then be summarized that the general debate in the EP was held in relation not only to the proposed Regulation, but also to political parties in general.

On another level of discussion, the project of strengthening political parties at EU level has always been regarded as an idea of the supporters of tightening EU integration. As Independent Belgian MEP Vanhecke observed, it has always been a "project of people who are hoping to create the European federal superstate" (European Parliament 2000a). Although this statement may be a bit exaggerated, it is true that the four biggest groups (EPP, PES, ELDR and the majority of the Greens) are known for their ardent integrationist views and for their warm support for the idea of European political parties. Furthermore, they have had the longest and most fruitful experience of transnational cooperation in the EU (Hix and Lord 1997). They would benefit from EU funding immediately, which might have been seen by the smaller political groups as yet another factor institutionalizing the domination of the grand parties (Beumer 2007). Eurosceptic Jans Peter Bonde pointed out in this context that for regional parties it could be impossible to set up a federation of political parties due to the above high representativeness criteria – being unable to gather representatives from 1/3 or 1/4 of the MSs. Furthermore, he added that Eurosceptics might never want to set up such a political party at EU level as a matter of principle, but they do represent the views of EU citizens, and that is why their interests should be also taken into account (European Parliament, 2001a). He therefore considered that "it is clear that those who preach servility to the EU's institutions are to be rewarded while those of us who still believe that constructive criticism is essential to real democracy are to be punished" (Agence Europe 19 June 2003). Finally, as has always been the case, very often the same personalities were active both in the political groups (as MEPs) and in Europarties. Most notably, Wilfred Martens in the 1994-1999 period used to be at the same time the president of the EPP outside the Parliament and the chairman of the EPP political group inside the Parliament. Therefore, the three biggest groups also had a direct personal motivation to advance the process of the institutionalization of Europarties.

Using extra parliamentary means, 25 MEPs, mostly from the French Front National, the Italian Lega Nord and the Belgian Vlaams Belang, applied to the Court of First Instance for the annulment of the Regulation on the grounds that it was unlawful, it infringed the principles of equality, transparency, political pluralism and subsidiarity. The Court, however, did not deal with their appeal relating to the content, but dismissed their claim as inadmissible, as the applicants did not have locus standi (Court of First Instance 2005).

Getting back to the analysis of the final vote over Regulation 2004/2003, if we analyse the relationship between voting pattern and nationality, we see that in the case of the MEPs from the MSs which rejected the Regulation in the Council, only the Danish MEPs almost unanimously voted against the Regulation, regardless of their group membership or whether at that time their parties were in government or in opposition. Therefore, taking into account the arguments used by the Danes both in the Council negotiations and in the debates in the Parliament, it might be said that there is wide agreement in Denmark about the advantages of their model of party law and consequent dissatisfaction with other models, such as the one applied in the Regulation. However, in the case of Italy and Austria, two other countries which opposed the adoption of the Regulation, the Italian and Austrian MEPs nevertheless supported it. Out of 48 Italian MEPs, only 4 Independents elected from the Lista Emma Bonino and Clemente Mastella from the EPP-ED voted against. None of the Lega Nord MEPs took part in this vote, but their opposition to this regulation is indisputable, given the application they brought before the Court of First Instance (above). However, all four MEPs of the National Alliance voted in favour. Out of 16 Austrian MEPs voting on that day, only three voted against (two from the FPÖ and one independent).

The table below presents the results of the roll-call vote on the adoption of Regulation 2004/2003 categorized by nationality. It reveals that the

Table 1. The results of the roll-call vote on the adoption of the Regulation 2004/2003 divided by nationality

MS	Yes	No	Abstentions	Agreement Index
Luxembourg	3	0	0	1
Denmark	0	10	1	0.95
Spain	48	2	0	0.94
Ireland	10	1	0	0.86
Germany	79	4	4	0.86
Italy	43	4	1	0.84
Portugal	14	1	1	0.81
Netherlands	27	4	0	0.8
Austria	13	3	0	0.71
Belgium	14	5	1	0.55
Greece	15	3	4	0.52
Finland	7	5	1	0.3
UK	31	37	1	0.3
France	34	19	14	0.26
Sweden	5	4	6	0.1

Source: own calculation based on the roll call vote in the EP (European Parliament 2003b)
The agreement index based on the method used by Hix, Noury and Roland (2007)

three most divided group of MEPs were the British (the Labour Party in favour and the other British MEPs against), the French (9 MEPs of the EDD Group were against, as well as the French members of the UEN and the independents, mostly from the Front National) and the Swedish (without any observable partisan divisions).

Subsequent developments

The process of the strengthening of Europarties has not finished with the adoption of the Regulation. The Regulation was primarily devoted to financing issues, leaving a number of other aspects of the legal status of political parties intact. From the very beginning, it was planned that revisions would be needed after the first experiences with the practical application of the Regulation. The Europarties were not calling for an increase in the amount of subsidies, but to make the rules governing their activities and finances less cumbersome. For example, given the rules set up by the EU Financial Regulation, Europarties had to spend all the subsidies they received in one budgetary year, which made long-term financial planning difficult. Such issues were the subject of the 2007 amendment to the Regulation. Additionally, this amendment provided a basis for the establishment of European political foundations affiliated to Europarties, aiming to complement their work. However, the most pressing problems pointed out by the representatives of the Europarties related to their status as Non-Profit-Making Associations based on Belgian law. The Regulation indicates that Europarties may freely choose a MSs in which they wish to have their seat. Given that most Europarties have their seats in Brussels, they must abide by the Belgian law. Accordingly, the only possibility for Europarties to obtain legal personality is to establish themselves as non-profit-making associations. In the opinion of the representatives of the main Europarties (interviews: 2006, 2007, 2011), such status gives a bad impression to the citizens about the real nature of Europarties and, secondly, leads to the situation in which they struggle to function in two different but complementary legal orders: one set up by the Regulation and another one specified by Belgian law. In January 2011, the EP discussed further steps to strengthen the legal position of Europarties. The Giannakou report adopted in March 2011 (European Parliament 2011) emphasized the need for Europarties to respect "the highest standards of internal democracy", inviting parties to involve ordinary citizens in their activities. It also proposed that EU parties should have the right to participate in national referendum campaigns linked to European integration. In June 2012, the European Commission was planning to present a draft of a new Regulation, one of whose most important novelties will be precisely European legal status for the Europarties.

However, it seems that the most important development, which facilitated subsequent amendment in 2007, and the one that was discussed in 2002, is that despite their fears the great opponents of the original Regulation 2004/2003, coming primarily from Eurosceptic circles, established their own Europarties. Since the entry into force of the Regulation, six new extra parliamentary political parties have emerged at the European level. Among these was the European Alliance for Freedom, uniting the Eurosceptics from such parties as the United Kingdom Independent Party (UKIP) and the FPÖ. The European Christian Political Movement was established as the first Europarty without a political group in the EP. However, probably the most interesting development took place in 2012. In that year, for the first time even the extreme-right parties such as the French and Belgian Fronts Nationals and the British National Party would receive EU subsidies for their newly created Europarty named the European Alliance of National Movements. The majority in the EP immediately reacted, demanding that EU law should exclude the possibility of funding racist and xenophobic parties, which was in turn received among the Eurosceptics as an attempt to remove them from the political scene (European Voice 2012). Overall, it seems that, although at a slightly lower temperature, future debates on the regulation of EU parties in law will combine very difficult and politicized questions (such as how to prevent the extreme right from benefiting from EU money) and some technical questions regarding the management and financial operations of Europarties.

Conclusions

To summarize the process of regulating European political parties in law, it is worth quoting Jean-Claude Juncker (quoted in Thomson & Hosli 2006:3), who described the EU's decision-making in the following way:

> We decide on something, leave it lying around and wait and see what happens…If no one kicks up a fuss, because most people don't understand what has been decided, we continue step by step until there is no turning back.

It seems that the process described above fits very well into Juncker's description. Through persistent, incremental steps, the process of regulating EU parties in law was a success. The results of the above analysis thus offer a number of crucial points in understanding party politics in the European Union, both from the perspective of EU studies as well as from perspective of comparative politics.

Our main hypothesis has been confirmed positively: in the matter discussed in this paper, and perhaps beyond, politicians use their national experiences as a source of inspiration to devise legislative solutions at EU level. Such mechanism was visible in relation to the MSs as well as regarding Members of the European Parliament. The arguments used in the entire debate had their sources, first, in given beliefs about the future of EU integration (since the process of party institutionalization was perceived as a step towards a more integrated EU), and, second, concerning the model of regulating political parties. Such a mix of influences resulted in the initial set of preference concerning MSs, individual MEPs and political groups in the European Parliament.

The above analysis has also shown that the conflict over the adoption of party law in the European Parliament did not divide the left and the right. It was rather a conflict between the large and small parties. In the same way, many examples of political finance reform in the nation state, for example in Germany in 1980s, highlight very similar lines of conflict (Scarrow 2004). In the EU, however, it happens that the big Europarties are at the same time very pro-European, whereas the small ones (or those political forces that did not establish a Europarty) exhibit negative or at least reserved views towards European integration.

While attempting to determine from which national tradition of regulating political parties subsequent proposals derived, it still seems worth arguing that the first European Parliament report (the Tsatsos report) reflected the prescriptive model, particularly by stipulating the conditions for party organization, the adoption and publication of their statutes and programmes, and in a practical aspect – the need to adopt a democratic programme and democratic mode of functioning. The Leinen and Dimitrakopolous report seems to operate in the same tradition, due to its emphasis on the procedure concerning loss of the status of European political party in cases where a party does not respect "democratic principles and fundamental rights". Those arguments were also present in the Commission's argument (European Parliament 2001c).

However, since the Tsatsos 1996 report, the subsequent drafts and proposals, looking for a wide compromise, softened their content, abandoning the detailed regulation of party structure, elements of its programme, etc. The draft was becoming less and less strict, to arrive in the final version only as a model for financing political parties. It seems that it is rather difficult to judge which model – prescriptive or permissive – prevails, since in the Regulation itself we have to do mostly with the financing scheme. We have still to wait, then, for when it will be possible to speak of party law at the EU level.

Appendix A: Grants from the European Parliament to political parties at European level 2004-2012

Party	Seat	Year	Maximum grant awarded to Europarty (in EUR)	Maximum grant awarded to affiliated European political foundation (in EUR)
European People's Party	Belgium	2004	1 587 587	-
		2005	2 863 693	-
		2006	2 929 841	-
		2007	3 271 810	-
		2008	3 354 754	1 500 208
		2009	3 485 708	2 294 292
		2010	4 959 462	3 288 663
		2011	6 183 988	4 075 836
		2012	6 482 715	4 197 068
Party of European Socialists	Belgium	2004	1 257 000	-
		2005	2 489 175	-
		2006	2 580 000	-
		2007	2 994 603	-
		2008	3 027 647	1 208 700
		2009	3 100 000	1 950 000
		2010	3 395 323	2 150 000
		2011	4 117 825	2 714 798
		2012	4 323 313	2 802 702

Party	Seat	Year	Maximum grant awarded to Europarty (in EUR)	Maximum grant awarded to affiliated European political foundation (in EUR)
European Liberal Democrat and Reform Party	Belgium	2004	618 896	-
		2005	894 454	-
		2006	883 500	-
		2007	1 133 362	-
		2008	1 115 665	233 750
		2009	1 179 191	725 200
		2010	1 553 984	818 438
		2011	1 815 770	942 819
		2012	1 950 344	1 075 703
European Green Party	Belgium	2004	306 000	-
		2005	568 261	-
		2006	581 000	-
		2007	631 750	-
		2008	641 534	302 678
		2009	643 562	414 895
		2010	1 054 999	684 419
		2011	1 298 539	850 767
		2012	1 333 372	872 042
Alliance of European Conservatives and Reformists	Belgium	2010	1 016 275	659 651
		2011	1 140 478	747 210
		2012	1 285 913	841 397
Party of the European Left	Belgium	2004	210 275	-
		2005	365 868	-
		2006	518 626	-
		2007	526 148	-
		2008	536 685	156 400
		2009	562 405	362 575
		2010	708 080	475 542
		2011	846 936	554 889
		2012	835 049	550 265

Party	Seat	Year	Maximum grant awarded to Europarty (in EUR)	Maximum grant awarded to affiliated European political foundation (in EUR)
European Democratic Party	Belgium	2004 2005 2006 2007 2008 2009 2010 2011 2012	340 425 459 530 514 797 526 148 496 291 492 487 505 617 598 555 550 293	- - - - 233 110 317 500 337 585 392 156 366 393
European Free Alliance	Belgium	2004 2005 2006 2007 2008 2009 2010 2011 2012	165 724 217 906 222 627 222 541 226 600 226 600 339 965 395 333 384 185	- - - - 106 608 147 929 212 544 252 450 259 134
European Alliance for Freedom	Malta	2011 2012	372 753 360 455	244 217 243 811
European Alliance of National Movements	France	2012	289 266	-
EUDemocrats	Denmark	2006 2007 2008 2009 2010 2011 2012	219 825 234 000 226 700 245 274 211 125 259 852 241 807	- - 103 530 153 170 152 008 170 248 167 198

Party	Seat	Year	Maximum grant awarded to Europarty (in EUR)	Maximum grant awarded to affiliated European political foundation (in EUR)
European Christian Political Movement	Netherlands	2010 2011 2012	209 500 259 852 241 807	- 150 000 167 198

Source: European Parliament (2012). In the years 2004-2007, the grant from the European Parliament amounted to 75 per cent of each Europarty's total budget. From 2008 onwards, according to the amended Regulation 2004/2003, it has amounted to 85 per cent of each Europarty's total budget. The national member parties added the remaining 25 (and later 15) per cent of each Europarty's total budget. With regard to European political foundations, in 2008 the grants for operation from the EP covered the period between September and December 2008, whereas the preceding period was covered by the European Commission.

Appendix B: Funding of Political Parties in EU Member States

Matrix on Political Finance Laws (1)

Country	1	2	3	4	5	6	7	8	9	10	11	12	13	14	15
Austria	yes	no	no	no	no	no	no	no	no	no	no	no	no	yes	no
Belgium	yes	yes	no	yes	yes	yes	no	yes	yes	no	yes	yes	yes	yes	no
Denmark	no	yes	no	yes	no	no	no	no	no	no	no	yes	no	yes	no
Finland	yes	no	no	no	no	no	no	no	no	no	no	yes	no	yes	no
France	yes	yes	no	yes	yes	yes	yes	yes	yes	yes	yes	yes	yes	yes	no
Germany	yes	yes	no	yes	no	yes	no	no	no	no	yes	yes	no	yes	yes
Greece		-	-	-	-	-								yes	
Ireland	yes	yes	yes	yes	yes	yes	yes	no	no	no	yes	yes	no	yes	no
Italy	yes	yes	yes	yes	yes	yes	no	no	yes	no	no	yes	yes	yes	yes
Luxemburg		-	-	-	-	-								yes	
Netherlands	yes	yes	no	yes	no	yes	no	no	no	no	yes	no	no	yes	no
Portugal	yes	yes	no	yes	yes	yes	yes	yes	yes	yes	yes	yes	yes	yes	yes
Spain	yes	yes	no	yes	yes	yes	no	no	yes	no	yes	yes	Yes	yes	yes
Sweden	no	no	no	no	no	no	no	no	no	no	no	no	no	yes	no
UK	yes	yes	yes	yes	no	yes	yes	no	no	no	yes	yes	Yes	yes	no
Summary	**yes: 11 no: 2**	**yes:10 no: 3**	**yes: 3 no: 10**	**yes: 10 no: 3**	**yes: 6 no: 7**	**yes: 9 no: 4**	**yes: 4 no: 9**	**yes: 3 no: 10**	**yes: 5 no: 8**	**yes: 2 no: 11**	**yes: 8 no: 5**	**yes: 10 no: 3**	**yes: 6 no: 7**	**yes: 15 no: 0**	**yes: 4 no: 9**
EU	**yes**	**yes**	**no**	**yes**	**yes**	**yes**	**-**	**no**	**yes**	**no**	**yes**	**yes**	**-**	**yes**	**No**

Source: Austin and Tjernström 2003, Funding of Political Parties and Election Campaigns, IDEA International (for EU Member States) and author's own work (for the EU).

Column 1: Is there a system of regulation for the financing of political parties?
Column 2: Is there provision for disclosure of contributions to political parties?
Column 3: Do donors have to disclose contributions made?
Column 4: Do political parties have to disclose contributions received?
Column 5: Is there a ceiling on contributions to political parties?
Column 6: Is there a ban on any type of donation to political parties?
Column 7: Is there a ban on foreign donations to political parties?
Column 8: Is there a ban on corporate donations to political parties?
Column 9: Is there a ban on donations from government contractors to political parties?
Column 10: Is there a ban on trade union donations to political parties?
Column 11: Is there a ban on anonymous donations to political parties?
Column 12: Is there provision for public disclosure of expenditure by political parties?
Column 13: Is there a ceiling on party election expenditure?
Column 14: Do political parties receive direct public funding?
Column 15: Are political parties entitled to special taxation status?

References

Austin, R. and Tjernstrom, M. (eds) (2003) *Funding of Political Parties and Election Campaigns*, Stockholm, International Institute for Democracy and Electoral Assistance.

Baldwin, T. (2001, 12/01). Prodi told to rethink subsidies for parties. The Times.

Bieber, R. (1999) 'Les perspectives d'un statut pour les partis politiques europeens', *Revue trimestrielle de droit europeen*, 35(3), 349-62.

Biezen, Ingrid van, and Kopecky, P. (2007) 'The State and the Parties: Public Funding, Public Regulation and Rent-Seeking in Contemporary Democracies', *Party Politics*, 13(2), 235-54.

Council of Europe (2004) Report on the Establishement, Organisation and Activities of Political Parties. *Study no. 247/2003*. Strasbourg: Council of Europe.

Council of the European Union (2001a) Proposal for a Council Regulation on the statute and financing of European political parties. No. 2001/0011 (CNS), 11667/01.

Council of the European Union (2001b) Proposal for a Council Regulation on the statute and financing of European political parties. No. 2001/0011 (CNS), 11960/01.

Council of the European Union (2001c) Proposal for a regulation of the European Parliament and of the Council on the statute and financing of European political parties: Report from Working Party on General Affairs. No. 2001/0011 (CNS), 12309/01.

Council of the European Union (2003a) The statute and financing of European political parties - Issues outstanding. No. 2003/0039 (COD), 10451/03.

Council of the European Union (2003b) The statute and financing of European political parties - Compromise text for Articles 3, 4 and 5(1). No. 2003/0039 (COD), 8133/03.

Council of the European Union (2003c) The statute and financing of European political parties - Presidency compromise text. No. 2003/0039 (COD), 10002/03.

Day, S. and Shaw, J. (2003) The evolution of Europe's transnational political parties in the era of European citizenship. in R. Chicowski and T.Borzel (eds) *State of the European Union Volume 6: Law, Politics and Society*. Oxford: Oxford University Press.

Day, S. and Shaw, J. (2005) Transnational Political Parties. in R. Bellamy, D. Castiglione and J. Shaw (eds) *Making European Citizens*. London: Palgrave.

European Commission (2001) Proposal for a Council regulation on the statute and financing of European political parties. OJ 2001 C 154 E, 29 May 2001.

European Commission (2003a) Proposal for a Regulation of the European Parliament and of the Council on the Statute and Financing of European Political Parties. No. COM (2003) 77 final, 2003/0039/COD.

European Commission (2003b). Commission proposes rules on statute and financing of European political parties, retrieved from http://europa.eu/rapid/pressReleasesAction.do?reference=IP/03/260&format=HTML&aged=0&lg=nl&guiLanguage=en, access date: 17.11.2008.

European Court of Auditors (2000) Special Report No 13/2000 of the Court of Auditors on the expenditure of the European Parliament's political groups, OJ C 181, 28.6.2000.

European Parliament (1996) Report on the constitutional status of the European Political Parties. Rapporteur: Dimitris Tsatsos. No. A4-0342/96.

European Parliament (2000a) Debate on European political parties, Wednesday, 14 June 2000. Retrieved 13 January 2007, from http://www.europarl.europa.eu/sides/getDoc.do?pubRef=- //EP//TEXT+CRE+20000614+ITEM-003+DOC+XML+V0//EN&language=EN.

European Parliament (2000b) Report on the European Parliament's proposals for the Intergovernmental Conference. Rapporteurs: Giorgos Dimitrakopoulos, Jo Leinen. No. A5-0086/2000European Parliament (2001a) Constitutional Affairs Committee, Monday 5 March, Point no.7 - 'The Status of EU Political Parties', Informal note.

European Parliament (2001b) Debate on the Statute and financing of European political parties, Wednesday, 16&17 May 2001. Retrieved 13 January 2007, from http://www. europarl.europa.eu/sides/getDoc.do?pubRef=-//EP//TEXT+CRE+20010516+ITEM-007+DOC+XML+V0//EN&language=EN

European Parliament (2001c) Report on the proposal for a Council regulation on the statute and financing of European political parties. Rapporteur: Ursula Schleicher. No. A5-0167/2001.

European Parliament (2003a) Debate on Wednesday, 18 June 2003 Statute and financing of European political parties. Retrieved 13 January 2007, from http://www.europarl.europa.eu/sides/getDoc.do?pubRef=//EP//TEXT+CRE+20030618+ITEMS+DOC+XML+V0//EN&language=EN.

European Parliament (2003b) Minutes Proceedings of the Sitting, Official Journal of the European Union, C 69E, Volume 47, p. 18.

European Parliament (2011) Report on the Application of Regulation (EC) No 2004/2003 on the Regulations Governing Political Parties at European Level and the Rules Regarding Their Funding (2010/2201(INI). Retrieved 2 July 2012 from http://www.europarl.europa.eu/sides/getDoc.do?type=REPORT&mode=XML&reference=A7-2011-0062&language=EN.

European Parliament (2012) Grants from the European Parliament to political parties at European level 2004-2012. Retrieved 2 July 2012, from http://www.europarl.europa.eu/pdf/grants/grant_amounts_foundations_per_01-03-2012.pdf.

European Political Parties (2001) Letter from Arnold Cassola (European Federation of Green Parties), Robin Cook (President of the Party of European Socialists), Werner Hoyer (President of the European Liberal, Democrat and Reform Party), Nelly Maes (Leader, Democratic, Party of the Peoples of Europe -European Free Alliance) and Wilfried Martens, President of the European People's Party to Guy Verhofstadt (President of the European Council), Louis Michel (President of the Council), Annemie Neyts (Minister attached to the Minister for Foreign Affairs, charged with Agriculture), Romano Prodi (President of the European Commission).

European Voice. "MEPs Want to Stop EU Funds Reaching Far-right Parties | European Voice", April 4, 2012. http://www.europeanvoice.com/article/imported/meps-want-to-stop-eu-funds-reaching-far-right-parties/74049.aspx.

Fletcher, M. (2001) EU stands firm on political subsidy. *The Times, 25 January.*

Hix, S. (2005) *The political system of the European Union,* Basingstoke, Macmillan.

Hix, S. and Lord, C. (1997) *Political parties in the European Union,* Basingstoke; New York, Macmillan; St. Martin's Press.

Hix, S., Noury, A. G. and Roland, G. (2007) *Democratic politics in the European Parliament,* Cambridge, Cambridge University Press.

Janda, K. (2005) *Political Parties and Democracy in Practical and Theoretical Perspectives.* Adopting Party Law, *Washington, National Democratic Institute for International Affairs.*

Johansson, K. M. and Raunio, T. *(2005) 'Regulating Europarties. Cross-Party Coalitions Capitalizing on Incomplete Contracts',* Party Politics, *11(5), 515-34.*

Judge, D. and Earnshaw, D. (2008) *The European Parliament,* Basingstoke; New York: Palgrave Macmillan.

Lehmann, W. (2003) Statut et financement des partis politiques européens. Luxembourg: Parlement européen Série Affaires constitutionnelles (AFCO 105FR).

MacShane, D. (2003) Letter from Denis MacShane, Minister for Europe, Foreign and Commonwealth Office to the Chairman of House of Lords Select Committee on European Union, 10 June 2003.

Mattila, M. (2004) 'Contested Decisions - Empirical Analysis of Voting in the EU Council of Ministers', *European Journal of Political Research,* 43(1), 29-50.

Moravcsik, A. (1998) *The choice for Europe: social purpose and state power from Messina to Maastricht,* Ithaca, N.Y Cornell University Press.

Nassmacher, K.-H. (2009) *The Funding of Party Competition: Political Finance in 25 Democracies*. Baden-Baden: Nomos.

Osiatynski, W. (2003) 'Paradoxes of Constitutional Borrowing', *International Journal of Constitutional Law,* 1(2), 244-68.

Pierre, J., L. Svåsand, and A. Widfeldt (2000) 'State subsidies to political parties: Confronting rhetoric with reality.' *West European Politics* 23(3): 1-24.

Regulation (EC) No. 2004/2003 of the European Parliament and of the Council of 4 November 2003 on the regulations governing political parties at European level and the rules regarding their funding. Official Journal of the European Union, 15 November 2003, L 297/1.

Ringe, N. (2010) *Who decides, and how? preferences, uncertainty, and policy choice in the European Parliament,* Oxford: Oxford University Press.

Scarrow, S. E. (2004) 'Explaining Political Finance Reforms: Competition and Context', *Party Politics,* 10, 653-75.

Taylor, S. (2012) 'MEPs Want to Stop EU Funds Reaching Far-right Parties', *European Voice,* April 4, 2012. http://www.europeanvoice.com/article/imported/meps-want-to-stop-eu-funds-reaching-far-right-parties/74049.aspx.

Thomassen, J., Noury, A. and Voeten, E. (2004) Political competition in the European Parliament: evidence from roll call and survey analyses. in G. Marks and M. R. Steenbergen (eds) *European Integration and Political Conflict.* Cambridge: CUP.

Thomson, R, and Hosli, M. O. (2006) 'Explaining legislative decision-making in the European Union' In R. Thomson, F. N. Stokman, C. H. Achen & T. Konig (Eds.), *The European Union Decides.* Cambridge: Cambridge University Press.

CHAPTER 7

The SGP Case: Did it Really (Re)Launch the Debate on Party Regulation in the Netherlands?

Hans-Martien ten Napel & **Jaco van den Brink**
Leiden University

Introduction

The Staatkundig Gereformeerde Partij (Political Reformed Party, hereafter, SGP), which was founded in 1918, is the oldest political party still functioning in the Netherlands. Since 1922 it has been represented continuously in the Lower House (Tweede Kamer) of the Dutch Parliament, with first one, then two or three seats (out of a total of 100 and, since 1956, 150 seats). It can be characterized as an Orthodox Protestant party, based on the Bible and the doctrinal so-called Three Forms of Unity.

According to Articles 7 and 10 of the SGP's Statement of Principles '[t]he Word of God holds that, on the basis of the order of creation, man and woman have each been given their own and distinct mission and place.... Every effort at emancipation that negates the God-given mission and place of men and women is considered revolutionary and has to be combated forcefully.' More specifically, Article 10 of the same Statement makes it clear that '[t]he notion of [the existence of] a right to vote for women which results from a revolutionary striving for emancipation is incompatible with woman's calling'.[1]

In 2005, legal proceedings were initiated against the SGP after the party had evoked anger from some feminist and other organizations because it did not nominate women on its election lists. The Council of State, the highest administrative court in the Netherlands, ruled in 2007 that the state could not exclude the party from receiving the regular political party subsidy. Three years later, however, the highest civil court in the Netherlands, the Supreme Court, ruled that the state was obliged to take (other) measures that would force the party to end the exclusion of women from its election lists.[2] In 2010, the party submitted an application to the European Court of Human Rights (ECtHR). In its decision on 10 July 2012, the Court declared the application to be manifestly ill-founded, and therefore inadmissible.[3]

This chapter will deal with the various legal proceedings in which the SGP has been involved both within the Netherlands and before the ECtHR. What considerations led to such different outcomes? And what have the implications been for party regulation? The internationally vibrant topic of party regulation has until recently been something of a taboo in the Netherlands. Traditionally, the idea was that political parties were essentially private associations in whose internal affairs the state ought not to interfere. However, the case of the SGP has led to a political and public debate on whether this view can be maintained. Section two will look at the national legal proceedings, section three at the European level. Section four will argue that the implications for the debate on party regulation have not been as significant as anticipated, and that the different considerations in the SGP case can be better understood against the backdrop of the so-called new institutionalism, whereby not just the historical and social sciences are characterized, but increasingly also the legal discipline.

National legal proceedings

Commencement

As was set out above, the legal proceedings against the SGP began in 2005 when both the SGP and the Dutch state were summoned before the civil sector of the District Court by the feminist Test Case Foundation Clara Wichmann and a number of other non-governmental organizations (Davies 2006).[4] According to these organizations, the differential treatment of men and women with respect to passive suffrage by the SGP violated not just their own goals as listed in their articles of association, but also the general interest of society in the elimination of discrimination as demanded by both the Dutch Constitution and a range of treaty obligations.

On 7 September 2005 the District Court declared the case against the SGP itself inadmissible. In their claim against the state, however, the claimant organizations were more successful: the Court ruled that by subsidizing the party pursuant to the Political Parties Subsidies Act, the Dutch state had violated Article 7 of the Convention on the Elimination of All Forms of Discrimination against Women (CEDAW) adopted in

1979 by the United Nations General Assembly. The Court therefore forbade the state to grant any further subsidies to the SGP (Davies 2006).

Administrative proceedings

The state discontinued the provision of subsidies to the SGP on 20 December 2005. The SGP challenged this decision by the Dutch Minister of the Interior and Kingdom Relations in new proceedings in the administrative law sector of the District Court, but on 30 November 2006 the court rejected the SGP's appeal. On 22 December 2006 the party then lodged a further appeal with the Administrative Jurisdiction Division of the Council of State, the highest administrative court in the Netherlands.

Almost a year later, on 5 December 2007, the Council of State quashed the lower court's ruling that the subsidies to the SGP had to be stopped.[5] Although according to Article 7 (c) of CEDAW the right of women to participate on an equal footing with men in non-governmental organizations and associations concerned with the public and political life of the country had to be ensured, this did not imply the right of women to participate in each and every such organization and association. Moreover, women who sympathized with the ideas of the SGP but nevertheless wanted to be candidates could relatively easily start a party of their own.

The SGP's rights to freedom of religion and conscience, freedom of assembly and association and freedom of expression, and hence central tenets of the Dutch democracy, were at stake because the measure against the SGP put the party at a disadvantage compared to other political parties. In its reasoning on whether the principle of gender equality, as enshrined in Article 7 of CEDAW, necessitated the state to end subsidies to the SGP, the Council of State noted that a democracy such as the Netherlands also needs a broad representation of all philosophical and religious streams of thought within society. Therefore, groups with views on the biblical vocations of men and women in public life that are rejected by the great majority of the population, including most fellow Christians, still ought to be given the opportunity to bring their ideas to the fore. It would undermine the basic principles of a democracy if the state disadvantaged certain groups because of their convictions; this would hamper the legitimacy of the outcome of the debate. As long as a party abides by criminal law, according to the Political Parties Subsidies Act the state should also remain impartial and relate in an even-handed manner towards all divergent political ideas. Therefore, according to the Council, the government ought not to interfere with the SGP's ideas and practices, and not disadvantage the party by withholding subsidies. This was also demanded by the case law of the ECtHR, which emphasized that a state should show restraint in interfering in the various freedoms of political parties because of their crucial role in achieving a pluralistic and democratic society, unless they constituted a danger to the democratic constitutional order (see Ten Napel 2009). According to the Council of State, this was not the case with the SGP.

Further civil proceedings

Meanwhile, the civil proceedings continued; the state and the SGP both lodged appeals against the District Court's ruling. In 2008, the Court of Appeal ruled, after balancing the principle of non-discrimination against the freedoms of the party, that the non-discrimination principle had to prevail in this case and that the state was under an obligation to take measures against the SGP.[6] The Court left the nature of these measures open, but as a result of the Council of State's ruling it was clear that these could not involve withholding subsidies from the party.

More specifically, the Court of Appeal stressed that the freedom of religion as protected by Article 9 of the European Convention on Human Rights (ECHR) was not an absolute right. In the case of the SGP, moreover, not even the core of this right would be touched upon if passive female suffrage were made compulsory. Neither would Article 11 on the freedom of association be infringed, as the party could organize itself in all other respects in accordance with its statutes. Finally, with respect to Article 10, the Court of Appeal once again failed to see how the party's freedom of expression would be restricted because of such a measure. The Convention, on the contrary, did not allow any exceptions with respect to the principle of non-discrimination on the basis of gender.

Like the Council of State, the Court of Appeal found it relevant that the case arose with respect to a political party. It interpreted this differently, however. The fact that political parties fulfil a crucial role in constitutional democracies did not keep the Court of Appeal from interfering in the internal affairs of the SGP, but made the violation of the non-discrimination principle even worse than it would have been in the case of a fully private association.

The state and the SGP appealed again to the Supreme Court, the highest judicial institution for civil cases in the Netherlands. On 9 April 2010 the Supreme Court upheld the Court of Appeal's conclusion.[7] The Court declared the voting rights of citizens to be the essential core of democracy. Therefore, it was not acceptable for a political party to act contrary to a clause that grants all citizens equal active and passive voting rights, even when this practice is rooted in a party's religious principles. This led the Supreme Court to the conclusion that the government needed to take effective measures against the SGP's disputed practice. Or, in the words of the Supreme Court itself:

> '4.5.3. The basic rights of freedom of religion and freedom of association – and of course also freedom of expression, which, for the matter now in issue, has little if any independent significance next to the basic rights just mentioned – guarantee that citizens may unite in a political party on the basis of a religious or philosophical conviction and may express their conviction and the political principles and programmes based thereon within the framework of that party.
> In a democratic state governed by the rule of law, however, those principles and programmes may only be given practical effect within the limits posed by laws and treaties.
> 4.5.4. The general representative bodies represent the entire population without making distinctions among the citizens of whom it is made up. They form the heart of the democracy and a guarantee for the democratic content of the State. The rights to vote and to stand for election are essential to guarantee the democratic content of these bodies. Both Article 4 of the Constitution and Article 25 of the International Covenant on Civil and Political Rights taken together with its Article 2 and, as far as women are concerned, Article 7 of the Convention on the Elimination of All Forms of Discrimination against Women guarantee to everyone, without any distinction based on gender, the right to elect members of these bodies as well as to be elected to them. The said provisions mention the right to vote and the right to stand for election in the same breath, thus expressing that in a democracy they are each other's necessary pendant, since the voters must be able to determine for themselves who among them should be eligible.
> 4.5.5. Seen thus, since the possibility to exercise the right to stand for election goes to the core of the State's democratic functioning, it is unacceptable that a political formation in composing its lists of candidates violates a basic right that guarantees the elective rights of all citizens, regardless of whether such action reposes on a principle rooted for that formation in its religious or philosophical convictions. To that extent, the prohibition of discrimination set forth in Article 4 of the Constitution, Article 25 taken together with Article 2 of

> the International Covenant on Civil and Political Rights and, in the particular context of the present case, Article 7 of the Convention on the Elimination of All Forms of Discrimination against Women outweighs the other basic rights in issue.
> It follows from the above that the SGP's violation of the basic right, guaranteed by the Constitution and the said treaties, to be allowed to stand for election on an equal footing with men is not justified by the fact that its view of woman's calling and place in society is directly rooted in its religious conviction. Admittedly the SGP cannot be denied its conviction and the civil courts are not even competent to express an opinion on the question whether that conviction is of greater or lesser importance in the faith of the members of the party, and admittedly a democratic legal order requires tolerance in relation to opinion rooted in religious or philosophical convictions. All that, however, does not prevent the courts from finding the way in which the SGP puts its convictions into practice in nominating candidates for general representative bodies unacceptable.'[8]

As a result, the Supreme Court upheld the judgment of the Court of Appeal in so far as it concluded that the Dutch state was under an obligation to adopt an effective measure to ensure that the SGP introduced passive female suffrage. At the same time, this measure should not infringe the party's rights any more than strictly necessary. Moreover, the Supreme Court did not want to decide for the state which particular measure would be best suited to achieve this double result.

The proceedings before the ECtHR

The SGP subsequently launched an application to the ECtHR under Articles 9, 10 and 11 of the European Convention. However, the ECtHR unanimously adjudged the complaint to be inadmissible as manifestly ill-founded.[9] The Court briefly expressed its doubts concerning the SGP being a victim, as the Dutch government had deliberately not yet taken any concrete measures against the party, but did not elaborate on this.[10] The reason was that, according to the ECtHR, the application was inadmissible for another reason.

The Court simply assumed that there had been an 'interference' with the party's rights, and that this interference had been 'prescribed by law' and pursued the 'legitimate aim' of protecting 'the rights of others'.[11]

Next, the Court referred to the Preamble to the Convention, in which the importance of democracy was clearly emphasized. It then went on as follows:

> '70. As the Court has stated many times in its case-law, not only is democracy a fundamental feature of the European public order but the Convention was designed to promote and maintain the ideals and values of a democratic society. Democracy, the Court has stressed, is the only political model contemplated in the Convention and the only one compatible with it. By virtue of the wording of the second paragraph of Article 11, and likewise of Articles 8, 9 and 10 of the Convention, the only necessity capable of justifying an interference with any of the rights enshrined in those Articles is one that may claim to spring from a "democratic society" ....
> 71. The Court has also held that a political party may, under the Convention, pursue its political aims on two conditions: firstly, the means used to those ends must be legal and democratic; secondly, the changes proposed must themselves be compatible with fundamental democratic principles.... Provided that it satisfies these conditions, a political party animated by the moral values imposed by a religion cannot be regarded as intrinsically inimical to the fundamental principles of democracy, as set forth in the Convention....
> 72. Turning to the present matter, the Court reiterates that the advancement of the equality of the sexes is today a major goal in the member States of the Council of Europe. This means that very weighty reasons would have to be advanced before a difference of treatment on the ground of sex could be regarded as compatible with the Convention....
> 73. Moreover, the Court has held that nowadays the advancement of the equality of the sexes in the member States of the Council of Europe prevents the State from lending its support to views of the man's role as primordial and the woman's as secondary....
> 75. No woman has expressed the wish to stand for election as a candidate for the applicant party. However, the Court does not consider that decisive....
> 77. The Supreme Court, in paragraphs 4.5.1 to 4.5.5 of its judgment, concluded from Article 7 of the Convention on the Elimination of All Forms of Discrimination against Women and from Articles 2 and 25 of the International Covenant on Civil and Political Rights taken together that the SGP's position is unacceptable regardless of

> the deeply-held religious conviction on which it is based.... For its part, and having regard to the Preamble to the Convention and the case-law ..., the Court takes the view that in terms of the Convention the same conclusion flows naturally from Article 3 of Protocol No. 1 taken together with Article 14.
> 78. That said, the Court must refrain from stating any view as to what, if anything, the respondent Government should do to put a stop to the present situation.'[12]

In an earlier, classic judgment, the Court had already stated that without 'pluralism, tolerance and broadmindedness ... there can be no democratic society'.[13] Furthermore, the Court attaches much weight to political parties' freedom of association, also because of the 'essential' or 'primordial' role of political parties within a democracy.[14] Nevertheless, this does not mean that diversity is completely unlimited: a democracy does not have to allow parties that threaten the plural democracy itself and want to replace it. In those cases, it can even be necessary, according to the ECtHR, to dissolve a party.[15] In the SGP's case, however, only one element of the party's ideology was at stake, raising the question whether or not this was compatible with fundamental democratic principles, notably gender equality *in politicis.* Furthermore, in the SGP case the equality principle collides with other fundamental rights such as the party's freedom of association and freedom of religion. Although it can therefore hardly come as a surprise that the ECtHR in the SGP decision attached so much weight to gender equality, it is less than obvious that state measures against the SGP had also to be regarded as justified.

Implications for party regulation?

After the rulings of the District Court in the civil proceedings, on 24 June 2006 the SGP amended its Principles to the extent that it would henceforth be possible for women to become members of the party. As the ECtHR had already noted, the Dutch Government had deliberately waited before taking any concrete measures against the party until after the judgment of the ECtHR, a decision that was backed by parliament.[16] It is an interesting question whether this was the right thing to do, given the subsidiarity principle that applies in the relationship between the ECtHR and national authorities. One explanation for this, however, is that the then Rutte I cabinet was a minority cabinet that needed the support of the

SGP to get legislation through the Senate. Meanwhile, in the summer of 2013 the party was changed from within, because a female member was nominated as a candidate for a municipal council.[17] In a sense this ended the Dutch debate on party regulation before it had actually truly begun.

According to legal scholars Schutgens and Sillen (2010), for example, what would perhaps have been most suitable was the addition of a provision to the Elections Act that prevents political parties' statutes from being discriminatory (see, however, B.P. Vermeulen and A.J. Overbeeke 2011: 147ff).[18] *De jure* exclusion of women by parties such as the SGP would then be ruled out, assuming that the parties wished to continue to participate in elections, even though it would remain possible in practice not to nominate women candidates. However at present not even this measure is being debated, let alone the possibly more effective measure of a legal obligation to nominate women candidates to election lists, a kind of quota requirement inspired by the Belgian example (Rodriguez Ruiz and Rubio-Marin 2008). In fact, even if made compulsory, the introduction of gender quotas in the Netherlands would not guarantee success, as it would be possible, for example, for the SGP formally to nominate women who would then give up their seats after being elected (Schutgens and Sillen 2010). It should be noted, however, that the measure suggested by Schutgens and Sillen – the introduction of a provision that obliges parties to admit both male and female candidates for elections – could also eventually result in the disqualification of a list submitted for elections and should therefore be considered a severe measure as well. Indeed, as Eva Brems has stated, 'it is a very serious measure, since it is the main purpose of a political party to compete in elections' (Brems 2006: 144). The seriousness of the measure is increased by the fact that, in this case, the disqualification of a list submitted for elections would take place largely because of the lack of internal party democracy. As Richard S. Katz has argued, ensuring appropriate forms of internal party organization and political behaviour is probably the most controversial purpose of state law concerning political parties (as cited in: Janda 2005: 3).

The main aim of this chapter has been to explain the SGP case, and indeed its potential significance to party regulation, to an (international) audience of non-lawyers. The central purpose has not been to present our own views on the attempts to balance fundamental rights that were undertaken by the various courts in the SGP case, as we have done both on an individual basis and together on other occasions. The first article asked how it was possible that two national high courts could, within a reasonably brief period, reach partly opposing conclusions, and what explained the then recent ruling by the Dutch Supreme Court. It sought to answer these questions with the help of a normative framework for balancing conflicting human rights, and problematized the legal-political choice in favor of the concept of positive liberty that the Supreme Court appeared to have made. In the article's conclusion, a form of constitutionalism for divided societies was suggested as a possible middle ground between positive and negative freedom, procedural and substantive democracy, and formal and substantive equality (Ten Napel 2011). A second article examined the case of the SGP particularly from the viewpoint of democratic theory. It concluded that, generally speaking, a light version of the substantial democracy conception, of which the Council of State's ruling is representative, is to be preferred over a proceduralist conception, by which both the Supreme Court's ruling and the ECtHR's admissibility decision in the SGP case are characterized. The difference is not so much that one conception of democracy or the other makes more moral choices. Rather, as can be learned from the SGP case, in a light version of the substantial democracy conception, a broader range of constitutional values is taken into account, whereas in a proceduralist conception, often one or two specific principles are singled out. From that perspective, a light version of the substantial democracy conception better guarantees the freedom and paradoxically the autonomy of both citizens and their associations. Therefore, it seems more suitable for a proper constitutional democracy (Van den Brink and Ten Napel (2013a).

It is worthwhile here, however, to point to the fact that, just as in the field of political science, among civil and constitutional lawyers different theoretical approaches can be discerned. These different approaches can lead to differences in outcome of the case law, over time or space. Thus, existing normative frameworks for balancing fundamental rights do not lead to an unequivocal result in the SGP case. The application of purely legal criteria is simply not sufficient to tip the scales to one side or the other. Consequently, the choice between conflicting fundamental rights in a case such as this becomes 'political'. It would be too simple to accuse the various courts of taking a party-political side. Nevertheless, court rulings can have important legal-political implications.

In the case of the SGP, what appears to be particularly relevant is the importance attached to the role of institutions. The so-called neo-institutionalism is gaining ground within the legal discipline as well. According to the underlying social pluralism theory we must recognize the variety of institutions that fulfill all kinds of roles in society and human life, including families, schools, organizations for charity or for the dissemination of (political) ideas, churches and other religious institutions, and of course the state. These institutions provide all kinds of goods that we need as human beings: food and shelter, love and company, mutual help and care, safety and security, livelihood, education, religious practice. Furthermore, each institution seems to be equipped with a particular authority structure, which suggests that we must prevent them from interfering in one another's internal business. This means that the state, or the political sphere, is not the sovereign and all-encompassing Leviathan, but only one sphere among others, albeit the only one with a monopoly on violence. The state is not plenipotentiary, and must be restricted to a limited area of legitimate interference (the public sphere). The other aspects of society must be left to the institutions, which are supposed to execute their proper authority and deliver their goods (Van den Brink and Ten Napel 2013b: 363-364).

The more 'the institutional turn' is taken, the more there will be a tendency, as one author recently put it, to 'treat ... religious entities as largely sovereign institutions, immunizing them from the application of civil rights laws and other statutes' (Horwitz 2013: 10). It is not too far-fetched to conclude that the Council of State is more representative of this approach than the Supreme Court or, for that matter, the ECtHR. Both latter courts emphasize rather the principles of individual autonomy and self-determination.

It is also possible to look at the debate on party regulation from this angle, and then conclude that the fact that the SGP case has thus far not led to a (re)launch of the debate on party regulation can at least in part be explained by this neo-institutionalism. Paradoxically, this neo-institutionalism is very much in line with Dutch traditions of tolerance and openness, according to which it is appropriate to regard the freedoms of conscience and religion, assembly and association, and expression as essential to democracy. In particular, the approach of the Council of State gives members of a religious community a maximum amount of freedom within the boundaries of the law to organize themselves, to define and practise their own preferences, according to their own principles.

As a result, the question is whether the Netherlands, in a comparative perspective, is indeed gradually moving away from the British approach of defining political parties as free associations of individuals, with a minimum of state regulation and oversight, towards the German model of political parties as specific associations with rather well-defined legal responsibilities, duties and prerogatives. This was suggested in the *Report on the participation of political parties in elections* by the Venice Commission

(2006, para. 6; cf. Ten Napel 2011: 69). Although tendencies in this direction can be seen in, for example, the ruling of the Supreme Court, it is too early to tell whether this development will continue or not, certainly as far as the legislature is concerned. From a constitutional law point of view this is not necessarily to be regretted, as '[i]t is vital for the nation that there be checks on the government, because government is not always right – and may be seriously wrong. The needed creative alternatives exist in a thriving civil society, a culture with institutions that can dissent from the society's – and governments' – popular views. A thriving civil society is one with strong and independent organizations that can protect and promote views that are unpopular, but may turn out to be right. To keep a necessary check on government, society needs alternative moral voices and those voices will only exist if their institutional framework is protected' (Carlson-Thies 2010: 18).

Notes

1 Translation taken from: ECtHR 10 July 2012, Case No. 58369/10 (admissibility decision), *Staatkundig Gereformeerde Partij* v. *the Netherlands*, para. 9.
2 The rulings of the Council of State and the Supreme Court are available (in Dutch) at www.rechtspraak.nl, under LJ-numbers BB9493, and BK4549 and BK4547, respectively.
3 Supra note 1.
4 In a sense, however, the history of the legal battle against the SGP actually dates back to the first half of the 1990s. See Ten Napel (2002).
5 Supra note 2.
6 The Court of Appeal judgment is available at www.rechtspraak.nl, under LJ-number BC0619.
7 Supra note 2.
8 Translation taken from: ECtHR 10 July 2012, Case No. 58369/10 (admissibility decision), supra note 1, para. 49.
9 Supra note 1.
10 Ibid., para. 67.
11 Ibid., para. 68.
12 Ibid., paras. 70-78.
13 *Handyside v the United Kingdom* Case no 5493/72 (ECtHR 7 December 1976), para 49.

14 Case nos 41340/98, 41342/98, 41343/98 and 41344/98 (Grand Chamber) (ECtHR 13 February 2003) *Refah Partisi (The Welfare Party)*, para 87; *United Communist Party of Turkey ao* v *Turkey* Case no 133/1996/752/951 (Grand Chamber) (ECtHR 30 January 1998), para 25.

15 *Refah Partisi (The Welfare Party)* (supra note 14), para 99.

16 Supra note 1, paras. 56-58.

17 'History was made as a woman could lead the orthodox Christian local party, www.dutchnews.nl, 21 August 2013; 'The brethren in black suits get their first female local leader', ibid., 27 August 2013.

18 Vermeulen and Overbeeke argue that the Constitution would need to be changed first before such a revision of the Elections Act could take effect.

References

Brems, Eva (2006) "Freedom of political association and the question of party closures", in: Wojciech Sadurski (ed.), *Political Rights under Stress in 21st Century Europe,* Oxford: Oxford University Press, pp. 120–195.

Brink, Jaco van den and Hans-Martien ten Napel (2013a), "The Dutch Political Reformed Party (SGP) and Passive Female Suffrage: A Comparison of Three High Court Judgments From the Viewpoint of Democratic Theory", in: *Merkourios. Utrecht Journal of International and European Law*, 29, no. 77, pp. 29-41.

Brink, Jaco van den and Hans-Martien ten Napel (2013b), "The State, Civil Society and Religious Freedom", *Oxford Journal of Law and Religion,* vol. 2, no. 2, pp. 354–370.

Carlson-Thies, Stanley (2010) 'Liberty or Liability: The Future of Institutional Religious Freedom', 3 *Cardus* 14-30.

Davies, Gareth (2006) "Thou Shalt Not Discriminate Against Women: Public Subsidies to Religious Parties Condemned in Clara Wichmann Foundation v. The Dutch State. Court of First Instance, The Hague. Judgment of 7 September 2005", *European Constitutional Law Review,* 2, pp. 152-166.

Horwitz, Paul (2013) *First Amendment Institutions* (Cambridge, MA: Harvard University Press).

Janda, Kenneth (2005) *Political Parties and Democracy in Theoretical and Practical Perspectives. Adopting Party Law,* Washington, D.C.: National Democratic Institute for International Affairs.

Napel, Hans-Martien ten (2002) "Een Nederlandse Taliban?", in: N.F. van Manen (ed.), *De multiculturele samenleving en het recht,* Nijmegen: Paul Scholten Instituut/Ars Aequi Libri, pp. 151-157.

Napel, Hans-Martien ten (2009) "The European Court of Human Rights and political rights: The need for more guidance", *European Constitutional Law Review*, vol. 5, no. 3, pp. 464–480.

Napel, Hans-Martien ten (2011) "Finishing the Work Begun by the French Revolution: A Critical Analysis of the Dutch Supreme Court Judgment on the Political Reformed Party and Passive Female Suffrage", *European Public Law*, vol. 17, no. 1, pp. 61-70.

Rodriguez Ruiz, Blanca and Ruth Rubio-Marin (2008), "The Gender of Representation. On Democracy, Equality and Parity", *International Journal of Constitutional Law*, vol. 6, pp. 287-316.

Schutgens, R.J.B. and J.J.J. Sillen (2010), 'De SGP, het rechterlijk bevel en het kiesrecht', *Nederlands Juristenblad*, vol. 85, pp. 1114-1117.

Vermeulen, B.P. and A.J. Overbeeke (2011), "Godsdienst, levensovertuiging en politieke gezindheid", in: C.J. Forder (ed.), *Gelijke behandeling: oordelen en commentaar 2010*, Nijmegen: Wolf Legal Publishers, pp. 139-161.

CHAPTER 8

Will it All End in Tears? What Really Happens when Democracies Use Law to Ban Political Parties

Tim Bale
Queen Mary University of London

The legal prohibition of political parties is 'a practice that exists with surprising regularity across the range of democratic societies' (Issacharoff, 2007: 1406) but one which continues to provoke controversy in both the real and the academic world, not only in different parts of Europe but also outside it (see Bourne and Casal, 2014, Bourne, 2012a and 2012b, Bogaards et al., 2010; also Reilly and Nordlund, 2008 and Mersel, 2006). Indeed, it often connects those sometimes separate spheres. At the end of 2007, for instance, a column in the Spanish newspaper *El País* (Gallego-Díaz, 2007) drew parallels between the banning of parties in Spain and Turkey; it also made explicit reference to the scholarly concept of 'militant democracy' – a term which captures the efforts on the part of some states to prevent elections being used by politicians who will then abolish them once they take power. The year before, as the EU had to make up its mind on how to deal with Hamas after it won a landslide in elections in Gaza, the *Jerusalem Post* treated its readers to a tour round some of the member and candidate states that can and have banned political parties, all in order to make the point that 'Europe has taken a much more forgiving position toward violent and terrorist organizations that form parties here than they do on their own continent' (Keinon, 2006). Looking at the problems of 'dealing with the Hamas within', to borrow from the *Post*'s arresting headline, is also interesting because it brings together scholars working in different disciplines, most obviously law and political science, who not only cross boundaries but also combine empirical enquiry and normative concerns (see – for a selection of recent examples – Sawyer, 2003, Sajó, 2004a, Brems, 2006, Minkenberg, 2006, Mersel, 2006, Capoccia, 2007, Issacharoff, 2007, Rosenblum, 2007, Cram, 2008, Thiel, 2009a and Bourne, forthcoming).

The banning of political parties in democratic states is commonly opposed, by politicians, pundits, lawyers and political scientists. Their opposition is sometimes philosophical: they may be supporters both of free speech and free association; they may take what is sometimes referred to as a 'procedural' rather than 'substantive' view of democracy.[1] But bans are also criticized on more practical grounds (see, for instance, the debates, past and present, outlined in Olsson, 2003 or the more contemporary concerns about banning certain parties in democratic Iraq cited by Randall, 2008: 251; see also Thiel, 2009b: 406). Both those whose objections are philosophical and those whose objections are practical suggest that bans may well prove pointless, counterproductive, or endanger hard-won achievements.

Not everyone, of course, agrees – including the present author. In an earlier study (Bale, 2007), I attempted to question the common wisdom, framed using Hirschman's perversity, futility and jeopardy theses (see Hirschman, 1991), by taking the trouble to look at what another scholar calls 'the actual experiences of functioning democracies confronted with [allegedly] antidemocratic challenges from within' (Issacharoff, 2007: 1415). A comparative empirical investigation of the consequences of recent bans on 'extremist' parties in three self-styled European democracies (Turkey, Spain and Belgium), selected in order to contrast what Pedahzur (2001, 2002) labels 'militant', 'defending' and 'immunized' democracies, found that those consequences were nowhere near as dire as predicted.[2] Firstly, bans in those countries saw no accentuation of the potentially existential threat apparently posed by the parties affected, whether that threat be religious, racist, or violent.[3] Secondly, those parties did not simply carry on as before. Thirdly, bans did not seem to undermine positive democratic development and achievements that took place prior to them coming into force. This suggested that closing down parties – while by no means always the only or the right thing to do – is not necessarily a mistake, at least on practical rather than on normative grounds.[4]

Like all studies which involve analysing recent developments, however, the study ran the risk of being proved wrong by time and chance. The bans it spoke about, after all, had occurred within just one decade of writing. Mao Zedong,a big fan of banning parties (other than his own of course) was once asked what he thought of the French Revolution – an event which at the time had occurred a hundred and fifty years previously – and famously (though possibly apocryphally) replied was that it was 'too soon to say'. On that reasoning, it may be premature, therefore, to revisit a study only a decade later in order to see whether the judgements made therein still hold good. Yet things have moved on apace in two of the three countries concerned (Turkey and Spain), while the lack of development in the other (Belgium) could be just as significant. This chapter looks at each country in turn before coming to an overall conclusion. Do those cases, then, still defy the philosophical and practical predictions that legal bans on parties will make no difference, that they will make things worse, or that they will put existing achievements at risk? Or, now that we have had more time to make up our minds, does it look instead like they will end in tears?

Turkey

'Mainstream' parties are often accused of using bans to deprive or even destroy small but still irritating opponents on the fringes of the party system – militant nationalists, ideological extremists, etc. The news coming out of Turkey in the spring of 2008 therefore came as quite a shock. The decision to initiate a case against the Kurdish nationalist Democratic Society Party (*Demokratik Toplum Partisi* – DTP), accused of having links to the outlawed paramilitary group, the PKK (*Partiya Karkeren Kurdistan*), was not the headline-grabber. Indeed, given Turkey's history of banning such parties, notwithstanding objections from the European Court of Human Rights (ECtHR), that particular move was par for the course (see Issacharoff, 2007: 1440-1). In fact, there were consequences, which we shall examine later. But what really attracted the attention of the world's media at the time was the unanimous decision, on 31 March, of the eleven-member Constitutional Court to hear a suit filed by the Chief Prosecutor of the High Court of Appeals to close down the AKP. AK, a religious party, had governed Turkey since winning 34 per cent of the vote in parliamentary elections in 2002 – a share that, in Turkey's disproportional electoral system, gave it 363 seats out of 550. The court also declared it would consider the Chief Prosecutor's request to bar seventy-one people from politics for five years – a group that included not only Recep Tayyip Erdoğan, the serving Prime Minister, but also Abdullah Gül, the serving President of the Republic, both of whom had been key players in the founding of AKP following the prohibition of two of its predecessors, *Refah* (Welfare) and *Fazilet* (Virtue) which had their origins in the Islamist *Milli Görüş* movement

The grounds for the ban were laid out in a 162 page indictment put together by the Chief Prosecutor, who, in contrast to the rules governing many other jurisdictions, can bring such a case entirely on his own initiative (see Özbudun, 2010: 138). The indictment alleged that, because of the AK government, what was officially a secular democracy had come to be seen throughout the world (and notably by the US) as 'a moderate Islamic republic'. Worse still, it said, the determinedly 'anti-secular' party was now attempting to take the Republic down a road that would end in its becoming an Islamic state on the lines of Iran. Interestingly enough, it also pointed out that 'The AKP was founded by a group that drew lessons from the closure of earlier Islamic parties and uses democracy to reach its goal, which is installing *Shari'a* in Turkey.'[5]

The legal basis for the charge was Turkey's constitution, which (in Article 68) makes it possible to ban any party whose 'statutes, programs, and actions' run counter to the country's territorial integrity and national sovereignty, or to 'human rights, the principles of equality and the rule of law,' or to the principles of the democratic and laic Republic'; this is then given effect by the 1983 Law on Political Parties, which, like the constitution itself, has been subject to forceful critique by those who argue it affords too much discretion to those determined at all costs to prevent any dilution of Turkey's assertively – even aggressively – secular and unitary state (see Özbudun, 2010). Under these rules, or those they came after, a host of parties have been banned.[6] Most were prohibited on the grounds that their support for minority (Kurdish) nationalism promoted the break-up of Turkey. Some, though, were broken up on the grounds that their Islamist ideals, if implemented, would undermine Turkey's commitment to secularism and even put democracy itself at risk, much in the way that fascist and communist parties in the 1930s and 1940s were elected to power but then did away with elections. This is a pre-emptive rationale that informs bans elsewhere and that has been backed by the European Court of Human Rights (ECtHR), not least in its decision (initially in 2001 and finally in 2003) to uphold the Turkish Constitutional Court's banning of one of AK's predecessors, *Refah* (see Bale, 2007, Issacharoff, 2007, Cram, 2008, Özbudun, 2010).

The ban on Refah, and in particular its upholding by the European Court, has been subjected to severe criticism on legal and human rights grounds, not least because it put more weight on remarks made by individual members of the party (which supposedly revealed its true intentions) than it did on the party's official position and its behaviour in office; the Court also came close not only to equating secularism with human rights but also to presuming that *shari'a* is essentially incompatible with democracy which, if true, would rule out the possibility of the latter in almost all Middle Eastern countries that have recently freed themselves from dictatorship (see Boyle, 2004 for the most detailed critique). However, a number of international scholars, whether they were academic lawyers or political scientists and irrespective of the fact that, as such, they were sometimes unaware of each other's work, opined that the bans handed out to AK's predecessors, however contestable their legal justification, may have benign rather than malign consequences: Issacharoff, in the course of an impressive international survey, even went so far as to suggest that 'under the circumstances, it is difficult to imagine a better outcome' (Issacharoff, 2007: 1447), while Randall, in a wide-ranging piece on party regulation, also sees Turkey as 'a success story'(Randall, 2008: 246). Moreover, most Turkish specialists, while making the point, quite rightly, that the bans on Refah and Fazilet, were by no means the only drivers of change which led the reformists (*yenilikçiler*) of the *Milli Görüş* towards a more moderate, democratic brand of religiously-inspired politics (see Gumuscu and Sert, 2009: 961 and n. 29-32; see also Cizre, 2008 and Çinar, 2006), acknowledge that they played a crucial part in the shift towards what the AKP calls 'conservative democracy' (see Çağliyan-İçener, 2009 and Adoğan, 2006), even if it might be more accurately labelled 'conservative globalism' (Öniş, 2009) or even 'post-Islamism'(see Duran, 2010). Has this positive interpretation been contradicted by more recent events?

When it comes to perversity, one could, when taking the long view, now argue that the banning of Refah in 1998 has had precisely the opposite effect to that which was intended. Instead of lessening the threat of political Islam by obliging its adherents to moderate, it has simply led to them pretending moderation in order to create a party that has ensured they are in a better position than ever to undermine the secular nature of the Turkish state. This was, after all, one of the implications of the Chief Prosecutor's indictment. However, to be convincing, those making an argument along such lines would have to show that political Islam had indeed achieved a sneaky and final victory over secularism. While, as we shall see, AK has acted in ways that have given adherents of the latter cause for concern, it has hardly, as we shall also see, had things all its own way.

The immediate trigger for the case being brought was AK's decision in Feburary 2008 to amend the Turkish Constitution to allow women in higher education to wear a headscarf – a measure which would mean that observant Muslim women would at last be able to attend university within Turkey, rather than, like the daughters of the Prime Minister and the President, having to do so overseas. The party's secular opponents, who have long claimed – not wholly without reason (see Wiltse, 2008 and Bayram, 2009) – that the headscarf issue is the thin end of an Islamist wedge managed to block the governments plans: in early June 2008 Turkey's Constitutional Court declared they violated the country's constitutional commitment to secularism. But this was insufficient to assuage simmering resentment on the part of the secularists at the parliamentary selection of the President. In the spring of 2007, AK had found its candidate for the presidency Abdullah Gül (whose wife, Hayrünnisa, famously wears the headscarf) blocked and had decided to call an early election as a show of strength. At the election AK won 341 seats in the 550 seat parliament increasing its vote share by over 12 per cent but leaving it some twenty-six seats shy of a two-thirds majority. It nevertheless succeeded (albeit on the third round of voting and by a simple majority) in getting Gül (formerly Turkey's Foreign Minister) elected and sworn in August 2007, even if the ceremony was boycotted by the army, which had, back in April, issued an 'e-memorandum' which many interpreted as threatening a *coup d'état* if AKP pushed its luck.

Survey research suggests that much of the vote for the AKP in 2007 was driven not by religious zeal *shari'a* for or a desire to dismantle the Kemalist state but by a combination of enthusiasm for the party's apparently successful stewardship of the economy and the distinctly unimpressive alternative offered by the main opposition, the CHP, which seemed intent on defending the interests of its core support – the secularist, urban, middle-class elite (Çarkoğlu, 2007, Öniş, 2009, and Kalaycıoğlu, 2010; see also Dagi, 2008: 29-30).[7] AK's leadership, however, seemed to many observers to interpret its victory almost as a mandate for regime change.[8] An initial post-election plan to build a consensus around a new Constitution drafted by academics was quickly derailed by the government's decision to push for just two amendments that would allow the wearing of headscarves. Just as seriously, the AKP wasted no time in exercising the executive's right to make appointments to all sorts of bodies that were hitherto the preserve of secularists, continuing a trend that began with its election to office in 2002.[9] It was the President of the Board of Higher Education, Yusuf Ziya Ozcan, chosen by President Gül and Prime Minister Erdoğan, who backed the government's campaign on the headscarf and who stood to gain greater control of universities as outgoing rectors were replaced. Gül, like the President of the USA, also gets to nominate judges to the highest court in the land as his predecessors' secularist choices begin to retire – the very judges who decide on constitutional issues, including party bans. Moreover, although the AKP government has not yet succeeded in getting the state to relinquish its control of mosques and sundry religiously endowed businesses and associations, it seems intent to exploit its tenure to move religiously inclined nominees into both high and low level posts, for example in the judiciary. The promotion of religious schools (*Imam-Hatip*) and an increase in the resources of the state's Directorate of Religious Affairs (*Diyanet*) have also worried secularists. Many liberals are no less alarmed by increased restrictions (often locally initiated) on alcohol sales and by the reduction in the number of women in top positions, not least in the AKP government itself (see Çağaptay and Perincek, 2010).

Opponents of such developments claim also point to the links between the AKP – a champion of privatization and in charge of public procurement – and the Islamist (but also neoliberal) business organization, MÜSİAD (see Şen, 2010: 71-76).[10] They point, as well, to the rising influence of the Islamist and nationalist Fethullah Gülen Movement (see Criss, 2010: 50-52) in both domestic and foreign affairs, where Turkey, without abandoning NATO, has clearly moved to improve relations with Arab countries and Iran while cooling considerably toward Israel (even before that country's botched boarding operation against Turkish vessels heading for Gaza in May 2010 and its subsequent refusal to apologize for the loss of life). The AKP's critics also claim that the government is exploitng its apparent success in exposing and tackling what is popularly known as the *Ergenekon* (a shadowy conspiracy linked to the military) to its advantage by hinting that those who criticize the AKP are somehow implicated in Turkey's *Derin Devlet*, the 'deep state' that supposedly 'really' runs the country (see, for a balanced view, Jenkins, 2009). Some also claim to have identified a politically motivated attempt by the government to bankrupt the Doğan media group, which in recent years has become something of a thorn in its flesh.

The AKP, then, might like to portray itself to the outside world as a responsible, conservative reformist party doing its democratic best in the face of what it calls 'totalitarian secularism'. It might even claim that it is no more integralist than its Christian Democratic counterparts (see Nasr, 2005; see also Hale, 2005). But its political opponents argue that such claims ring hollow when the reality of the regime's actions, and indeed its populist rhetoric, is examined more closely. Academic observers are naturally less inclined to buy wholesale into the idea that the AKP's leaders are 'theocrats in neckties,' not least because many of them have a pedigree as reformers which predates their founding of a party which, it has been persuasively argued, represents a genuine break with its predecessors and one motivated not simply by political expediency but by profound political and social change that has created space and demand for a party committed not to *shari'a* but to governing competence, free markets, and 'conservative democracy' (see Dagi, 2008, Gumuscu and Sert, 2009 and Dönmez, 2010). On the other hand, the party's actions in office have clearly provoked considerable concern about 'creeping Islamization' both among Turkish and foreign observers (see for example, Yeşilada and Rubin, 2010, Çağaptay, 2009).

Some of these – particularly those who argue (not unreasonably it should be emphasized) that there is a fundamental and possibly ineradicable incompatibility between Islamism and liberal democracy – were never particularly inclined to give AKP the benefit of the doubt (Tibi, 2008 and 2009).[11] Yet even some of those who are prepared to do so admit that the party 'has yet to clarify its position on the role of religion in social life' (Gumuscu and Sert, 2009: 958) and 'is open to criticism on the grounds that it has a narrow majoritarian and instrumental understanding of democracy and has ignored the sensitivities of the secular segments of society' during a fraught post-election period which has exposed 'the limits of liberal Islam and the underlying tensions between [its] globalist and conservative elements' (Öniş, 2009: 35, 37; see also Yavuz, 2009). And even those who are most inclined to believe in the transformation of the AKP wonder whether the party's need to borrow Western liberal rhetoric to defend itself against militant secularism has actually prevented it from finding a genuinely novel, Islamic, and therefore stable, synthesis (see Duran, 2010; see also Jenkins, 2008 for an excellent overview).

On balance, however, no objective observer could conclude that bans on its Islamist predecessors have perversely backfired by leading to the creation of a party, AKP, that is clearly interested in, or has yet succeeded in overthrowing Turkey's secular republic by stealth in order to bring into being some sort of Islamic republic. Indeed, more recent events – involving crackdowns on protesters and social media, the harassment of journalists, and the justification of such actions on the part of the prime minister by his pointing to the fact that his party is still capable of winning big majorities in various second order elections – smack less of a regime on the road to theocracy and more of the sort of depressing tactics the world is all-too-used to seeing from secular politicians tempted by more 'managed' forms of democracy.

But if the charge of perversity can be dismissed on the grounds that it was the threat to secular democracy that provoked Turkey's bans, actual or putative, what about futility? One could, after all, argue that attempts to ban AK itself implies that previous bans have been pointless, not simply (or even mainly because) some of the banned entities have survived in other guises, but because such bans have done nothing to resolve the continuing tension between political Islam and militant secularism. This, however, is to place too much of a burden on one legal instrument. The conflict between AK and its supporters and Turkish secularists, be they in the military, the bureaucracy or simply in civil society and the general population, is a profound political cleavage which no single measure can hope to 'cure'.

What about jeopardy – the idea that bans endanger previous achievements? If anything, one effect of the threat to ban was, firstly, to encourage AKP publically to place even more stress on liberal values like human rights, the rule of law, and democracy in order to defend its actions in the court of international opinion.[12] Secondly, and not unrelatedly, the threat of a ban temporarily resuscitated the AK's enthusiasm for Europe (see Çinar, 2006: 480-1) which, since the general election of 2007, had appeared to be cooling, notwithstanding (or possibly because of) the opening of so far pretty fruitless accession negotiations in 2005. Both Prime Minister and President clearly decided that cosying up once again to the EU would be their best hope of deterring the Turkish Courts from an unfavourable judgement, EU diplomats having made it very clear since the case was accepted that a ban on AK would constitute a serious obstacle to good relations. On the other hand, this is to assume that people both inside and outside Turkey really set much store by the thinly veiled warnings issued by, among others, High Representative Javier Solana and Enlargement Commissioner Olli Rehn who was quoted in the media as saying that 'In EU member states, the kinds of political issues referred to in this case are debated in the parliament and decided through the ballot box, not in court rooms.'[13]

The unconscious irony of Rehn's words, given that Europe is no more immune than anywhere else from the (often politically-driven) 'judicialization of mega-politics' (Hirschl, 2008), may have escaped some, even if the superiority complex which they betray is far from subtle. But suggestions that the EU would have trouble dealing with a state which bans parties was slightly difficult to credit given that (as the *Jerusalem Post* acidly observed when writing about how Europe was 'dealing with 'the Hamas within') its own members are no slackers when it comes to proscription or other measures designed to hobble parties deemed to be threats to democracy. Nor is it true, as Turkey's Foreign Minister (echoing Rhen) asserted in an interview aimed at both an international as well as a domestic audience (Babacan, 2008), that states strictly limit bans (or actions which try to achieve similar results by apparently lesser measures) to parties that advocate or employ violence. As one recent study notes, there are at least three additional rationales (including the prevention of incitement to hatred, of an existential change to the character of the state, and of outside interference) – not surprisingly so, given we live in an ever more complicated and ever more democratic world where fascism is no longer the only or even the most imminent danger (see Rosenblum, 2007). And, as a comprehensive survey of both international conventions and national codes (Brems, 2006) shows, these other rationales are built into and thereby acknowledged by both domestic and international law.

In the event, Turkey's Constitutional Court did not end up banning the AKP when it announced its decision in July 2008. Although it believed that that the party was 'a focal point' for anti-secular activities, this appeared to be offset for a sufficient number of the justices by the lack of either incitement to violence or clear and present danger; equally significant was AK's support for the legislative and constitutional reforms urged on the country by the EU (see Vidal Prado, 2009: 307). Instead of banning, the Court made use of 'wiggle room' which allowed it to 'discipline' the government without bringing it down and making an already serious situation even worse. Two amendments to the constitution in 2001 left open the possibility that a party could be fined rather than closed down (Article 69, paragraph 7) and required any ruling on such matters would henceforth require a three-fifths majority (seven out of eleven) instead of a (six out of eleven) simple majority (Özbudun, 2010: 136-7). The new decision-rule saved the AKP in 2008, it was widely attested, precisely because of the availability of the alternative sanction (agreed by ten of the eleven judges). Handing down a fine equivalent to half the party's state funding for that year (an amount approaching US$20 million), the Head of the Court, Haşim Kılıç, made it clear, that the AKP should regard the judgement as 'a serious warning' and professed the hope that it would 'get the message'.

This is likely to be the absolute limit of any leeway granted to the Court (and therefore to the political parties on whom it sits in judgement) in the foreseeable future: providing any more room for manoeuvre would in all likelihood involve amending the so-called 'unamendable' articles of the Constitution, such as its staunch commitment to secularism – a move that would require two-thirds of MPs and therefore the support of opposition parties. AK's hopes that it would gain a big enough majority at the general election of June 2011 to allow it to submit its proposals to a referendum without consulting its opponents were dashed when, although it increased its share of the vote to 49.8 per cent, it actually lost seats – an irony given its continued support for a system whose 10 per cent threshold clearly favours big, national parties and discriminates against smaller formations, ensuring, for example, that even the biggest Kurdish party is best off sponsoring supposedly independent candidates in individual constituencies in order to make it into parliament. AK's ambitions for a new constitution however, have not faded and its efforts continued to alarm secularists, who noted that, of the package of 'minor' amendments approved in a referendum in September 2010, progress on implementation was greatest on those measures (like changes to judicial appointments) which arguably favour AK. They can, of course, be seen as illustrative of a less worrying and not uncommon tendency (see Hirschl, 2008: 109-10) among those elected politicians who have suffered at the hands of courts to take steps – sometimes involving institutional changes – to minimize the risk of it happening again.

In Turkey, of course, it already has. After the AKP was 'spared' in July 2008, the world turned its attention away from the country. As a result, it largely ignored the Constitutional Court's decision in the other case brought by the Chief Prosecutor, namely his call for the closure of the Kurdish nationalist DTP, which continued to call for more autonomy, as well as doing nothing to undermine the assumption that it was effectively the political wing of the outlawed PKK. In December 2009, the Court, citing articles 68 and 69 of the Constitution and the Party Law, ordered DTP be shut down on the grounds that it threatened the state's integrity and was linked to terrorist violence – links which probably explain the muted reaction to the news from the EU, whose revolving presidency (like the AKP) did little more than express its concern. The DTPs assets were seized, two of its parliamentarians removed from parliament, and nearly forty of its members barred from political activity for five years.

That opponents of the ban in Turkey insisted this was bound to set back a peaceful resolution to the Kurdish problem, while the party's remaining MPs promptly followed form and joined a successor party, *Barış ve Demokrasi Partisi* (BDP), already set up a 'lifeboat' for them, inevitably throws up questions, if not of perversity, then of jeopardy and futility. In the elections of June 2011, the BDP (effectively the eighth party of its kind) and the independents it sponsored made it into parliament only to find that several of them were denied their seats after being imprisoned for links with the PKK while another, Hatip Dicle, was barred on the grounds of a previous conviction for spreading terrorist propaganda – an offence not so very different, some argued, from the one which saw the Prime

Minister Erdoğan banned from parliament back in 2002 until a change was made to the law (with cross-party support) to rectify the situation. In Dicle's case no such change was forthcoming, despite widespread concern that the country's Supreme Electoral Council (YSK) had acted arbitrarily in his and other cases. As a result, 169 MPs – most of them from the main secularist opposition party who were protesting about two of their would-be colleagues being barred on the grounds of alleged involvement in a putative military coup – refused to take their oath of office.

Sympathy for the plight of the BDP, however, is qualified in many quarters by the suspicion that many of those elected on its slates are indeed linked to the PKK, which ended a ceasefire in the summer of 2011 and returned to a strategy of violent provocation of the army and an AK government – a government which had looked determined to pursue a more liberal policy toward the Kurds. That the return to violence and the barring and refusal of the BDP coincided suggested to some that the BDP's actions were all of a piece with the PKK cooling on the idea of a political rather than a warfighting strategy, although others argued that it was the proscription of elected candidates that caused (or at the very least reinforced) the decision to return to violence. Ironically, the civilian deaths that occurred as a consequence so outraged the general public in Kurdish areas that some prominent BDP politicians felt obliged to come out against them. Moreover, at the beginning of October 2011, those BDP MPs not subject to a ban (ie the vast majority of them) decided to take up their seats, primarily in order to be able to join in all-party talks on a new constitution.

In the Kurdish case, then, the arguments are more finely balanced than they are in the case of the AKP and the banned religious parties it took over from. While the decision to ban the BDP's predecessors, and to disbar some of its elected candidates from actually taking up their seats, may not have made things worse, it can hardly be said to have made them better. Moreover, the fact that the BDP would still appear not to have put clear blue water between itself and the PKK suggests that previous bans can, with some reason, be said to have been futile. The possibility of progress towards an all-party agreement on a new constitution – a document which may well make it less easy to ban parties in the future – means it would be premature to say that the proscription of yet another Kurdish formation (or at least some of its MPs) has ended in tears. But if, in the end, tears are shed they are likely to be triggered not so much as the result of the bans but as a consequence of the ongoing failure to solve (or at least manage) the tension between the Kurds' desire for independence and Turkey's determination to preserve its borders intact.

Spain

Some of the same issues, of course, have been thrown up in Spain, although in that case the argument against futility (and jeopardy and perversity) would appear to be stronger – and to have grown stronger as time moves on. The supposedly 'permanent' ceasefire declared by the Basque terrorist group ETA in March 2006 lasted only just over a year – a year during which socialist politicians were prepared (in the end to no avail) to risk opposition accusations that they were secretly negotiating with ETA's political wing, *Batasuna*, whose prohibition in 2003 they had supported and whose successors they had, as a government, similarly shut down (see Ferreres Comella, 2004 and Vidal Prado, 2009). Although the ceasefire formally finished on 6 June 2007, it had effectively ended in December 2006 when an explosion at Madrid airport 'accidentally' killed two people. ETA mounted numerous attacks thereafter, some of them deadly. Given that in the period immediately before the ban on Batasuna, ETA had generally tried (not always successfully) to avoid fatalities, opponents of the ban could claim jeopardy – put bluntly, to suggest that things have got worse. They also argued that one of the reasons that ETA called off its ceasefire was the Government's stubborn refusal during secret negotiations, firstly, to allow Batasuna to take part in all-party talks in the Basque Country on a political solution to the conflict and, secondly, to take steps to facilitate its re-legalization in time for the municipal elections of 2007 and the general election of 2008 – supposedly more proof, if proof were needed, that the Spanish state's uncompromising stance made a settlement of the Basque question much more difficult than it really needs to be (see Guittet, 2008: 284; see also Woodworth, 2007).

These criticisms, however, are flawed. With regard to the apparent increase in fatalities, ETA's willingness (and capacity) to take lives always fluctuated but actually declined in recent years, though not of course simply as a result of the ban on Batasuna (see de la Calle and Sánchez-Cuenca, 2009: 214). With regard to frustration at the ban being responsible for ending the ceasefire, this ignores the fact that, when the bomb went off at Madrid airport, it clearly took not just the government but some of its ETA and Batasuna interlocutors by surprise. Indeed, the latter scrambled, in the days and weeks that followed, to keep the peace process on track – all in vain because it became clear that (younger) hardliners within the terrorist organization had (temporarily at least) triumphed over the moderates or simply taken matters into their own hands, forcing their internal opponents either to disown them and admit disunity or (as they eventually did) hang together and, however reluctantly, call off the ceasefire. It was clear, then, that at the time of the airport attack, Batasuna's leadership was still hopeful that it might allowed to contest the municipal elections; indeed, they were probably well aware that, if history was anything to go by, their fortunes were likely to be much improved if they could stand during a lull in the bombings and shootings. The end of the ceasefire, then, had more to do with disputes over strategy within ETA than it did with the ban on Batasuna *per se*.

Such oscillation between violence and negotiations will be familiar to anyone tracking the behaviour of the IRA in the initial phase of the Irish peace process even though its 'political wing', Sinn Féin, was not banned (see Richards, 2008). The Irish example, of course, is now even more relevant than ever since, in late October 2011, ETA (following a few months of ceasefire) finally declared a definitive (and according to most observers genuine) end to its armed struggle, following a peace conference in Donostia-San Sebastián attended by, among others, former Irish Prime Minister Bertie Ahern, Tony Blair's former Chief-of-Staff, Jonathan Powell, and Sinn Féin's Gerry Adams. Although decommissioning of weapons and disbandment of the organization itself were still apparently some way off, and polls suggested scepticism among many Spaniards, this development, above all, suggests that the ban on Batasuna did not, as many predicted, prove counterproductive. Whether that ban actually contributed to peace is, of course much harder to assess. It would be easy to fall into the *post hoc ergo propter* hoc fallacy and assume that because a permanent peace followed the ban, that the latter led to the former. But that is a temptation that must be avoided.

In the light of this, how, then, should we consider futility? Has the ban really made no difference? Even if we forget the possibly specious argument that it has, in fact, led to peace, there are ways of assessing the question, the most obvious being the extent to which the banned party has been able simply to continue its political-electoral activities by, for example, creating 'lifeboat' or 'spare' parties which carry on its work as if nothing had happened. Early critics of the ban, for example, pointed to the way in which a tiny party formed just prior to the ban, EHAK-PCTV (*Euskal Herrialdeetako Alderdi Komunista – Partido Comunista de las Tierras Vascas*), openly appealed, in the 2005 elections for the Basque parliament, to voters who would otherwise have voted for the *Aukera Guztiak* list that was proscribed as simply a front for Batasuna – an appeal that saw them come from nowhere to win 12.3 per cent of the vote and nine (out of 75) seats. Following the election, critics of the ban pointed to evidence of links between that party and Batasuna, especially after one of EHAK's MPs was discovered at a September 2007 meeting of Batasuna leaders broken up by police, as well as to the seizure of documents which appeared to show payments from EHAK to members of Batasuna. On the other hand, the fact that it took the authorities until February 2008 to prevent it participating at the forthcoming general election is testimony to the fact that EHAK was very careful until then to avoid publicly giving aid or comfort to a terrorist organization, in other words to avoid doing anything the ban was designed to prevent.

Possibly because of this reluctance, Batasuna – ETA made several attempts to put together other formations that would facilitate its involvement in elections and municipal and regional government. The most obvious of these – so obvious in fact that it may have been more a symbolic gesture than a genuine attempt – was the planned launch of *Abertzale Sozialisten Batasuna – Unión de Socialistas Patriotas* in March 2007, less than two months before the 27 May municipal elections. Given its use of the Bastasuna brand and those who were involved, some of whom were facing criminal charges, its swift proscription prior to the elections in question came as no surprise. In fact, the Supreme Court (whose ruling was then upheld by the Constitutional Court) banned all 246 lists (containing thousands of candidates) presented by ASB, but also 133 lists presented by another outfit, the EAE-ANV (*Eusko Abertzale Ekintza – Acción Nacionalista Vasca*). EAE-ANV, like ASB, with which it stood in an electoral alliance called *Abertzale Sozialistak*, was deemed to be a 'fraudulent successor' of Batasuna; the fact that it had been around (if not particularly active) for decades made no difference since it had clearly been 'infiltrated' or colonized by Batasuna.

Only those EAE-ANV lists that contained three or more candidates deemed to be 'infiltrators' were proscribed in 2007 but even this denied them a presence in over half of all Basque local contests as well as the regional elections in Navarra, an autonomous community that many Basques see as an integral part of their homeland. The so called 'votantes huérfanos' of the banned formations either stayed at home or provided an unexpected windfall for other parties, such as the *Nafarroa Bai* electoral alliance in Navarra, which scored 24 per cent on its first outing. Nevertheless, the remaining lists of the EAE-ANV netted the party over

70,000 and 20,000 votes in local elections in the Basque Country and Navarra respectively – results which gave it effective control of 33 councils in the former and 9 in the latter. EAE-ANV was, however, effectively prevented by the Supreme Court from standing in the 2008 general election (see below) – a decision which, once again, probably saw votes transferred to Nafarroa Bai, which won one seat.

This action in particular illustrates that, even for those who support them, bans continue to throw up dilemmas or even injustices. One of the most obvious of these relates to the prevention of individuals standing for election simply because they appear on the same party list as others who in the past stood (quite legally at the time) either for Batasuna or one of its predecessors. Worse still, they might be prevented from standing if anyone on their list previously appeared on a list along with candidates belonging to Batasuna or its predecessors – all of which means that it is perfectly possible that lists have been banned even though none of the individuals on them have ever stood for Batasuna or its predecessors. Although one might argue that the candidates concerned could always have stood on a different list (that is, for parties that clearly reject violence), this is a serious and perhaps undue restriction on individuals' political rights.

Given that the stakes are so high, and that Spanish courts have continually proved themselves willing to back bans on Batasuna and its supposed successors, it is hardly surprising that the ECtHR has become involved in the Spanish as well as the Turkish case. In December 2007 the Court declared that it was prepared to hear Batasuna's claim that the Spanish government had violated its right to freedom of expression (article 10) and its right to freedom of association (article 11). Even though it ruled out a claim under article 13 (that the plaintiff had no effective remedy before a national authority) – thereby agreeing that the Spanish legal process was watertight – this represented encouraging news for opponents of the ban since only a tiny minority of claims even make it so far as a hearing.

By no means all legal scholars believed that the Strasbourg Court would find in favour of Spain (see Cram, 2008: 90-5), although some observers suspected that the state's case may well have been strengthened by the fact that, in February 2008, Spanish judges had rejected urgent requests by the government and prosecutors simply to impose a blanket ban on EHAK and ANV in advance of the general election to be held the following month. Instead, they chose the lesser (but immediately effective) option of cutting off the parties' funding and preventing them from presenting candidates, declaring, interestingly, that the latter was designed to prevent parties claiming some kind of parliamentary immunity in the face of a future application to ban them completely. This – allowing the party to continue but preventing it contesting elections – mimics the 'smarter' sanctions employed for some time by Israel (which like Spain now permits the banning of parties supporting terrorism), arguably to good effect (Issacharoff, 2007: 1447-51 and Navot, 2008). Whether, however, it had any impact on the ECtHR is a matter for speculation, but in June 2009 the Court upheld the dissolution of Batasuna; it also upheld the Spanish legal system's right to prevent successor parties running candidates in elections (running all the way up from local to European) in an attempt to render the initial ban useless, although it stressed that it would have to be able to show strong links between those candidates and the dissolved party (see Černič, 2010, for a critique).

Although Spanish courts' decisions preventing certain lists and candidates from being put before the electorate led to demonstrations in the Basque country (and even to a clandestine meeting called to organize another party by Batasuna members who were promptly arrested by police), it gained a good deal of support in the rest of Spain. Yet the precautionary principle on which it was based, however reasonable and pragmatic, again raises thorny questions since, in effect, the 'defendants' are presumed guilty until proven innocent. Also problematic is the extent to which being seen to pursue the same objective as that pursued by the men of violence may by itself be enough to create a link between a candidate or a party and such men: the danger of 'guilt by association' (one, in fact, raised in the Spanish case by a UN Special Rapporteur) is blatantly obvious (see Černič, 2010: 11). The common response to such concerns, namely that ETA hardly gives the benefit of the doubt to its victims (one of whom, a former Socialist councillor was gunned down in front of his wife and five-year old daughter less than forty-eight hours before polling day in March 2008) is understandable, but not perhaps wholly convincing. More persuasive perhaps is the argument – one floated in debates about the prohibition of Nazi-inspired parties in Germany (see Niesen, 2002: 34-5) – that the intimidation resulting from such attacks creates a climate of fear in which alternatives to the party which instils such fear, fail to emerge or at least to thrive to the extent that one might expect in a fully-fledged democracy.

At the regional elections of 2009, Batasuna – already under pressure from *Aralar* (the secessionist but non-violent party founded by some of its disillusioned partisans in 2000) – again tried to get together a new party that would run lists on which its activists would stand. However,

D3M (*Democracia Tres Millones* or *Demokrazia Hiru Milioi*), was banned, obliging Batasuna to call on its supporters to vote for it anyway – votes which have to be totted up even if they count for nothing. The response from nationalists was not unimpressive: had D3M been running it would almost certainly have gained over 100,000 votes or around 8.5 per cent. On the other hand, this still represented a significant drop compared to the 12.3 per cent which went to EHAK-PCTV when the same seats were fought in 2005. Of course, not all of those who chose to cast a ballot that counted went straight over to Aralar (or indeed more mainstream nationalists) but many of them did (see de la Calle and Sánchez-Cuenca, 2009: 218-222).

In February 2011, however, in anticipation of municipal and regional elections, a new party, explicitly rejecting violence and promising an exclusively political campaign for Basque independence, *Sortu*, was founded. In late March 2011, though, it was denied the chance to stand candidates by a majority decision of the Supreme Court on the familiar grounds that it was, effectively, a ruse by which Batasuna activists could participate in the upcoming elections. In response, yet another electoral coalition, *Bildu*, was announced. Composed of the *Eusko Alkartasuna* party (originally a splinter party from the mainstream PNV) and the smaller (and more left-leaning) *Alternatiba*, as well as some supposedly non-affiliated 'independents', it was formed just before the election campaign began. It too was banned by the Supreme Court in early May; but a few days later the Constitutional Court (on a 6-5 majority vote) overturned the decision, arguing that, although there were concerns about two or three of the independents having Batasuna connections, they were not sufficient to permit the banning of two parties with an unblemished record of non-violence. This decision outraged the conservative *Partido Popular* but was greeted with relative equanimity by the *PSOE* minority government in Madrid – not surprisingly perhaps in view of the fact that the Supreme Court's initial decision looked like costing it the vital parliamentary support of the mainstream Basque Nationalists, the PNV.

The Constitutional Court's decision allowed Bildu to contest the elections, at which it performed impressively, winning, for example, 25 per cent of the vote in the city of San Sebastián and 13 per cent in the Navarre regional contest. In late September 2011, Bildu's main components, Eusko Alkartasuna and Alternatiba, announced that they would be getting together with Aralar to form a coalition (called *Amaiur*) in order to contest the general election of 2011. It won seven seats in parliament that November, fielding candidates in the Basque Country and Navarra.

To argue, however, that all this means the ban on Batasuna was futile would be inaccurate. The new electoral coalition, while still separatist and left-wing, seems genuinely committed (or at the very least reconciled) to peace and no longer prepared to act as a front for, or to try to excuse, ETA violence, even it its stands on prisoners offends some Spaniards. In any case, there is now no violence (apart from the violence of the past) to excuse. If that continues to be the case, then there is no longer any justification for a ban.

Belgium

In Belgium, things do not seem to have got any worse. When it comes to elections, Vlaams Belang, the successor to the banned Vlaams Blok has, if anything, lost rather than gained support. In the municipal elections of October 2006, VB improved its performance in many places in Flanders but, despite a slightly increased share of the vote in its 'home-city', Antwerp, where it took 33.5 per cent, it actually suffered a reverse – this despite VB's claim (heavily disputed) that it could now count on the support of large numbers of Antwerp's 20,000 strong Orthodox Jewish community, now supposedly prepared to forgive its past links with the Nazi occupation in common cause against the cities growing Muslim population.[14] At the June 2007 general elections, the party won 17 out of 150 seats in the Chamber of Representatives (down one seat albeit on a marginally increased vote share of 18.9 per cent) and 5 out of 40 seats in the Senate (the same as in 2003). VB also performed relatively poorly in the EP elections of 2009, its 15.9 per cent of the vote representing a drop of over seven points compared to its share in 2004. And at the general election of June 2010, VB was clearly outperformed by its separatist (non-far-right) rival N-VA (*Nieuw-Vlaamse Alliantie*), taking just 12.3 per cent of the vote and losing five and two seats in the lower and upper house respectively. In 2014 it performed even more poorly, winning only 3 seats (out of 150) in the lower house in the federal election and just 1 seat (out of Belgium's 21) in the European Parliament. This could even be a party on its way out.

Of course, strictly speaking, even if Vlaams Belang had instead made big electoral strides this would not constitute an argument against a ban on its predecessor: after all, bans are designed to rid the public sphere of parties whose infringement of basic human rights or whose advocacy of such infringement poses a real threat to democracy or public safety; they are not designed – or at least should not be designed – to drain sympathy from parties we simply do not like or disagree with. Likewise they are not intended to prevent such parties gaining publicity. Some would see the invitation extended to two of VB's then leading figures, Filip Dewinter and Frank Vanhecke, to address the Washington-based Robert A. Taft Club as evidence that the ban had backfired by conferring upon the party an aura of martyrdom and respectability. But if America's so called 'paleoconservatives' thought it worth flying over representatives of what they claimed was 'the most successful true right wing party in Europe' to talk to them about 'the threat that multiculturalism, radical Islam, and mass immigration bring to the fundamental European and American values of free speech, tolerance, and representative government in Europe', then that (as well as the hope that VB's success 'can be duplicated by a genuinely right wing movement' in the US) is their business.[15] It is unlikely that it harmed anybody back home in Belgium.

But if perversity and jeopardy can be relatively easily dismissed, what about futility? Has the effective banning of Vlams Blok been pointless? This, it seems, is a greyer area than we first thought: while it remains broadly true that the name-change to Vlaams Belang allowed the Flemish populists to drop some of their baggage, our initial findings arguably overstated the moderation involved. Inasmuch as VB's overt ethnocentrism and racism have receded, their replacement by an equally aggressive (and socially divisive) Islamophobia has continued apace. Outside of Belgium, too, the transmogrification of the Blok into the Belang has made little difference to how it is perceived, for instance, in the international media where it continues to be routinely referred to as 'extreme-' or 'far-right'. This is partly inertia but partly because of the causes (sometimes the lost causes) that the VB champions and the company it keeps.

In March 2008, the party's president, Bruno Valkeniers, caused a storm by appearing to suggest in a TV appearance that he hankered after apartheid-era South Africa. Meanwhile, Filip Dewinter was busy launching a charter to 'fight the Islamization of West-European cities', focusing in particular on a moratorium on mosque building. Given that the latter is a controversial issue exploited by radical right wing populist parties all over Europe, it is interesting that the Austrian FPÖ was the only high-profile member of that party family to attend a meeting on the topic in Antwerp organized by the VB, suggesting perhaps that the latter, at least at that stage, remained rather too unreconstructed for some of its supposedly like-minded counterparts in other countries The absence of Geert Wilders of the Dutch PVV (*Partij voor de Vrijheid*) –

Freedom Party) no slouch himself when it comes to criticizing Islam – was particularly noticeable. The fact that other parties of that ilk also stayed away also seemed to point to an ongoing distinction between radical right wing populist parties as a whole and those parties who joined the Identity Sovereignty and Tradition (ITS) group in the European Parliament – a group that split after just ten months of existence (from January to November 2007) when it could no longer contain the possibly predictable tensions between ultra-nationalists from East European gypsy-bashing parties and West European parties (such as the French *Front National*) which, at that point anyway, continued to flirt with fascism and even holocaust denial. The latter, incidentally, is something that VB itself would recoil from, having made a huge effort to portray itself as a friend of Israel in recent years, although its stance is somewhat qualified by its campaign for an amnesty for those who collaborated with the Nazis in wartime Belgium. Its outreach to Israel, however, is very much of a piece with its obsessive concern with the threat supposedly posed by Islam – a threat that is used as justification for the oft-made observation by party leaders that Flemish cities are starting to resemble Morocco or Mecca, proven, they say, by official lists of residents of certain suburbs apparently showing over ninety per cent of have African and Arabic names, or by school canteens serving *halal* meat and no pork. Concern apparently runs so deep that the party leadership expressed solidarity with the campaign against building a 'mosque' at Ground Zero in New York, with Filip DeWinter continually referring in remarks on the matter to the US President as Barack *Hussein* Obama.

Following elections to the European Parliament in 2009, VB declared itself interested in some form of cooperation, especially with the Austrian Freedom Party (FPÖ), the Sweden Democrats (both of whom have joined the VB in declaring their heartfelt support for Israel against Islamist terror), as well as the Danish People's Party, the Italian Northern League, and the Slovak National Party, all of whom decided to distance themselves from more extremist outfits like Jobbik (Hungary) and Ataka (Bulgaria). Such cooperation, however, was to begin with largely limited to initiatives like the campaign against Turkish membership of the EU, the latter issue being quite high up in the mix for VB, with the Party courting controversy in the spring of 2011 by releasing a poster (modelled on a similar one from Switzerland) showing a white sheep standing on a collage of European flags kicking out a red sheep embossed with the flags of Turkey and Morocco. Later that year, however, the European Parliament recognized the 'far-right-lite' European Alliance for Freedom, in which VB joined with the newly 'detoxified' French FN, the FPÖ, the Dutch PVV and the Northern League. VB will, however, play a very small role in any such group after 2014 since it performed so poorly in European elections that year.

In short, the VB might not be successful but it continues to hold and express views that border on the extreme. As such, our initial conclusion that the Belgian ban avoided futility might require some qualification. This has led some of the same groups (including *Kif Kif* and the Movement against Racism, Anti-semitism and Xenophobia) that brought the action which saw Vlaams Blok disband to consider doing the same to Vlaams Belang by getting the courts to deprive it of state funding on the grounds that it opposes rights granted under the European Convention. They know that the federal government is already under international pressure to fulfil what many states, regard as the obligation to prohibit racist organizations embodied in article four of the 1966 International Convention on the Elimination of All Forms of Racial Discrimination, to which 177 countries have signed up (see Brems, 2006). On the other hand, they also realize that, given the apparently chronic difficulties it has in even forming an administration that can hold the country together, the Belgian political class has had other things on its mind. In any case, bans are almost always responses to domestic rather than international pressure, and tend to occur when regimes face threats from parties that look like they are on the up rather than on the wane.

Conclusion

The motives for banning parties are rarely beyond question wherever in the world such bans are allowed for, proposed and enacted. They include 'sheer partisan self-serving, prejudice, an expressly exclusionary national ideal, a unitary political identity hostile to multiculturalism, or simply a disproportionate response to fear of disorder' (Rosenblum, 2007: 25; see also Randall, 2008). But nor are those motives wholly ulterior: there are good reasons, recognized by a host of international conventions and ranging well beyond the possibility of violence, for states to take such action or at least to assert their right to do so if they deem it necessary – and as long as it is proportionate and done within the law (see Brems, 2006).

These noble (or at least less base) motives do not necessarily give rise to outcomes which are perverse or futile or which jeopardize previous achievements. But those outcomes, being political and being of only recent provenance, remain as disputed and debateable as the 'necessity' of banning parties in the first place (see Rosenblum, 2007: 71-3). In no small part this is because outright prohibition is by no means the only (and definitely not the first) weapon that states keen to contain internal threats should reach for (see Rummens and Abts, 2010). We would of course be wrong to claim that the consequences in every country in which a ban is actually implemented (rather than simply kept on the books as a deterrent) are uniformly positive. Research both from Europe and further afield suggests mixed results (see Minkinberg, 2006, Bieber, 2008: 109-110, Moroff, 2010, Moroff and Basedau, 2010), as well as 'unintended – and not so unintended – consequences' (Randall, 2008: 252-58). However, we would clearly be mistaken if we were to suggest that they are always and everywhere malign – evidence, if you like of some kind of iron law of institutional interference. After all, those consequences not only take time (if not necessarily as much time as Mao supposedly implied) to emerge but also vary considerably between polities. This is also the case, incidentally, for another of the strategies sometimes employed by 'mainstream' parties to discipline their more extremist counterparts, namely an attempt to ostracize them politically rather than legally via a *cordon sanitaire* (see Van Spanje and Van der Brug, 2009: 375-6; see also Rummens and Abts, 2010).

Looking again at developments in Turkey, Spain, and Belgium, it seems clear that different judgements apply in each country and might even had been different had events taken a different turn. In Turkey, for instance, both the perversity and futility arguments can on balance be dismissed when it comes to the AKP; so too can jeopardy – but only because the judges' decision to avoid an outright ban on the governing party meant that the country's long-sought EU candidature was not put at risk. The less high-profile case of the DTP, however, should prevent us from making too sweeping a judgement in that case. In Spain, perversity and jeopardy can be dismissed and, although some might like to argue that the eventual decision to allow the Bildu and Amaiur electoral coalitions to stand candidates in 2011 constitutes futility, this ignores both the degree of separation with ETA and even Batasuna, and the fact that the former has now apparently ended its terrorist campaign for good. On the other hand this rather more sanguine conclusion should not blind us to the fact that previous bans throw up injustices (particularly those done to individual candidates) which may or may not be possible to mitigate. In Belgium, neither perversity nor jeopardy is the problem, but, given the continued ethno-cultural extremism of the Vlaams Belang, futility might be.

Our earlier findings, then, need not be thrown overboard but they may require some qualification – not only right now but in the future, too. Whether, as political scientists or legal scholars, rather than, say historians, our findings can ever be much more definitive than that is a moot point. Only slightly less moot is an additional finding made possible by this return visit to two of the cases concerned – Turkey and Spain. This is that 'the authorities', especially where the bans in question are seen to have 'worked', tend not to repeat them *holus bolus* but instead to employ rather more sophisticated or 'surgical' (Issacharoff, 2007: 1446) methods: where previously they might have reached for the cosh, they now prefer the scalpel. States, then, would appear to travel along a learning curve, albeit one characterized not so much by cool consideration of abstractions but instead (and rather appositely) by trial and error. This process, not surprisingly perhaps, gets more attention from academic lawyers (see Sajó, 2004b: 217 and Thiel, 2009b: 420) than from political scientists, who, despite their increased interest in path-dependence, are always anxious to avoid explanations that seem to smack of particularism. That said, as the different treatment handed out to AKP and DTP (and BDP) in Turkey reminds us, we are dealing with a trend that, even within a single polity, is far from linear or unqualified. Speaking normatively, that is perhaps how it should be: as recent work on combating racism, for example, emphasizes (see Bleich, 2011), solutions – presuming there are solutions – have to be contextually appropriate as well as proportionate.

Notes

1 Put briefly, the adherents of 'procedural democracy' value pluralistic political competition primarily for its capacity to determine and give effect to the preferences of the electorate, irrespective of what those preferences may be; the adherents of 'substantive democracy', on the other hand, fear that goods such as liberty, human rights, equality, etc., will not necessarily be protected by a majority vote, especially if that vote brings to power actors that will ignore them. Arguably, the former is a 'thinner' conception of democracy than the latter.

2 For an interesting critical discussion on whether such labels really help us, given how difficult it is to come up with categories or clusters that are

genuinely mutually exclusive, and attempt to come up with an alternative, see Thiel, 2009b.

3 Strictly speaking, it would be more accurate to use the formulation 'and/or' because, as Issacharoff (2007: 1434) rightly notes, the perceived threats and resulting rationales 'cannot be hermetically walled off from each other.'

4 Pragmatists, of course, can always seek refuge in the (not necessarily philosophically illegitimate) 'lesser of two evils' argument – one that bleeds into a consequentialist logic (see Darwall, 2002) that an action's morality cannot, indeed should not, be separated from its outcome.

5 Translation by Sinan Ikinci, 'Turkey's chief prosecutor seeks to ban the ruling AKP', *WSWS*, 2 April 2008, available at http://www.wsws.org/articles/2008/apr2008/turk-a02.shtml.

6 Some 27 parties have been banned in Turkey since 1923 – 19 of them since 1983. Not all attempts to ban parties, however, have been successful: up to and including the two most recent cases, 17 have escaped that fate.

7 The CHP may now present more of a threat to the AKP after its uncompromising leader, Deniz Baykal, was forced to step down after a sex-scandal and replaced by the potentially more popular Kemal Kılıçdaroğlu.

8 For a series of increasingly critical articles on AKP rule, see the Turkish Research Program pages of the US think-tank, http://www.washingtoninstitute.org.

9 Technically, a new Constitution would actually be an amendment to the 1982 document and, in order to stand any chance of being accepted without a full-blown crisis, would have to leave in place its unamendable articles which, among other things, protect Turkey's territorial integrity and its secular nature.

10 It should be noted, in all fairness, that the organization has long been an important – and open –ally of the party (Gumuscu and Sert, 2009: 954). Moreover, its involvement hardly makes AKP an outlier: one only has to look to the US to see a centre-right party winning backing from groups that are liberal on economics but conservative (often religiously so) on almost everything else under the sun (see Insel, 2003).

11 Islamism must of course be distinguished from Islam. According to one uncompromising definition (Tibi, 2008) 'Islam itself is basically a faith, a cultural system, and an ethics', whereas 'Islamism…is a political ideology, albeit one based on religion' held to by those who 'seek to "*shari'a*-tize" Islam' and to 'establish an "Islamic state" or "Islamic order"' in which 'difference appears as heresy and politics is placed within the ambit of that which is sacred and hence nonnegotiable.' For a detailed discussion, see Ayoob, 2008.

12 Sceptics, of course, may very well claim that the AK's resort to such values is instrumental rather than because they have been internalized – after all,

one man's attempt finally to get a supposedly 'fascist' military under civilian control is another's plot to dupe Western liberals and neutralize the one force that, when it comes to the crunch, stands a chance of preventing Turkey from falling into the hands of 'fundamentalists' (see, for example, Tibi, 2009).

13 See 'EU slams Turkish Court's decision to hear AKP ban', *EurActiv*, 1 April 2008, available online at http://www.euractiv.com/en/enlargement/eu-slams-turkish-court-decision-hear-akp-ban/article-171240.

14 For evidence of the Jewish community's resistance to VB's overtures, (but also perhaps of concern lest they strike a chord) see 'De 10 Hoofdzonden van het Vlaams Belang' ('trans: VB's ten deadly sins'), *Joods Actuell*, January 2008.

15 See http://www.youtube.com/view_play_list?p=7B81CB2087830F6D.

References

Adoğan, Yalçın (2006) 'The meaning of conservative democratic identity', in M. Hakan Yavuz (ed) *The Emergence of a New Turkey: Democracy and the AK Party* (Salt Lake City: University of Utah Press), pp. 49-65.

Ayoob, M. (2008) *The Many Faces of Political Islam. Religion and Politics in the Muslim World* (Ann Arbor: The University of Michigan Press).

Babacan, Ali (2008) Interview with the *Financial Times*, transcript published 14 April and available on www.ft.com.

Bale, Tim (2007) 'Are bans on political parties bound to turn out badly? A comparative investigation of three "intolerant" democracies: Turkey, Spain and Belgium', *Comparative European Politics*, 5 (2), 2007, pp. 141-157.

Bayram, Salih (2009) 'The Justice and Development Party's Conception of "Conservative Democracy": Invention or Reinterpretation?', *Turkish Studies*, 10 (4), pp. 511-538.

Bieber, Florian (2008) 'Regulating Minority Parties in Central and Southeastern Europe', in Benjamin Reilly and Per Nordlund (eds.) *Political Parties in Conflict-Prone Societies: Regulation, Engineering and Democratic Development* (Tokyo: UNU Press) pp. 95-125.

Bleich, Erik (2011) *The Freedom to Be Racist? How the United States and Europe Struggle to Preserve Freedom and Combat Racism* (Oxford: Oxford University Press).

Bourne, Angela (2012a) 'Democratization and the Illegalization of Political Parties in Europe', *Democratization*, 19 (6), pp. 1065–1085.

Bourne, Angela (2012b) 'The proscription of parties and the problem with "militant democracy"', *Journal of Comparative Law*, 7 (1), pp. 196–213.

Bourne, Angela (forthcoming) 'Why Ban Batasuna? Terrorism, political parties and democracy' *Comparative European Politics.*

Bourne, Angela and Casal Bértoa, Fernando (2014) 'Prescribing democracy? Party proscription, militant democracy and party system institutionalization', Paper presented at the 42nd ECPR Joint Sessions of Workshops, University of Salamanca, 10-15 April.

Brems, Eva (2006) 'Freedom of political association and the question of party closures', in Wojciech Sadurski (ed) *Political Rights Under Stress in 21st Century Europe* (Oxford: Oxford University Press).

Bogaards, Matthijs, Basedau, Matthias and Hartmann, Christof, eds. (2010) *Ethnic Party Bans in Africa*, special issue of the journal *Democratization,* 17 (4).

Boyle, Kevin (2004) 'Human Rights, Religion and Democracy: The Refah Party Case', *Essex Human Rights Review,* 1 (1), pp. 1-16, available online at http://projects.essex.ac.uk/ehrr/V1N1/Boyle.pdf.

Çağaptay, Soner (2009) '7 Years of AKP Rule', *The Majalla,* 27 November, available online at http://www.majalla.com/en/cover_story/article11110.ece.

Çağaptay, Soner and Perincek, Rüya (2010), 'No Women, No Europe', *Hurriyet Daily News,* 20 January, available online at http://www.cagaptay.com/6863/no-women-no-europe.

Çağliyan-İçener, Zeyneb (2009) 'The Justice and Development Party's Conception of "Conservative Democracy": Invention or Reinterpretation?', *Turkish Studies,* 10 (4), pp. 595-612.

Capoccia, Giovanni (2007) *Defending Democracy: Reactions to Extremism in Interwar Europe* (Baltimore: Johns Hopkins University Press).

Çarkoğlu, A. (2007) 'A new electoral victory for the "pro-Islamists" or the "new centre-right"? The Justice and Development Party phenomenon in the July 2007 parliamentary elections in Turkey', *South European Society and Politics,* 12 (4), pp. 501–519.

Černič, Jernej Letnar (2010) ' National Security – a Trump Card?', EUI Working Papers, Max Weber Programme, MWP 2010/02, available on line at http://hdl.handle.net/1814/13343.

Çinar, Menderes (2006) Turkey's Transformation Under the AKP Rule, *Muslim World,* 96 (3) pp. 469-486.

Cizre, Ümit, ed, (2008) *Secular and Islamic Politics in Turkey: the Making of the Justice and Development Party* (London: Routledge).

Cram, Ian (2008) 'Constitutional responses to extremist political associations – ETA, Batasuna and democratic norms, *Legal Studies,* 28 (1), pp. 68-95.

Criss, Nur Bilge (2010) 'Dismantling Turkey: The Will of the People?', *Turkish Studies,* 11 (1), pp. 45-58.

Dagi, Ihsan (2008) 'Turkey's AKP in Power', *Journal of Democracy*, 19 (3), pp. 35-30.

Darwall, Stephen (ed.) (2002) *Consequentialism*. (Oxford: Blackwell).

de la Calle, Luis and Sánchez-Cuenca, Ignacio (2009) 'The End of Three Decades of Nationalist Rule: The 2009 Regional Elections in the Basque Country', *South European Society and Politics*, 14 (2), pp. 211-226.

Dönmez, Rasim Özgür (2010) 'The Justice and Development Party between Islam and modernity', *Religion Compass* 4 (6), pp. 365-375.

Duran, Burhanettin (2010) 'The experience of Turkish Islamism: between transformation and impoverishment', *Journal of Balkan and Near Eastern Studies*, 12 (1), pp. 5-22.

Ferreres Comella, Victor (2004) 'The New Regulation of Political Parties in Spain, and the Decision to Outlaw Batasuna' in Sajó, *op cit*, pp. 133-156.

Gallego-Díaz, Soledad (2007) 'Una sentencia necesaria' *El País*, 14 December.

Guittet, Emmanuel-Pierre (2008) 'Is Consensus a Genuine Democratic Value? The Case of Spain's Political Pacts against Terrorism', *Alternatives* 33, pp. 267–291.

Gumuscu, Sebnem and Sert, Deniz (2009) 'The Power of the Devout Bourgeoisie: The Case of the Justice and Development Party in Turkey', *Middle Eastern Studies*, 45 (6), pp. 953-968.

Hale, William (2005) 'Christian Democracy and the AKP: Parallels and Contrasts', *Turkish Studies*, 6 (2), pp. 294-310.

Hirschl, Ran (2008) 'The Judicialization of Mega-Politics and the Rise of Political Courts, *Annual Review of Political Science*, 11, pp. 93-118.

Hirschman, A.O. (1991) *The Rhetoric of Reaction: Perversity, Futility, and Jeopardy* (Cambridge, MA: Belknap Press).

Issacharoff, Samuel (2007) 'Fragile Democracies', *Harvard Law Review*, 120, pp. 1405-1467.

Jenkins, Gareth (2008) *Political Islam in Turkey: Running West, Heading East?* (Basingstoke: Palgrave Macmillan).

Jenkins, Gareth (2009) *Between Fact And Fantasy: Turkey's Ergenekon Investigation* (Washington, DC: Central Asia-Caucasus Institute & Silk Road Studies Program, Johns Hopkins University), available on line at (http://www.silkroadstudies.org/new/docs/silkroadpapers/0908Ergenekon.pdf.

Kalaycıoğlu, Ersin (2010) 'Justice and Development Party at the Helm: Resurgence of Islam or Restitution of the Right-of-Center Predominant Party?', *Turkish Studies*, 11 (1), pp. 29-44.

Keinon, Herb (2006) 'Background: How Europe deals with the Hamas within', *Jerusalem Post*, 31 January.

Mersel, Yigal (2006) 'The dissolution of political parties: the problem of internal democracy', *I-CON*, 4 (1), pp. 84–113.

Minkenberg, Michael (2006) 'Repression and reaction: militant democracy and the radical right in Germany and France', *Patterns of Prejudice*, 40 (1), pp. 25-44.

Moroff, Anika (2010) 'Party Bans in Africa – An Empirical Overview'. *Democratization* 17 (4), pp. 618-641.

Moroff, Anika, and Basedau, Matthias (2010) 'An effective measure of institutional engineering? Ethnic party bans in Africa', *Democratization* 17 (4), pp. 666-686.

Nasr, Seyyed Vali Reza (2005) 'The Rise of "Muslim Democracy"', *Journal of Democracy*, 16 (2), pp. 13-27.

Navot, Suzie (2008) 'Fighting Terrorism in the Political Arena: the Banning of Political Parties', *Party Politics*, 14 (6), pp. 745-762.

Niesen, Peter (2002) 'Anti-Extremism, Negative Republicanism, Civic Society: Three Paradigms for Banning Political Parties', German Law Journal, 3 (7), available online at http://www.germanlawjournal.com/index.php?pageID=11&artID=164 and http://www.germanlawjournal.com/index.php?pageID=11&artID=169.

Olsson, Stefan (2003) 'Countering Extreme Parties without Prohibition: the Swedish Case', paper delivered to the ECPR General Conference in Marburg.

Öniş, Ziya (2009) 'Conservative globalism at the crossroads: the Justice and Development Party and the thorny path to democratic consolidation in Turkey', *Mediterranean Politics* 14 (1), pp. 21-40.

Özbudun, Ergun (2010), 'Party prohibition cases: different approaches by the Turkish constitutional court and the European Court of Human Rights', *Democratization*, 17 (1), pp. 125-142.

Pedahzur, A. (2001) 'Struggling with the challenges of right wing extremism and terrorism within democratic boundaries: a comparative analysis', *Studies in Conflict and Terrorism*, 24, pp. 339–359.

Pedahzur, A. (2002) *The Israeli Response to Jewish Extremism and Violence: Defending Democracy* (Manchester: Manchester University Press).

Randall, Vicky (2008) 'Party Regulation in Conflict-Prone Societies: More Dangers than Opportunities?', in Reilly and Nordlund, *op cit.*

Reilly, Ben and Nordlund, Per, eds. (2008) *Political Parties in Conflict Prone Societies: Regulation, Engineering and Democratic Development* (New York: United Nations University Press).

Richards, Anthony (2008) 'Terrorist Groups and Their Political Fronts', in James Dingley (ed) *Combating Terrorism in Northern Ireland* (London: Routledge).

Rosenblum, Nancy L. (2007) 'Banning Parties: Religious and Ethnic Partisanship in Multicultural Democracies,' *Law & Ethics of Human Rights*, 1 (1), pp. 17-75 Available at: http://www.bepress.com/lehr/vol1/iss1/art3.

Rummens, Stefan and Abts, Koen (2010) Defending Democracy: the Concentric Containment of Political Extremism, *Political Studies*, 58 (4), pp. 649-665.

Sajó, András, ed (2004a) *Militant Democracy* (Utrecht: Eleven International Publishing).

Sajó, András (2004b) 'Militant Democracy and Transition towards Democracy' in Sajó, *op cit.*, pp. 209-230.

Sawyer, K.A. (2003) 'Rejection of Weimarian politics or betrayal of democracy? Spain's proscription of Batasuna under the European Convention on Human Rights', *American University Law Review*, 52, pp. 1531-1581.

Şen, Mustafa (2010) 'Transformation of Turkish Islamism and the Rise of the Justice and Development Party', *Turkish Studies*, 11 (1), pp. 59-84.

Thiel, Markus, ed (2009a) *The 'Militant Democracy' Principle in Modern Democracies* (Aldershot: Ashgate).

Thiel, Markus (2009b)'Comparative Aspects', in Thiel, *op cit.*, pp. 379-424.

Tibi, Bassam (2008) 'Why They Can't Be Democratic', *Journal of Democracy*, 19 (3), pp. 43-48.

Tibi, Bassam (2009) 'Islamists Approach Europe', *Middle East Quarterly*, Winter, pp. 47-54, available online at http://www.meforum.org.2047/islamists-approach-europe.

Van Spanje, Joost and Van der Brug, Wouter (2009) 'Being intolerant of the intolerant. The exclusion of Western European anti immigration parties and its consequences for party choice', *Acta Politica*, 44, pp. 353–384.

Vidal Prado, Carlos (2009) 'Spain', in Thiel, *op cit.*, pp. 243-262.

Wiltse, Evren Çelik (2008) 'The Gordian Knot of Turkish Politics: Regulating Headscarf Use in Public', *South European Society and Politics*, 13 (2), pp. 195-215.

Woodworth, Paddy (2007) 'The Spanish-Basque Peace Process', World Policy Journal, 24, pp. 65-73, available online at http://www.pixelatedorange.com/PADDYWOODWORTH/article04.pdf.

Yavuz, M. Hakan (2009) *Secularism and Muslim Democracy in Turkey* (Cambridge: Cambridge University Press).

Yeşilada, Birol A. and Rubin, Barry, eds. (2010) *Islamization of Turkey under AKP Rule*, a special issue of the journal *Turkish Studies*, 11 (1).

CHAPTER 9

Ethnic Party Regulation in Eastern Europe

Ekaterina R. Rashkova
University of Innsbruck
Maria Spirova
Leiden University

Introduction

The representation of minorities – ethnic and others – in the political process is an important indicator of the quality of democracy and can take various forms. Minorities can have their own representatives in the legislative institutions at both national and regional level; they can have minority "experts" in various consultative bodies to the government. Alternatively, minorities can also be given a right to self-government. Achieving legislative representation can also be done in several ways – minorities can participate in the political process through non-minority-specific parties or they can try to form their own parties and achieve representation along ethnic lines. There are also various ways in which the state, through its political institutions and legislative framework, can encourage or discourage the representation of its minorities. It is this relationship which we examine.

The chapter investigates the link between one of the forms of ethnic political representation – ethnic parties – and one of the possible ways through which state policy can impact upon it – the type and nature of regulation of ethnic parties found in the Constitution, Party Law, and Electoral Law of a given country. Ethnic parties – parties that aim to represent a specific ethnic minority group – exist in virtually all East-European states, but the legal and institutional frameworks of these countries treat such parties in several quite different ways. Albania and Bulgaria, for example, ban ethnic parties, while the Czech and Slovak Republics allow ethnic parties to exist and subject them to equal treatment by their electoral laws. Hungary and Poland, on the other hand, not only permit ethnic parties to form and run in parliamentary elections but also make it easier for them to gain representation at different levels of government. Finally, Romania and Slovenia provide the most extreme form of positive discrimination by guaranteeing seats to minorities (subject to some limitations). As the countries of Eastern Europe countries have substantial proportions of their population belonging to minority groups – about 15% on average – the legal treatment of political parties based on ethnicity has important consequences for the political representation and participation of these groups.

The chapter offers a comparative analysis of the legal regulations of ethnic minority parties. Concentrating on the EU10 East-European states, we trace the development of regulation on parties' activity and identity. As we shall see, Romania proves to have increased the amount of regulation in that category most significantly.

To delve more deeply into the differences and contextual specificity of regulation of minority parties we further examine the Party and Electoral Laws, as well as the Constitutions, to find that the most *restrictive* and most *encouraging* in their regulation towards minority parties are, respectively, Bulgaria and Romania. Finally, the chapter provides a comparison between these two most different forms of minority electoral arrangements and analyses the impact they have had on the success of ethnic parties in the two countries. Our analysis concentrates on the political parties of the Hungarian and the Roma minorities in Romania and on the Turkish and the Roma minorities in Bulgaria. We conclude that the electoral arrangements have made a significant and consequential difference in the case of only one minority – that of the Roma – in both countries. The larger minorities, on the other hand, have done similarly well in both Romania and Bulgaria despite differences in the institutional constraints on their behaviour.

Finally, in an attempt to link institutional arrangements with the political behaviour of individual members of minority groups, the paper investigates whether the different electoral fates of Roma parties have had any impact on the levels of political participation of the Roma minorities in the two countries. For this purpose, the paper uses survey data from the UNDP *Avoiding the Dependency Trap* database (UNDP 2003) and the *Legal Regulation of Political Parties in Post-war Europe* database (van Biezen 2009).

The Regulation of Ethnic Parties

Many of the methods used to promote the representation of minorities have been controversial, in large part because many appear to be opposed to the basic "individualistic" principles of liberal democracy. One in particular – the formation of "ethnic," "minority" or "ethno-regionalist" political parties – has been particularly contentious. These are parties which, formally or in practice, speak for the interests of a particular group, which are delineated in ethnic terms (Chandra 2011). As such, ethnic parties aim to fulfill a descriptive representative function for these groups in the national political arena.

The ethnic party is an interesting nexus of group-driven efforts to achieve representation and the state's policies regarding representation. No party can form without individuals willing to be part of it, making ethnic parties a reflection of the minority group's cohesiveness, socio-economic situation, and political ambition. However, the party's existence is often subject to differential treatment by the Constitution and other laws of the state. While many African and some European states (such as Albania and Bulgaria) simply ban ethnic parties, others, such as Romania and New Zealand, provide for the preferential treatment of those organizations. The presence of ethnic parties in contemporary democracies has recently been encouraged by the policy recommendations of international organizations such as the OSCE, which has included "establishing political parties based on communal identities" as part of a minority group's right to freedom of association (OSCE Lund Recommendation, article 8, 2000).

However, academic research provides divergent conclusions about the link between ethnic parties and democratic stability. In his works on consociational democracy, Arend Lijphart, for example, saw the existence of group-based parties as a positive and necessary institutional mechanism to provide for the representation and participation of the various segments of society (Lijphart 1977). Quite in contrast, Donald Horowitz (1985) has made a strong argument against ethnic parties by maintaining that ethnic parties tend to divide a divided society even further. As ethnic parties often represent strictly group interests, they are unable to concern themselves with issues of national importance and their behaviour is dangerous for the good government of the country (Horowitz 1985, 294). States that fear secessionist movements can, therefore, choose to ban ethnic parties. Bulgaria and Albania are examples of systems in which ethnic-based parties are banned in the Constitution or the Law on Parties and where their activities are discouraged by the electoral laws (Juberias

2000, 37). Reilly (2003) has similarly argued that because ethnic parties make their political appeal specifically on ethnicity, their emergence 'often has a centrifugal effect on politics.' The resulting fragmentation of the party system has a detrimental effect on the stability of democracy and government in such situations.

In contrast, other authors have argued that ethnic parties pose challenges to democratic government only in deeply divided societies. Stroschein, for example, has maintained that ethnic parties "domesticate" ethnic issues into institutional forms, thus allowing them to be resolved in parliament rather than through violence. Conflicts between these and other parties are routinized and the political process allows the parties to "find a way to bargain over heated issues and negotiate alternatives" (Stroschein 2001, 61). Birnir has made an even stronger argument: ethnic parties might in fact help the stabilization of the party system in the early years of democracy by providing a stable link between voters and parties for at least some part of the electorate at a time when such links are not well developed overall. Chandra (2005) has argued that, even in deeply divided societies, ethnic parties might not lead to centrifugal tendencies in the party system, while van Cott (2007) maintains that the formation and success of ethnic (indigenous) parties in Latin America has had a very beneficial effect on the quality of democracy in the region.

A natural extension of either of these two positions is the legal and institutional framework which states impose on all political actors. Constitutional provisions and electoral and party legislation are the most common instruments of state policy that can influence the success or failure of any political party, including an ethnic minority party. The actors that make the policies, however, are the parties themselves – something, which Rashkova and Biezen (2014) refer to as the 'paradox of regulation'. Thus, in an era of growing party regulation, and especially considering the areas of spoils for successful competitors and gate-keeping for potential entrants, Katz and Mair (1995) argue that the link between the parties and the state has gained strength, and thus the party has become a public, rather than a private, utility (Biezen 2004). That political parties are increasingly managed by the state, in that their activities are to a larger extent subject to regulations and state laws, is also the focus of Biezen and Kopecký's (2007) study of the dimensions of the party-state link.

To estimate the extent to which ethnic minority parties are regulated, we begin by using the data from the *Party Law in Modern Europe (PLME)* database. The PLME database consists of detailed coding of European party laws. The content of party laws is codified in twelve major categories ranging from 'democratic principles' to 'party organization' and 'party finance'. Each category is further broken down into additional, more specific, sub-categories – for example, the 'democratic principles' category includes texts related, but not limited, to principles of competition, equality, participation and pluralism. The database provides an overview of the *range* and *magnitude* of regulation (more detailed explanation of the coding scheme and the database is provided in Casal Bértoa, Piccio and Rashkova, chapter 6).

For our purposes here, we are interested in the 'party activity and identity' category, as it refers to what parties do or seek to do; it offers rules governing the activity, goals and behaviour of parties. We make a comparison between the *raw* magnitude of regulation, that is the number of times a particular category is mentioned in a given country's Party Law, the *weighted* magnitude or how much of the regulation in a country's Party Law relates to party activity and identity, and, finally, how the magnitude of regulation *changes* over time. The results show that not much attention is devoted to the 'party activity and identity' in any of the ten East-European democracies. In fact, the highest percentage of regulation devoted to 'party activity and identity' in any Party Law is 14.1 per cent in Lithuania's 1995 Party Law. This figure however drops to less than 10 per cent for all states in their current Party Laws, which shows that states are increasingly less interested in regulating the activity and identity of their parties. In addition to the amount of regulation, we also examined the change in regulation over time. We observe a general low regulation of parties' activity and identity, which throws up no clear pattern of how the regulation changes. Bulgaria, Slovakia and Slovenia are decreasing the amount of regulation; Estonia, Poland and Romania are increasing it, while the remaining four states remain neutral.

Despite providing a useful overview of the extent and directional change of regulation of a party's activity and identity, the figures reported in table 1 leave the regulatory puzzle unsolved as we do not know how specific rules are worded and to what extent they are truly restrictive. Furthermore, table 1 presents an overview of regulation found only in the Party Law, while political parties are regulated also in the Constitution and the Electoral Law of a given country. To complete the picture, we go on to examine the actual content of legislation in both the Party and Electoral Laws, as well as the Constitutions of our countries. An in-depth analysis of the contents of all these legal documents reveals that there is a lot of variation on the regulation of ethnic, religious or other national minorities among the EU10. To encompass the differences in a way which is useful for further investigation into how ethnic minorities are treated in the political arena in East-European states, we make a fourfold classification of the types of minority references found in legal texts. The first and to some extent least telling type is what we call the *no reference* category; simply, this category reflects a legal document that makes no reference to minorities.[1] The second category is what we call *neutral*, or in other words some references to minorities do exist, however they do not discriminate against these groups, nor do they strengthen their position in the political arena. The final two categories reflect the existence of positive discrimination, which we call *encouraging*, and negative discrimination references which we term *restrictive*.[2] The four categories thus aid us in making an overall classification of the political treatment of minority parties in East-European legal texts. The results of this examination are summarized in table 1.

Table 1: Regulation of national minority electoral participation

Country	**Constitution**	**Party Law**	**Electoral Law**
Bulgaria	*restrictive*	*restrictive*	--
Czech Republic	--	*restrictive*	*encouraging*
Estonia	*neutral*	--	--
Hungary	*encouraging*	--	--
Latvia	*neutral*	--	*neutral*
Lithuania	--	*neutral*	--
Poland	*encouraging*	--	--
Romania	*encouraging*	*encouraging / restrictive*	*encouraging*
Slovakia	*encouraging*	*restrictive*	--
Slovenia	*neutral*	*restrictive*	--

Of the three types of laws examined, the Constitution appears to be the legal document in which minorities are referred to the most.[3] As we see, only the Czech and the Lithuanian Constitutions have no reference to minorities and their participation in the political process. In terms of the overall variation in the regulation of minority representation, Romania and Bulgaria appear to be the two countries with consistent types of reference across all legal texts – the former strongly encouraging the representation of minorities, and the latter quite restrictive in that regard. Romania gives special treatment to its national minorities – they are guaranteed representation under some very basic conditions and they are referred to in many places in the law (Constitution Art. 62.2 and in multiple places in the Electoral Law). In Bulgaria, on the other hand, both the 1990 Party Law (Art. 3.2.3) and the Constitution (Art. 11.4) state that a political party based on a religious or ethnic principle may not be established. Thus, Bulgaria is the only European Union member state which openly bans the existence of ethnic parties. While the clause prohibiting the existence of ethnic parties was removed from the 2009 Party Law, multiple mentions restricting links to religious institutions and the prohibitive ethnic clause in the Constitution still remain. Besides in Bulgaria and Romania, restrictive clauses about ties with religious groups, propaganda promoting religious inequality, and the acceptance of funding from religious entities are also found in the Party Laws of the Czech Republic, Lithuania, Romania, Slovakia and Slovenia. Other states treat all their citizens equally and therefore pay little attention to specifically addressing minorities in their legislation. Finally, we have a group of states which mention ethnic or religious minorities but in clauses that do not in any way encourage or impede their political participation and are therefore considered to have no specific electoral effect on the minority – an example here is Latvia.

In addition to the regulation established by the Constitution and the Party Law, the specific relations between the electoral rules and ethnic parties also have substantial consequences for the ability of those parties to function in the political systems. Assuming that ethnic parties are not banned, the nature of the electoral laws can significantly influence the chances of success or failure of ethnic parties, even without providing them with any special treatment. That electoral systems have an impact on who is represented in the legislative bodies is a long-standing law in political science. According to Duverger's original formulation, in systems where winners take all, smaller parties are discouraged from competing, while proportional representation systems provide little or no reward for fusing and no punishment for splitting (Duverger 1951, 248-254) and are therefore beneficial to both small and large parties alike. As proportional representation lowers the hurdles for smaller parties, ethnic parties are more likely to gain representation in those systems, thus providing for peaceful resolution of ethnic issues and, ultimately, for greater support for the political system by the members of the minority (Lijphart 1999, Norris 2004, 113-5).[4]

Interestingly, our analysis of legal texts shows that no restrictions on minorities are applied in the Electoral Laws in any of the 10 East-European states. Moreover, in the three instances where minority groups are mentioned at all, the law is either *encouraging* minority representation in some way or *neutral* towards it. Examples of the former treatment are the obligatory rule that municipalities establishing committees for national minorities must issue election announcements also in the language of the national minority concerned (Art 15.4 Czech Electoral Law) and guaranteeing legislative representation to all minority groups which have failed to get a member elected but have gathered at least 10% of the average vote awarded to an elected MP (Art 9.1 Romanian Electoral Law). The Latvian electoral law provides an example of *neutral* treatment. The *restrictive* treatment of ethnic parties by the Electoral Law is more difficult to discern since, in addition to what we may term 'descriptive discrimination', i.e. direct bans on parties of ethnic minorities, they can also be subject to 'substantive discrimination.' That is, the very features that distinguish electoral systems within the PR family are likely to influence the chances of success of ethnic parties even when the rules are not directed at minorities *per se*. As ethnic parties are usually small, the nature and presence of an electoral threshold are probably the most important. Not only do higher thresholds hurt small parties (Rashkova and Spirova, forthcoming) and thus by default also minorities, but thresholds set around the percentage point that reflects the minority proportion of the population also reduce the chances of an ethnic party gaining seats. Similarly, when substantially raised thresholds apply to coalitions, minority parties are hurt especially as the vote is limited by the size of the minority (Juberias 2000, 35). In terms of the classification scheme established above in those cases the electoral law is *restrictive* towards ethnic political participation.

Most of the East-European countries discussed here use proportional representation with thresholds of 4-5% for individual parties. Romania, Slovakia, Poland and the Czech Republic have thresholds of between 7 and 11% for political coalitions. Hungary is the only country with a mixed electoral system, with a 5% threshold in its PR part. Thus, even though electoral legislation does not *de facto* restrict ethnic parties from participating in the political competition, the existence of high electoral thresholds has a *restrictive* effect. Due to the (small) size of minorities in these countries – with the exception of the Russian minorities in the Baltic countries – their representation in the political process is often challenged by such thresholds.

Electoral arrangements can provide for the positive discrimination of ethnic parties by easing their requirements specifically for minority parties. As Juberias notes (2000, 38), countries may relax the requirements for fielding and registering candidates, running national campaigns, and they may even ignore the electoral threshold in the case of minority parties. Such measures have been introduced by Poland where the party of the German minority which receives between 0.4% and 1.2% of the total vote has been able to secure a proportional number of seats in the Polish Sejm, and by Hungary, but only for local elections. Finally, the most direct way to *encourage* minority participation in the political process is to provide minority parties or minorities as a whole with guaranteed representation in the national legislative body. Thus, groups officially recognized as minorities by the state or minorities that have a political party competing in the elections can be granted seats. Slovenia, for example, provides for the representation of two minorities that are constitutionally recognized as such, while Romania, as is also reflected in table 2 above, provides the strongest system of positive discrimination as it does not limit the number of minorities that can obtain representation (Juberias 2000, 44-49) and it has *encouraging* references to national minorities in all three legal texts examined.

Both positive and negative discrimination of minorities – banning their parties or granting them special privileges – have been criticized by democratic theorists; the former for not allowing a basic right to all citizens, the latter for violating the equality of representation, one of the basic principles of democracy. Moreover, the impact of electoral arrangements is not as clear-cut as electoral engineers sometimes claim it to be. A close examination of these electoral arrangements and their impact on the success or failure of ethnic parties is thus necessary before any conclusions can be made.

Comparing Bulgaria and Romania

Ethnic Party Regulation and Ethnic Composition

Bulgaria and Romania provide a suitable comparison in an effort to look for the impact of ethnic party regulation on party behaviour since they represent the most restrictive and most encouraging modes of regulation of ethnic parties, but also have relatively similar ethnic make-ups and quite comparable histories of inter-ethnic relations and democratic transition.

As noted by the examination of the Constitutions and Electoral and Party Laws of the ten East-European EU member-states, Bulgaria and Romania represent the two extremes of the policy options discussed here. Bulgaria's restrictive form of institutional arrangements for ethnic parties makes any other electoral arrangement for minorities impossible, while Romania's generous guarantee of a seat to every legally recognized minority organization circumvents the otherwise restraining effect of its high electoral threshold.

The restriction of certain types of parties is in line with the general spirit of the Bulgarian constitution which avoids any mention of the word minority and does not provide for any collective rights (Vassilev 2001, 43). In general, Bulgarian political actors seem fearful of the association of the word *national minority* with *secession* and generally refuse to use the word in public discourse, calling national minorities "minority groups" (CEDIME 1999 and 2001). Despite allegations by minority rights advocates that the constitutional ban on ethnic parties is discriminatory and violates international laws, there has been no discussion about amending the constitution in any relevant way (Bulgarian Helsinki Committee, various years). Bulgaria operates under a proportional representation electoral system,[5] with a 4% national threshold which treats political parties and coalitions identically.

In contrast, Romania, as noted above, not only allows ethnic parties, but has introduced special provisions to guarantee that they have a seat in Parliament. Its general electoral rules until 2007 were proportional representation with 5% for parliamentary representation of political parties, which became larger for political alliances depending on the number of valid votes cast across the country (Law for the Election of the Chamber of Deputies and the Senate in Romania, 1992). Since 2008, a system mixed system with a 5% threshold for individual parties and 8% threshold for two-party alliances has been used (Stan and Zaharia 2009). Most importantly, since 1990, legally constituted organizations of citizens belonging to a national minority which have not obtained at least one seat through the general rules of the elections have had the right to a seat in Parliament with the only restriction that only one organization per minority group can obtain a seat. Since 2004 it has become more difficult for such organizations to obtain a seat, since they need to meet a "symbolic threshold" of 10% of the average number of valid votes required for the election of one deputy on national level (Romanian Government Department of Interethnic Relations). Despite this qualification, the Romanian system of positive discrimination of minorities is extremely strong, as it does not limit the number of minorities that can obtain representation.[6] Through that system about fifteen minorities, on average, and 18 at present, have gained representation in Parliament.

In terms of their ethnic make-up, both countries have a clear dominant majority, a single, large and concentrated minority (Turks in Bulgaria and Hungarians in Romania) and a substantial but scattered second minority (Roma). Table 2 presents basic data on the ethnic composition of the two countries.

Table 2: Minority Groups in Bulgaria and Romania

Ethnic group	**Bulgaria**		**Romania**	
	Size	**Percent of total population**	**Size**	**Percent of total population**
Armenians	6 552	0.10%	-	-
German	-	-	60 088	0.28%
Hungarians	-	-	1 431 807	6.6%
Roma	325 343	4.9%	535 140	2.5%
Russians	9 978	0.15%	35 791	0.17%
Serbs	-	-	22 561	0.10%
Tatars	-	-	23 935	0.11%
Turks	588 318	8.85%	32 098	0.15%
Ukrainians	1 789	0.03%		
Vlachs	3 684	0.06%		
Others	19 659	0.29%		

Source: Bulgarian Statistical Institute, Census 2011, http://censusresults.nsi.bg/Reports/2/2/R7.aspx; Romanian Statistical Institute, Census 2002, http://colectaredate.insse.ro/phc/aggregatedData.htm

In Bulgaria, the majority group constitutes around 85 % of the total population. The largest minority – the Turks – makes up 8.8% of the population and is concentrated in five of the 28 administrative regions of the country, in two of which they are a majority. The Roma (Gypsies) who constitute about 4.9% of the population according to official statistics, although Roma experts provide estimates of their number that are almost twice as large (CEDIME 1999), are the second largest minority and are territorially dispersed (National Statistical Institute 2011). The Russian, Armenian, Vlach and Ukranian minorities each make up less than 1% of the population and do not have a specific territorial concentration.

Romania has a similar ethnic composition: Romanians constitute a clear majority, amounting to 89% of the population. The country has two large and several smaller minorities. The largest minority are the Hungarians, which make up around 6.6% of the total population and, like the Turkish minority in Bulgaria, the Romanian Hungarians are concentrated in six of the 32 counties of the country (Romanian Government Department of Interethnic Relations). The second largest minority, the Roma of Romania, are the most numerous Roma minority in Eastern Europe. However, given the size of Romania's population, they constitute only 2.5% of it, which makes them a smaller proportion than the Roma in Bulgaria. However, just as in the case of the Bulgarian Roma, experts estimate their population to be much bigger than shown in official data. Some 1.8 million or 7.9% of the total population is the unofficial estimate of the Roma count in Romania (CEDIME 2001). Like all Roma communities, the Romanian Roma are scattered throughout the country and therefore do not encourage any special electoral strategies of the political elite wishing to compete for their vote. Germans, Russians, Turks, Tatars and Serbs are minorities that make up less than 1% of the population.

We focus currently on four minorities – the Turks, the Hungarians and the Roma in the two countries. Until 1990, all four minorities were subject to various policies of assimilation and discrimination by the Communist parties. The Bulgarian experience of forcibly re-naming and re-locating the Turkish minority during the 1970s and 1980s is probably more brutal, but it is fair to say that both countries imposed the majority dominant culture and system on all ethnic groups in the two states. Democratic reforms in the two countries were also similar: the first part of the 1990s was dominated by the successor parties – the Bulgarian Socialists and the Romanian PSDR. Still, and irrespective of the quite diverse legal treatments of politically mobilized ethnicity, all minorities of interest here have established their own political parties, making an examination of the comparative trends of ethnic party development an important insight into the ability of party regulation to impact upon party behaviour.

The Turkish and Roma Parties in Bulgaria

The presence of a constitutional ban on ethnic parties has not meant that no ethnic parties have existed in Bulgarian politics. Using Chandra's (2011) multifaceted definition of ethnic party, which uses the party's name, platform, source of support, and political behaviour as alternative indicators of ethnic natures, ethnic parties have maintained a stable position in Bulgarian politics by not openly registering as ethnic political entities. However, for most of the 1990s, this was possible only for the relatively numerous and powerful Turkish minority in Bulgaria. The Turkish-dominated Movement of Rights and Freedoms (DPS) was founded officially in January 1990. Although it does not have an openly stated ethnic platform and it includes ethnic Bulgarians in both its membership and its leadership, it represents the interests of the Turkish minority in Bulgaria and its support is heavily concentrated in the regions populated by the minority. As figure 1 illustrates, the party has been present in all legislatures since 1990. Its share of the vote was well below the proportion of the Turkish minority in society, but this changed substantially after 2001. This happened not only because of the stability of the DPS's voters and their turnout in comparison to the substantial decline of the general voter turnout in the country, but also because of an increase in the actual number of DPS votes. In addition, the party's position and support were considered instrumental for the changes of government in 1991 and 1994 while from 2001 to 2009 the DPS was an official coalition partner in the Bulgarian government. The 2009 election left the party and its latest partner, the Bulgarian Socialist Party, in opposition, yet this was reversed in 2013 when early elections put the BSP-DPS coalition back in power.

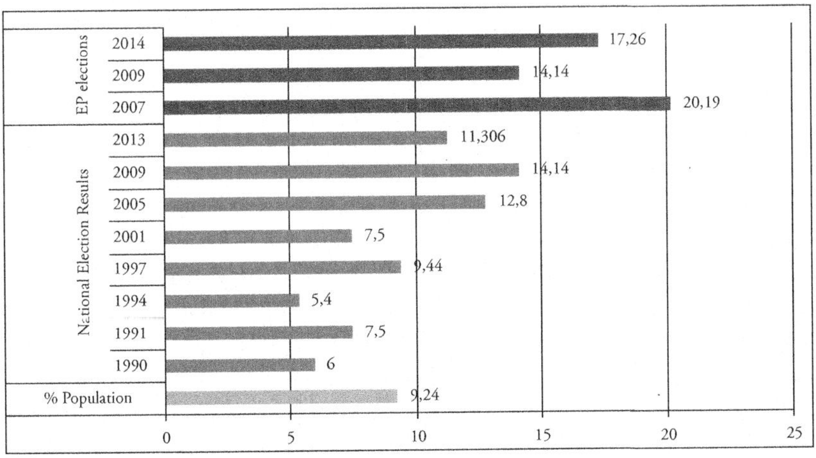

Figure 1. DPS Electoral Support, 1990-2014

The ability of the DPS to function freely in Bulgarian politics was challenged in the early 1990s. In 1991, 93 members of Parliament, virtually all affiliated with the former Communist Party, petitioned the Constitutional Court to declare the DPS unconstitutional because of its *de facto* ethnic base (Ganev 2004, 66). The Court rejected the petition with the argument that there was nothing in the formal documents of the party that made it exclusively Turkish, although its decision is considered to have been prompted by broader considerations of keeping the ethnic peace. The decision of the Bulgarian Constitutional Court ensured the party's persistence in the system and thus greatly influenced political life and ethnic relations in the country. By the late 1990s, there was no major concern that the constitutional provision could prevent either the DPS or the fledgling Roma political parties from participating in the political process (Vassilev 2001). This enabled the Turkish party to function in Bulgarian political life despite the constitutional ban and the absence of special electoral treatment of ethnic parties in Bulgaria.

This has also been made possible by factors beyond the regulatory regime. The Turkish minority is not only of substantial size, well above the electoral threshold of 4%, but the party and its leader (until 2013) Ahmed Dogan have also managed to cultivate a strong loyalty in a large part of the minority. The DPS has a very well encapsulated electorate – 17% – measured as the ratio of its members to its voters; it is second only to the BSP in Bulgaria and way above any averages for non-ex-communist parties in the region (Spirova 2007, 130; van Biezen 2003). Its membership has continued to grow through the 2000s, uniquely among the Bulgarian parties, or indeed European parties more generally.

The DPS thus does not appear to have been substantially hurt by the constitutional or the electoral arrangements in Bulgaria. The 4% electoral threshold came close to posing a threat to the DPS only once, when in the 1994 elections the party received just over 5% of the vote. In response, the DPS formed pre-electoral coalitions with other, not exclusively ethnic parties (these included the Green Party, three small centrist parties and one royalist party in 1997 and the Liberal Union and *EuroRoma* in 2001). This was an indication of a realization that the DPS could not expand its vote further unless it reached outside the Turkish minority (Dal 2003). Consequently, since 2001 the party has been making a conscious effort to transform itself into a "liberal" party concerned generally with minority rights. It has included more ethnic Bulgarians is its leadership, and joined the Liberal International. However, as Horowitz has suggested for ethnic parties in general (Horowitz 1984, 282), achieving broader electoral support has proven extremely challenging because most Bulgarians do not associate the DPS with liberal values but, rather, with strong commitment to defending the interests of the Turkish minority. Yet, the party itself, as well as numerous commentators and analysts, has praised the "Bulgarian ethnic model", despite the restrictive legal framework, for the incorporation of the DPS in mainstream democratic politics, the moderation of the party's policy positions, and its law-abiding behaviour and considers it as a major factor for the preservation of ethnic peace in the country (Vassilev 2001, Tatarli 2003, Petkova 2002; Krasteva and Todorov 2011).[7] However, the model has excluded all other minorities, a fact that is painfully obvious in the situation of the Roma. Roma parties were unable to secure a stable place in Bulgarian politics throughout the post-communist period. Several factors account for this. First, the initial registration of one Roma party – the Democratic Roma Union was not permitted in 1990 based on the Constitutional ban on ethnic parties, which stymied political mobilization early on. Second, the Roma minority is much more heterogeneous than the Turkish one, and is also scattered around the country. This makes it almost impossible for them to mobilize and support a single national party. Finally, the Bulgarian Roma represent just about 4% of the population, equivalent to the threshold of the electoral system, making the success of an even well-organized and unified Roma party doubtful.

The Bulgarian Roma parties are not unique in this regard. As Stroschein has argued (2001, 61), in order to be successful an ethnic party must obtain a high percentage of votes from a finite political base – the groups that it represents. Ethnic parties thus require a lot of consensus-minded politicians, which is hardly feasible option for the diverse, internally heterogeneous and politically fragmented Roma communities and organizations throughout Eastern Europe (Baranyi 2001, 3). The absence of any special electoral encouragement for ethnic parties in Bulgaria, however, has made Roma representation in Parliament even less likely than in most other post-communist systems.

For most of the 1990s the only political representation the Roma in Bulgaria got was through the mainstream political parties. This was a very limited form of representation in which one or two Roma had a symbolic presence in Parliament during each term.[8] It was not until 1997-1998 that Roma organizations again began to show genuine political ambition and to take the first steps towards organizing for elections (Mladenov 2003) but, due to the constitutional ban on ethnic political organizations, Roma organizations are either not registered as parties or have non-Roma-specific names. In the period between 1997 and 2003 some twenty one Roma political organizations were found in Bulgaria, including *Free Bulgaria, the Party for Social and Democratic Change* (PSDC), *Evroroma and Citizens' Union Roma* as the more visible and active ones.[9]

Roma parties' first elections were the 1999 local elections where *Free Bulgaria* got three Roma elected as mayors and placed over 60 Roma as local councillors. The successful Roma participation led to quite high optimism about the impending parliamentary elections in 2001. However, the heterogeneity of the Roma population, which is divided into several self-enclosed sub-groups, and infighting among its leaders prevented a unified Roma party from emerging despite numerous NGO efforts to encourage this. Two of the main parties – *Free Bulgaria* and the *PSDC* – appeared in a coalition called *National Union Tzar Kiro* with six smaller organizations and parties. The Roma coalition received 27,000 votes (0.6%). Very few Roma voted for the party although Roma participation in elections is estimated at around 65% (UNDP). After this defeat the coalition fell apart (Mladenov 2003). *Evroroma* chose to run in a coalition with the DPS, while *Citizens' Union Roma* joined the BSP coalition. In the 2005 elections, *Evroroma* ran alone and managed to achieve electoral support of 1.25 per cent,[10] enough to provide it with state subsidies, but in 2009 *Evroroma* joined the BSP coalition and secured one seat in Parliament through that coalition. The trend of uniting with the BSP continued in 2013, but neither *Evroroma* nor the other Roma party in the Socialist coalition was given an electable position in the electoral lists of the coalition and, consequently, failed to secure seats in Parliament.

The development of the Roma representation in Bulgaria has thus been characterized by individual representatives here and there elected on larger parties' lists and fluctuating enthusiasm about unifying all Roma parties and seeking to win their own electoral support. These trends have also been influenced, among others, by the legal treatment of ethnic parties. The Constitutional ban on ethnic parties prevented the initial registration of a Roma party, while the absence of special electoral treatment of minority parties ends any hope for the representation of the heterogeneous and not very well organized group along ethnic party lines.

The Hungarian and Roma Parties in Romania

Like the DPS in Bulgaria, the party of the ethnic Hungarians in Romania, the Hungarian Democratic Union (UDMR/RMDSZ) has played a substantial role in Romanian political life. As ethnic parties are not banned in Romania the party has never had problems with displaying its ethnic basis, and it has managed to preserve itself as the exclusive party of the Hungarian minority. The UDMR has gained representation in all post-1989 parliaments at a level roughly corresponding to the Hungarian proportion of the population, while in the EP elections it has even achieved slight over-representation (Figure 2). In addition it has remained the only stable party in Romanian politics, apart from the communist successor party. It was part of the governing coalitions from 1996 to 2000, a fact that many saw as a major step towards achieving ethnic harmony in Romania. Its support is also very highly encapsulated. Its membership to electorate ratio was about 65% in 1996, a level that is much higher than in the DPS and any other party in the region as well. A large proportion of the Hungarian minority also voted for it, an important fact given how close the proportion of Hungarians in Romania is to the electoral threshold of the electoral system (Stroschein 2001).

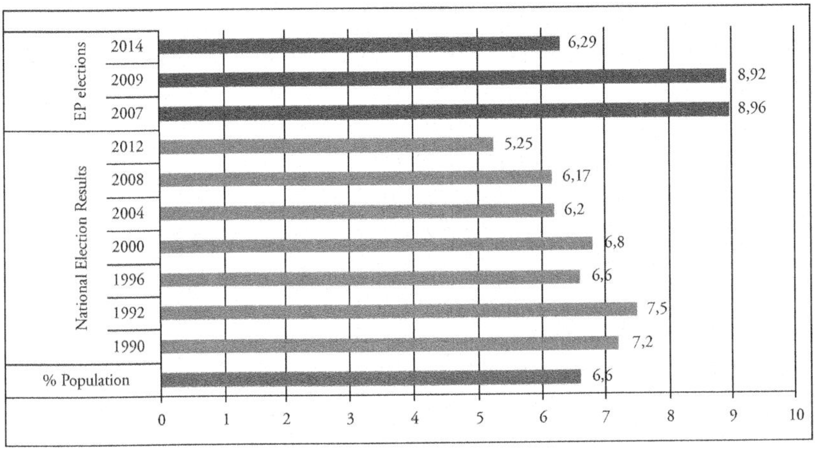

Figure 2. UMDR Electoral Support, 1990-2014

Overall, the UDMR has benefited from the provisions of Romania's PR system and mixed electoral systems, but not from the positive discrimination system that exists for other minorities in the Romanian system. The electoral system has discouraged it from forming electoral alliances so, unlike the DPS, the UDMR has never attempted to ally with other parties. It can be argued that given the nature of the minority and the experience of the DPS in Bulgaria, the UDMR would have done equally well under a typical PR system with no ethnic element. In fact, the demands of the UDMR have at times reached much more extreme levels than those of the DPS. It threatened to leave the governing coalitions in 1997 and 1998 "if demands for state funded Hungarian university were not met" and has repeatedly called for some degree of autonomy for the Hungarian-majority regions (Stroschein 2001, 61). This trend was exacerbated by the internal split in the UDMR in 2003. The more radical, the Hungarian Citizens' Party (MPP) supported territorial autonomy for Transylvania and presented itself as a "purer Hungarian alternative" (Stroschein 2011, 192). Fractionalization was somewhat stymied after 2009 with the joint actions of the MPP and the UDMR, but the debate on what the real issue and demand of the Hungarian minority are continues (Spirova and Stefanova 2012).

The higher degree of radicalization along ethnic lines might be attributed to the acceptance of ethnicity as a legitimate political cleavage in Romania's general legislation. The same feature has also allowed the Roma in Romania to do much better in terms of political mobilization and representation in comparison to their Bulgarian counterparts. Roma political activity has clearly been dominated by the *Partida Romilor* (PR), which "receives government subsidies, allowing it to further strengthen its network and better prepare for its next electoral campaign" (Roma Rights 2003).[11] Roma parties have competed from the very first democratic elections and *Partida Romilor* has obtained the guaranteed one seat in the legislature at every election. Its leader, Nicolae Paun, has served as Chairman of the Committee for Human Rights, Religious Affairs and National Minorities in Parliament since 2000.

The Roma Parties in Romania seem to enjoy higher levels of support amongst the Roma minority than do Bulgarian Roma parties. Electoral results show that about twice as many of the Roma in Romania vote for Roma parties as do the Roma in Bulgaria. However, it can also be argued that the Romanian system of positive discrimination has caused the Roma minority to be underrepresented, while many others are overrepresented. The vote-seat ratio for the Roma parties ranges from 0.22 in 1996 to 0.48 in 1990, with 1 being perfect proportionality. Electoral arrangements of the kind that exist in Poland (which allow ethnic parties to gain representation proportional to their vote no matter whether they have passed the electoral threshold or not) would have allowed for much stronger representation of the minority in the Romanian legislature.

Overall, however, the level of representation of Roma parties in the Romanian Parliament is still infinitely larger than that of Roma parties in Bulgaria, and the Romanian Roma parties have gained much more visibility in political life than have the Roma parties in Bulgaria. While in terms of numbers of Roma in Parliament there is no significant difference between Bulgaria and Romania, the ability of the Romania Roma to achieve representation through their own parties has allowed them to gain more influence in Romanian politics. For example, as a result of the pre-election agreement between the PSD, the winning party in the Romanian 2000 elections, and *Partida Romilor*, the latter received a position in the state administration – under Secretary of State and Head of the National Office for Roma – as well as one Presidential advisor position. *Partida Romilor* also negotiated the appointment of members of the Roma minority to regional and local government offices throughout the country (NDI 2003a). Clearly, these achievements go well beyond what the Roma in Bulgaria have managed to do, where Roma affairs are entirely subject to the will of the governing majority parties. This suggests that even the token representation of Roma ethnic parties in the legislature can make a difference when compared to token representation of Roma leaders only.

Consequences for Minority Political Representation

The final question that this chapter addresses is whether having Roma parties in Parliament elected on their own terms has had any effect on the political attitudes of the Roma minority in Romania. For this purpose, the research uses data from the 2001 Survey of Roma in Bulgaria, Romania, Hungary and the Czech and Slovak Republics carried out by the UNDP (UNDP 2001).[12] The data show that Roma in both Bulgaria and Romania exhibit high involvement in the electoral process – in both countries the voter turnout for the Roma is just around or above the national turnout rate, a fact that is remarkable, given the low education level and economic status of the Roma in society. However, the voter turnout of Romanian Roma is markedly higher than that of the Roma in Bulgaria – a difference of about 14 per cent.

Further, Romanian Roma exhibit a substantially higher familiarity with and trust in their own political parties. About 27 per cent can name a Roma party they trust in Romania, while only about 5% of the Bulgarian Roma can do the same. The contrast is even more striking when we compare these figures to the percentage of Roma who could name any other party that they would trust. About the same number of Roma in Romania could do so – a little over 28%, while the number of Roma who would name a trusted party in Bulgaria was more than three times more than the number of people who could name a trusted Roma party.

The results clearly indicate much greater familiarity with Roma parties at a similar level of general familiarity with political parties. When asked directly about the source of support for the Roma in their country, the Roma in Romania indicated that they can rely on the Roma parties at almost twice the rate of the Bulgarian Roma. Intriguingly, the Romanian Roma also exhibit much lower rates of relying on the state to support them.

However, the difference in familiarity with Roma parties might be a result of the fact that there have been many more Roma parties in Romania and they have been much more active over the years than their counterparts in Bulgaria. A more interesting question is whether there is a difference in how the Roma feel about the political process in general. Regretably, the only survey question that taps into the efficacy of the Roma is the question "Do you feel your interests are well represented (at different levels of government)?". Romanian Roma show much higher levels of satisfaction with the way their interests are represented at all levels of government. The active presence or absence of Roma parties in the political system seems to make a difference to the political attitudes and behaviour of the Roma minority in Bulgaria and Romania.

Conclusion

This chapter has provided an overview of the regulatory regimes of ethnic political parties in post-communist Europe through a comparison of the ways they are treated in the Constitutions, Party Laws and Electoral Laws of the states in the region. The policies vary substantially from positive discrimination for ethnic parties to outright bans on their existence. The chapter focused on two extreme examples of regulatory positions – those in Bulgaria and Romania – and examined the ways the regulation of ethnic parties and their activities has impacted on their existence in both polities. The general conclusion is that regulatory regimes matter for the ability of political parties to function in the political system. However, there are two major qualifications to this: (1) their effect is felt more by smaller minorities than by larger ones, and (2) their effect is often indirect: it acts to set up the dimensions of political competition rather than directly to pressure political actors.

While the constitutional ban on ethnic parties in Bulgaria has not hurt the Turkish minority, it seems to have at least originally impeded the development of Roma political parties. In addition, the absence of any positive discrimination with respect to ethnic minorities and the 4% electoral threshold have further prevented the Bulgarian Roma from sending their own representatives to Parliament. In Romania, the arrangements of positive discrimination do not appear to have made much of a difference to the electoral fate of the Hungarian minority party, but have influenced the development of Roma parties. Electoral arrangements thus seem to matter, but to do so mostly in situations where other factors of political mobilization make representation uncertain. The effect of electoral arrangements on the success of ethnic parties is clearly mitigated by the size and dynamics of the minority they represent.

The differences in political attitudes and behaviour between Bulgarian and Romanian Roma lend further support to the argument that constitutional treatment and electoral rules can influence the nature of politics in a country. The politicization of ethnicity, attributable to the *encouraging* treatment of minorities in the Constitution and electoral legislation in Romania, may have allowed the development of more radical nationalism in the case of the Romanian Hungarians than the *officially* non-ethnic representation of the Turkish minority in Bulgaria. While DPS policy positions have been moderated over the 1990s and 2000s, those of the UMDR seem to have become more radical. Clearly, there is a plethora of other factors that have influenced these developments, but the regulatory frameworks have clearly influenced them as well.

Notes

1 Estonia, Hungary, Latvia and Poland, for example, do not mention ethnic parties in their Party Laws.

2 Our *no reference*, *encouraging*, and *restrictive* categories are similar to Janda's (2005) *proscriptive*, *promotional* and *prescriptive* models of party regulation.

3 Party Finance Laws, which are the fourth main legal document in which parties and party competition are regulated were also examined. However, with the exception of two articles classified as 'neutral 'in the Romanian PFL, no other country's PFL refers to minority representation.

4 It has to be mentioned, however, that in cases when the ethnic minorities are highly concentrated in only several regions, SMD electoral systems can also benefit them. However, cases like this are relatively rare (Norris 2004).

5 Prior to the 2009 elections one plurality-elected seat was introduced in each electoral district, reducing the number of seats elected through the PR part (Kolarova and Spirova 2011).

6 The breadth of the rule has been criticized for allocating the same status to minorities of various sizes and positions in society (Juberias 2000, 44-49).

7 This position was somewhat challenged during the 2005-2009 tenure of the party as coalition partner, when its engagement in clientelistic patron-dominated and corrupt networks brought its behaviour under closer scrutiny. For many (ethnic) Bulgarians the problem the DPS posed in 2011 was not its ethnic nature but its rent-seeking behaviour (Krasteva and Todorov 2011, 35).

8 Cooperation with the party of the Turkish minority, the Movement for Rights and Freedoms (DPS), seemed to be a natural choice for some of the Roma leaders. The argument that the two minorities faced common problems as well as the proclaimed desire of the DPS to defend the rights of all people, minorities and individuals in Bulgaria made this an alluring possibility. Cooperation between the two ethnic groups did not pick up again until the 2001 elections when the DPS formed an electoral coalition with Evroroma, an important Roma organization in Bulgaria, and placed a number of Roma representatives on its ticket, yet at unelectable positions (Illiev 2001). By 2003, the DPS dismissed any possibility of future cooperation with the Roma party (Dal 2003). Cooperation with the Bulgarian Socialist Party (BSP) has also been a common policy for the Roma political leaders and was relatively welcomed by the BSP leadership through most of the 1990s. Given that the problems of the Roma mostly call for active state involvement, they are placed on the left side of the political continuum and thus naturally expected to support the major political actor on the left – the BSP (Sega 2002). However, the cooperation between the BSP and the Roma people has been far from fair to the minority, because the concern of the BSP with the situation of the Roma minority has been minimal despite the couple of Roma leaders who achieved representation through the BSP over the years (Illiev 2001).The Union of Democratic Forces, as the major anti-communist political organization in Bulgaria, was also a partner of some of the new Roma political organizations in the early 1990s. Manus Romanov – the first Roma representative in Parliament after 1989 was elected on the UDF list. However, for the rest of 1990s the UDF became "notorious for disregarding Roma as possible partners during elections (Iliev 2001).

9 *Free Bulgaria* was originally led by Tzar Kiro – the self-proclaimed tsar of the Roma in Bulgaria and was established in 1997. It is currently led by his son, Prince Angel. ROS Kupate is an organization primarily concerned with the economic development of the Roma and has an ideology that is close to the "democratic idea" (i.e. the UDF). (Mladenov 2003) The organization's leader established the *Party for Social and Democratic Change* (PSDC) in 2000. In

1998, Tzvetelin Kunchev established *Evroroma* after being elected to the National Assembly through the Bulgarian Business Block lists in 1997. By 2000, his immunity as a member of Parliament was removed to allow the courts to prosecute him for several crimes.

10 Public funding of political parties in Bulgaria was previously provided for parliamentary parties only (Smilov 1999, IDEA 2004). Currently, parties that have received more than 1 per cent of the national vote are entitled to state subsidy equal to 5 per cent of the minimum wage per vote (Rashkova and Spirova 2014).

11 Public funding for Romanian political parties is rather complex, but most recently the parties which have more than 50 councilors have been eligible for some state funding (previously the barrier was 2, then 4 per cent). For more detail see Ghergina et al. (2011).

12 The data used here are somewhat outdated, but with the refocusing of the UNDP toward discrimination against rather participation of the Roma, this is the most recent available report.

References

Barany, Zoltan. 2001. "Romani Electoral Politics and Behavior." *JEMIE*. Autumn 2001.

BHC, Bulgarian Helsinki Committee (1996). *Annual Report: Human Rights in Bulgaria in 1995*, (Sofia: BHC).

BHC, Bulgarian Helsinki Committee (1997). *Annual Report: Human Rights in Bulgaria in 1996*, (Sofia: BHC).

BHC, Bulgarian Helsinki Committee (1998). *Annual Report: Human Rights in Bulgaria in 1997* (Sofia: BHC, February 1998).

Biezen, Ingrid van and Petr Kopecky. 2007. "The State and the Parties: Public Funding, Public Regulation and Rent-Seeking in Contemporary Democracies." *Party Politics* 13 (2): 235-254.

Biezen, Ingrid van. 2003. *Political Parties in New Democracies: Party Organization in Southern and East-Central Europe.* Basingstoke: Palgrave.

Biezen, Ingrid van. 2004. 'Political Parties as Public Utilities', *Party Politics* 10 (6): 701-722.

Bingham Powell, G. 1982. *Contemporary Democracies: Participation, Stability and violence.* Cambridge, MA: Harvard University Press.

BTA. 2003. BTA News. 30.08. 2003 http://www.bta.bg/site/elect2003/archive-form/08aug/24-31.htm.

CEDIME. 1999. Roma in Bulgaria. http://www.greekhelsinki.gr/pdf/cedime se - bulgaria-roma.doc.

CEDIME. 2001. Roma in Romania. http://www.greekhelsinki.gr/pdf/cedime-se- romania-roma.doc.

CEDIME. http://www.greekhelsinki.gr/pdf/cedime-se-romania-roma.doc.

Constitution of the Republic of Bulgaria available at http://www.oefre.unibe.ch/law/icl/bu00000_.html.

Cox, Gary. 1997. *Making Votes Count*. New York and London: Cambridge University Press.

Dal, Kasim. 2003. *Interview*.

Danova, Savelina. 2001. "More Empty Promises? The state of Roma affairs in Bulgaria." *Central European Review* 21 May 2001. http://www.ce- review.org/01/18/danova18.html.

Duverger, Maurice. 1951. *Political Parties: Their Organization and Activity in the Modern State*. London: Meuthen and Co. Ltd.

ERRC, 2003. *Roma Rights*. http://www.errc.org/rr_nr4_2003/noteb1.shtml).

European Roma Rights Center. 1999. *Roma Rights*. Snapshots from Around.

Europe. http://www.errc.org/rr_nr4_1999/snap14.shtml.

European Roma Rights Center. 2001. *Political Participation and Democracy un.*

Europe: a short Guide for Romani Activists. Budapest.

Friedman, Eben. 2002. "Political Integration of the Romany Minority in Macedonia." *South-East European Politics Online*, III(2-3O).

Ganev, Venelin. 2004. "History, Politics, and the Constitution: Ethnic Conflict and Constitutional Adjudication in Postcommunist Bulgaria." Slavic Review, 63 (1): 66-89.

Gherghina, Sergiu, Mihail Chiru and Fernando Casal Bértoa (2011). 'State Resources and Pocket Money: Shortcuts for Party Funding in Romania', Working Paper Series on the Legal Regulation of Political Parties, No. 8.

Grofman, Bernard and Arend Lijphart. 1986. *Electoral Laws and Their Political Consequences*, eds., New York: Agathon Press.

Horowitz, Donald. 2000. *Ethnic Groups in Conflict*. Berkeley: University of California Press.

Huber, Evelyne, Dietrich Rueschemeyer, and John D. Stephens. 1997. "The Paradoxes of Contemporary Democracy: Formal, Participatory and Social Democracy," *Comparative Politics* 29 (3): 323-42.

IDEA 2004. IDEA Handbook on Funding of Political Parties and Election Campaign. Stockholm. http://www.idea.int/publications/funding_parties/index.cfm.

Ikstens, Janis, et al. 2002. "Political Finance in Central Eastern Europe: An Interim report." *Austrian Journal of Political Science* 31 (1).

Illiev, Andrei. 2001. "Participation of Bulgarian Roma in the 2001 General Elections and prospects for political representation." Roma Rights 4(21). http://www.errc.org/rr_nr4_2001/noteb4.shtml.

Janda, Kenneth. 2005. *Political Parties and Democracy in Theoretical and Practical Perspectives*. NDI.

Juberias, Carlos Flores. 2000. "Post-communist electoral systems and national minorities: a dilemma in five paradigms." in Stein. op.cit.

Katz, Richard and Peter Mair. 1995. "Changing Models of Party Organization and Party Democracy: The Emergence of the Cartel Party", *Party Politics*, vol. 1 (1): 5-28.

Kymlcika, Will. 2002. 'Multiculturalism and Minority Rights: West and East.' *JEMIE*. Special Issue, available at http://www.ecmi.de/jemie/special_4_2002.html.

Kymlicka, Will and Magda Opalski, eds.. 2001. *Can Liberal Pluralism Be Exported?* Oxford University Press.

Law for the Election of the Chamber of Deputies and the Senate (1992). http://www2.essex.ac.uk/elect/electjp/ro_el92.htm#c2.

Law for the Election of the Chamber of Deputies and the Senate (1992). http://www2.essex.ac.uk/elect/electjp/ro_el92.htm#c2g.

Lijphart Arend, 1999. *Patterns of Democracy*. New Haven: Yale University Press.

Lijphart, Arend, 1994. *Electoral Systems and Party Systems: a Study of Twenty Seven Democracies, 1945-1990*. New York: Oxford University Press.

National Democratic Institute (NDI). 2003a. *Roma Political Participation in Romania*. Available at: http://www.romanothan.ro/engleza/reports/docs/1629_ro_romaparticip_022803.pdf.

National Democratic Institute (NDI). 2003b. *Roma Political Participation in Bulgaria*. Available at: http://www.accessdemocracy.org/library/1611_romaassess_020803.pdf.

National Statistical Institute. 2001. *Official Census of the Republic of Bulgaria* available at http://www.nsi.bg/Census/Ethnos.htm (in Bulgarian).

National Statistical Institute. 2011, Census 2011 Results Accessed May 30, 2012. http://www.nsi.bg/EPDOCS/Census2011final.pdf.

Norris, Pippa. 2004. Electoral Engineering: Voting Rules and Political Behavior. Cambridge University Press.

Ordeshook, Peter and Olga Shvetsova. 1994. "Ethic Heterogeneity, District Magnitude, and the Number of Parties." *AJPS* 38(1): 100-123.

Parushev, Georgi. 2003. Interview.

Petkova, Lilia. 2002. "The Ethnic Turks in Bulgaria: Social Integration and Impact on Bulgarian-Turkish Relations, 1947-2000". *Global Review of Ethnopolitics* 1 (4).

Powell, G. Bingham. 1982. *Contemporary Democracies*. Cambridge: Harvard University Press.

Project on Ethnic Relations (PER). 1998. *Political Participation and Roma in Hungary and Slovakia*. http://www.per-usa.org/

Project on Ethnic Relations (PER). 2000. *State Policies Towards Roma in Macedonia*. http://www.per-usa.org/

Przeworski, Adam. 1986. "Some Problems in the Study of the Transition to Democracy," in Guillermo O'Donnell, Phillipe C. Schmitter, and Laurence Whitehead, eds. *Transitions from Authoritarian Rule: Prospects for Democracy*, Part III. Baltimore: Johns Hopkins University Press, pp. 47-63.

Przeworski, Adam. 1991. *Democracy and the Market: Political and Economic Reforms in Eastern Europe and Latin America*. New York: Cambridge University Press.

Rae, Douglas. 1971. *The Political Consequences of Electoral Laws*. New Haven: Yale University Press.

Rashkova, Ekaterina R. and Maria Spirova. 'Party Regulation and the Conditioning of Small Political Parties: Evidence from Bulgaria', *East European Politics*, 30 (3), pp 315-330.

Rashkova, Ekaterina R. and Ingrid van Biezen. 2014. "The Legal Regulation of Political Parties: Contesting or Promoting Legitimacy", *International Political Science Review* 35 (3): 263-272.

Reilly, Benjamin. 2003. "Political Engineering of Parties and Party Systems." Paper presented at the 2003 APSA Annual meeting, Philadelphia, August 28-31, 2003.

Romanian Government Department of Interethnci Relations. Statistical Data 2012. Accessed June 1, 2014. http://www.dri.gov.ro/en.

Roper, Steven. 2003. "Explaining party system development: a cross-national comparison of post-communist party finance." Paper presented at the 2003 APSA Annual meeting, 28-31 August 2003.

RrAJE. 2003. Roma political representation in Slovakia.

Sega 2000. http://www.segabg.com/05092000/p0050007.asp.

Sega. 2003. http://www.segabg.com/06092003/p0020011.asp.

Sega.2002. 27 November, 2002. "Romite i bledolikite vozhdove na chervenite [The Roma and the pale-faced leaders of the Reds.]"

Shafir, Michael 2000. "The Hungarian Democratic Federation of Romania" in Stein, op.cit.

Simard, Carolle. "Political participation by ethno-cultural and visible minorities." Canada Policy Research Initiative. www.recherchepolitique.gc.ca.

Smilov, Daniel. 1999. "Structural corruption oaf party funding models: governmental favoritism n Bulgaria and Russia." Paper presented at the

Princeton University /CEU Joint conference on Corruption, Budapest 30 October-6 November 1999.

Stan, Lavinia and Razvan Zaharia. 2009. "Romania 2008." EJPR Political Data Yearbook 2008. 48 (7-8) 1087-1100.

Stein, Jonathan P. ed. 2000. *The Politics of National Minority Participation in Post-Communist Europe.* Armonk: M E Sharpe.

Stroschein, Sherrill. 2001. "Measuring Ethnic Party Success in Romania, Slovakia and Ukraine." *Problems of Post-Communism*, 48 (4), pp 59-69.

Tarashleva, Svetlana. 1994. *Standart.* December 3, 1994.

Tatarli, Ibrahim. 2003. *Dvizehnie za Prava I Svobodi: Studii* [Movement for Rights and Freedoms: Essays]. Sofia.

Tomov, Toma. 2002. Interview. http://www.bgns.net/Bg/actual/med/arhiv/drugi/190702.html.

UNDP, 2002. *Avoiding the Dependency Trap*, Regional Data Set http://roma.undp.sk.

Vasssilev, Rosen. 2001. "Post-Communist Bulgaria's Ethnopolitics" *Global Review of Ethnopolitics* 1 (2).

Vermeersch, Peter. 2001. "Advocacy Networks and Romani Politics in Central and Eastern Europe." *Journal and Ethnopolitics and Minority Issues in Europe.* Autumn 2001.

Vermeersch, Peter. 2002. "Ethnic Mobilization and the Political Conditionality of the European Union Accession; the Case of the Roma in Slovakia." *Journal of Ethnic and Migration Studies* 28 (1), pp 83-101.

Vermeersch, Peter. 2003. "EU Enlargement and Minority Rights Policies in Central Europe: Explaining Policy Shifts in the Czech Republic, Hungary and Poland." Paper presented at the 8th Annual World Convention of the Association for the Study of Nationalities, Columbia University, 3-5 April 200.

Wolf, Stephen. *JEMIE.* 2002. 'Multiculturalism and Minority Rights: West and East.' Special Issue. available at http://www.ecmi.de/jemie/special_4_2002.html

Zhivkova, Ljudmila. 2003. *Interview.*

CHAPTER 10

On the Engineerability of Political Parties: Evidence from Mexico

Imke Harbers
University of Amsterdam
Matthew C. Ingram
University at Albany, SUNY

Introduction

As the contributions to this volume make clear, laws regulating political parties have become increasingly common in new democracies. In this context, Mexico stands out with regard to the depth and breadth of party regulation as well as the frequency of reforms. Over the course of the last four decades, particularly since 1977, party regulation has grown steadily. Detailed legal provisions now govern all aspects of party behaviour, including the organizational structure of parties, finances, and electoral campaigns. The number of articles in the electoral code alone has quintupled, from 115 in 1954, to 394 in 2007, and most recently to an excess of 600 articles across the three electoral laws that replaced the electoral code as of May 2014.[1] Parties are recognized by the constitution, which explicitly defines them as "entities of public interest" (*entidades de interés público*, Art.41). During Mexico's gradual transition to democracy, changes in the regulation of party competition were one of the major dimensions along which the democratization of the regime took place. Substantial changes to electoral laws occurred frequently in the last three decades of the authoritarian regime (1970s-1990s), and have continued into the democratic era. With each new reform, additional aspects of party life came under the umbrella of legislation.

The Federal Electoral Institute (IFE) – an autonomous monitoring body established in 1990 (and replaced, as of 2014, by the National Electoral Institute (INE) – is credited with cleaning up the electoral process in a country where electoral fraud and vote rigging were commonplace. Yet, after initial enthusiasm about democratic progress the sense that democracy was incomplete remained widespread. In the public debate about the nature of Mexican democracy, this stagnation was at least partially attributed to insufficient regulation of party behaviour since the perception was that inadequate laws left room for parties to violate democratic norms. Thus, even after a major reform in 2007 – the fifth major reform of its kind in 30 years – there were increasing calls for yet another round of reforms, which then took place in 2014.

Both the depth of party regulation and rate of change over time make Mexico a compelling case in the study of the regulation of parties. The success of the IFE in organizing clean elections meant that the institute became a model for electoral institutions. Representatives from the IFE were frequent guests in the capitals of other democratizing countries. Yet, even though changes in public law have been associated with progress towards democracy, the Mexican case also illustrates forcefully that even extensive and detailed regulation is insufficient to guarantee responsible party government. It therefore provides a note of caution to the debate about the "engineerability of political parties" and the hope that all-encompassing and "good" regulation by itself can induce parties to behave as responsible democratic actors. The debate about party regulation in Mexico is often characterized by an enduring formalist faith that all will be well if we can just "get the laws right".

This excessively formal, technical approach to party regulation stands in sharp contrast to the political motivations that have underpinned regulatory reforms in Mexico over the past decades. During first the consolidation and later the democratization of the authoritarian regime, the regulation of political parties in public law has been an important arena of political struggle. For instance, in the earlier hegemonic era, the Institutional Revolutionary Party (PRI, by its Spanish initials) used public law to safeguard its position against outside challengers, but also to maintain party discipline and internal cohesion. Legal provisions rendered defection from the PRI extremely costly. Rather than outright repression of dissent, the PRI shaped the formal rules so as to limit political opportunities for independent actors, especially parties. What is noteworthy about the Mexican case is the extent to which the PRI succeeded in stifling opposition by codifying specific normative ideals of what a party should look like. Regional antagonisms during the Mexican Revolution, which led to considerable bloodshed, were used, for instance, to justify the notion that parties wishing to compete in elections should have a nationwide support base. In practice, however, high spatial registration requirements were an effective means to exclude potential challengers.

This chapter examines how provisions in public law regarding political parties have changed over time, and how the extent of regulation has grown from the consolidation of the authoritarian regime to the present day. More specifically, while we provide an overview of changes in the regulation of parties since the 1950s, we focus on legal barriers to party formation and how they have been employed by political actors. In the historical sketch we highlight the dual motivation underlying the growth in regulation, i.e., the political motivations of elites and the technical desire to 'fix' past abuses through increasingly detailed regulation. Looking ahead, we show that party regulation has increased steadily since the 1950s and that it has had mixed effects on contestation, cleaning up elections while simultaneously generating an electoral landscape that is markedly unfair and tilted in favour of major parties. We close by highlighting successes of party regulation, remaining challenges, and possibilities for future research, including research that examines the still undetermined consequences of the most recent set of reforms in 2014, some of which are not scheduled to become effective until after 2018.

From Authoritarianism to Democracy: The Development of Party Regulation

Any exploration of party politics in Mexico has to begin with an acknowledgement of the extraordinary position of the PRI, the long-term 'goliath' of Mexican politics (Bruhn 1997). The PRI was forged in the aftermath of the Mexican Revolution (1910-1929) with the explicit goal of holding power. In fact "from the time it was founded as the National Revolutionary Party (PNR) in 1929 until 1988, the PRI had never lost a presidential, gubernatorial, or federal senatorial race it contested" (Klesner 2005: 105). This is all the more remarkable in light of the constitutional ban on consecutive re-election, one of the legacies of the Revolution, which essentially eliminated all candidate-specific advantages of incumbency.[2] The PRI dominated all levels of government, and its organization extended even into the remote corners of the country. How did the PRI manage to establish and maintain its hegemonic position? Why did challengers find it so difficult to take on the PRI at the polls? A closer look at party regulation and specifically at the rules governing party formation can help to answer these questions. The PRI skillfully employed public law to promote internal discipline and to prevent the formation of viable opposition parties. The PRI thus used public law to serve its organizational needs. During the process of democratization, major opposition parties also found that they stood to benefit from maintaining some of these provisions. This section traces the development of the regulation of parties through public law.

During the early years of the hegemonic party the organizational imperative was the consolidation of centralized one-party rule. Presidential succession was a particularly difficult time for the revolutionary party, as there was always the threat that those who considered themselves *presidenciables*, but who were not chosen as the party's nominees, would break away and go it alone. The post-revolutionary electoral law did not deter this kind of behaviour. It allowed for independent candidacies, and the bar for registering new political parties was low. Under the Federal Electoral Law of 1918, parties merely had to have the support of 100 citizens and publish governing rules in order to appear on the ballot (Edmonds-Poli & Shirk 2009: 168–170). The main restriction imposed by the law was a ban on parties that had a religious or racial denomination (Molinar Horcasitas 1991: 27).

After a few tumultuous years, the electoral law of 1946 reduced the space for electoral challenges to the PRI through stricter ballot access requirements. The new law banned independent candidacies and raised the bar for parties wishing to appear on the ballot. Only legally registered parties were now eligible to compete in federal elections. The authorities also enshrined a particular normative ideal of what constitutes a political party into law. To obtain the required registration aspiring parties had to demonstrate that they were national political parties and, as such, that they possessed broad and territorially dispersed membership bases. Specifically, only parties able to prove a minimum of 30,000 members and at least 1,000 members in two-thirds of Mexico's federal entities could register (Story 1986: 46). However, even parties that could meet these requirements were not necessarily guaranteed a place on the ballot. The 1946 law had also centralized the organization of electoral processes in the hands of the powerful and PRI-controlled Ministry of the Interior (*Secretaría de Gobernación*). The recognition of registration was, therefore, in the hands of the PRI.

Registration requirements became even more stringent in 1951, when aspiring parties had to demonstrate 30,000 supporters, and then again in 1954, when parties had to demonstrate 75,000 supporters nationwide, and a minimum of 2,500 members in at least two-thirds of Mexico's states and territories (Navarro 2010: 225, n. 118; Edmonds-Poli & Shirk 2009: 168–170; Ley Electoral Federal 1955, art. 33).[3] These measures stifled the development of opposition parties. They also limited the exit options for disgruntled *priístas* because there were no viable electoral alternatives (Ward et al. 1999: 31; Langston 2006b: 151). While the requirements of nationwide organization and national orientation were normatively justified as a way to overcome the territorial divisions of the Revolution, they clearly served the needs of the hegemonic party by preventing challenges at the ballot box. The PRI thus found a way to exclude opposition groups because they fell short of a specific normative ideal.

During the hegemonic period the PRI, with its supermajorities at all levels and in all branches of government, controlled the rules of the game. Yet in using electoral law as an instrument to define the terms of competition, it had to strike a delicate balance (Crespo 2004). On the one hand, the cohesion of the party depended on its monopoly on power and access to the resources of the state. This ensured that all political career ambitions were focused on the hegemonic party. Party recalcitrants were discouraged from defecting because there was essentially no political life outside the party – at least, not for an ambitious politician hoping to win office. The PRI's access to public resources meant that the playing field was biased against opposition parties, even those that had been able to meet the high registration requirements. Mizrahi (2003) aptly described the motivation of the early opposition leaders organized in the National Action Party (*Partido Acción Nacional*, PAN) as a form of martyrdom. They had few illusions about their political career prospects, but stayed in the game for programmatic and ideological reasons.

On the other hand, to maintain the legitimacy of the regime, it was crucial that "the opposition neither leave the field nor perish in electoral terms, thereby turning the regime into a single-party system and depriving it of internal and international legitimacy" (Crespo 2004: 59). The opposition thus had to have sufficient incentives to participate, but could not be successful enough to launch a credible threat against the PRI. Electoral legislation was designed with this dual goal in mind: "When there was a danger of their disappearance or withdrawal, the electoral system would be opened up sufficiently to provide oxygen to the opposition; when it appeared that opposition forces might become strong or unite, the electoral system was closed off in order to weaken or contain them" (Crespo 2004: 64).

Given the high registration requirements, only the best-organized opposition parties, or those with help from the regime, were able to overcome the hurdles and obtain party registration. To maintain a semblance of political pluralism, the PRI propped up certain opposition parties, such as the Socialist Popular Party (*Partido Popular Socialista*, PPS) and the Authentic Party of the Mexican Revolution (*Partido Auténtico de la Revolución Mexicana*, PARM). These parties have been described as "PRI satellites" because they were financially and organizationally linked to the PRI.[4] During the presidency of Carlos Salinas de Gortari (1988–1994), the PRI also appears to have supported the foundation of the Worker's Party (*Partido del Trabajo*, PT). To critical questions about the young party's remarkable resource base, its leader, Alberto Anaya, nonchalantly replied: "In this country, the government pays for everything – even to be criticized" (Oppenheimer 1996: 142).

The PAN was the main independent opposition party and jealously guarded its autonomy from the regime. From its foundation in 1939, the party's founding fathers emphasized strong organization as the basis for the advancement of their conservative doctrine (Shirk 2005). The PAN started fielding candidates for municipal office in 1940 and ran its first gubernatorial candidate in 1944 in the state of Aguascalientes. By 1977 the PAN was nominating candidates for federal deputies in all 300 electoral districts (Lujambio 2001).

Yet even though the territorial extent of the opposition grew, it remained weak electorally. The opposition may have been able to register and field candidates, but they generally did not win. Through the introduction of "party deputies" in 1963 the PRI sought to revive its ailing opponents. The reform was the first of a series of measures that introduced elements of proportional representation (PR) into what had previously been a purely majoritarian system. It granted parties that won at least 2.5 but less than 25 per cent of the national vote special seats in the Chamber of Deputies.[5] That these reforms were first and foremost an attempt to revive the opposition in order to ensure the legitimacy of the hegemonic system is underlined by the fact that the PRI was slightly underrepresented in three of the five legislative periods between 1964 and 1976. Even though the PRI controlled virtually all seats in the Chamber, due to the introduction of party deputies it had fewer seats than it would have been entitled to under pure PR (Díaz-Cayeros & Magaloni 2001: 283–285).

While the introduction of proportional elements lowered entry barriers, it did not solve the PRI's legitimacy problems. In 1976, due to internal differences, the PAN failed to nominate a presidential candidate. As the satellite parties PPS and PARM generally supported the official party's candidate, the PRI contender José López Portillo ran unopposed. This was a painful embarrassment for a regime trying to maintain the appearance of competitiveness. One of the first legislative projects undertaken by the new president was, therefore, the constitutional reform of 1977 and the introduction of the Federal Law of Political Organizations and Electoral Processes (LOPPE). LOPPE constituted yet another expansion of regulatory detail, as illustrated by the number of articles in the law. While the 1954 electoral law had 115 articles, this had increased to 151 in 1970, 204 in 1973, and 250 in 1977.

In addition, this reform granted parties a privileged place in the political system by recognizing them as "entities of public interest" (*entidades de interés público*). With this reform, the trend towards increasingly restrictive registration requirements for political parties was reversed and, for the first time in decades, obtaining legal registration became easier for opposition parties. Under the new law, organizations now had two avenues available for party registration: conditional and permanent (*condicional* and *definitivo*). First, those organizations able to demonstrate four years of continuous political activity could appear on the ballot with conditional registration. If they then won at least 1.5 percent of the national vote, they would qualify for permanent registration (Edmonds-Poli & Shirk 2009: 168–170). Second, the signatures requirement for permanent registration was adjusted. Previously, aspiring parties had been required to collect a minimum of 2,000 signatures in each of two-thirds (20) of the states, and in no case could the total number of signatures be lower than 65,000 (LFE 1973, art. 23(I)). However, the 1977 LOPPE opened the political space for parties by reducing this barrier to 3,000 signatures in each of only half (15) of the states, adding the alternative of 300 signatures from each of half of the electoral districts (150). Thus, the 1977 law increased the required number of signatures in each state from 2,000 to 3,000, but reduced the spatial distribution requirement – dramatically reducing the burden of geographical extension throughout the country – by reducing the total number of states in which aspiring parties needed to collect signatures from two-thirds to half.

The 1977 reform also marks (a) the expansion of proportional representation, and (b) the introduction of direct public funding to political parties. First, the "party deputies" of 1963 were replaced with a true proportional system. Specifically, the Chamber of Deputies would now be composed of 300 deputies elected by majoritarian, first-past-the-post rules, and up to an additional 100 deputies elected based on PR rules. These PR seats would be filled by members on regional party lists according to the percentage of votes received in those regions (LOPPE 1977, art. 3).

The introduction of public funding is another illustration of how the PRI used public law for its own needs. Normatively, the new availability of public funding can be seen as an attempt to acknowledge the inequality of the playing field.[6] However, access to public resources – in the form of direct public funding and free television time – was supposed to offer opposition parties incentives for continued participation in elections.[7] The PRI itself, which had almost monopolistic access to the resources of the state, was not dependent on party financing at this time. Even though hard evidence is difficult to come by, it was widely understood that PRI-controlled executives at all levels of government made use of government resources to shore up electoral support for the hegemonic party (see, e.g., Greene 2007).

The 1983 reform was yet another initiative to breathe life into the struggling opposition, as it opened up possibilities for the introduction of PR seats in state legislatures (González Casanova 1995: 593). In Mexico's federal system, the 31 states and the federal district have their own legal framework for elections. The process of political democratization thus extended over multiple levels of government to include the subnational level. In 1987 the PR component of the federal electoral system was also strengthened by increasing the number of PR seats from 100 to 200, while the 300 single-member districts were maintained (Código Federal Electoral 1987, art. 14).[8] While the electoral system moved closer to a mixed system, the reform discouraged the unification of opposition forces against the PRI. It determined that voters were to cast only one vote in the single-member district race, which would automatically be counted for the allocation of PR seats. Voters were therefore unable to split their ballot, which rendered the coordination of opposition parties against the PRI in district races extremely costly (Díaz-Cayeros and Magaloni 2001).[9] Moreover, the reform of the ballot also made the PRI eligible for PR seats.

In the run-up to the 1988 presidential election, one of the PRI's worst nightmares came true. For decades, the hegemonic party had succeeded in resolving the contentious issue of presidential succession internally. In 1987, amidst controversy about the party's economic course, the so-called Democratic Current (*Corriente Democrática*, CD) and its leader, Cuauhtémoc Cárdenas, broke away from the PRI after an unsuccessful attempt to challenge the presidential nomination.[10] Cross-party endorsements, which had benefited the PRI when its satellites backed the official party's candidate, facilitated the formation of a broad electoral alliance of small left-wing parties to support Cárdenas's bid for the presidency. In this sense, this episode highlights one of the elements of the transition era, namely that even carefully crafted laws are likely to have unintended consequences.

After early vote counts on election night showed the challenger in the lead, the computer system tabulating the vote mysteriously "collapsed", and when it was started up again, the PRI was ahead. This episode is known in Mexico as the *caída del sistema* or "breakdown of the system". Whether the PRI "stole" the election from Cárdenas, or if his initial lead was just due to an urban bias in early counting, is a subject that still provokes heated debate in Mexico. In any case, it was clear that the incoming president, Carlos Salinas de Gortari, would have to restore confidence in the regime in order to gain legitimacy. As his predecessors did before him, Salinas drew on the time tested tool of revising public law. The reform of 1990, which took place during his presidency, brought the number of articles in the electoral code to an all-time high of 410.

In the aftermath of the 1988 presidential elections the PRI reached out to the PAN. The two parties shared an interest in curbing the rise of the new leftist party formed by Cárdenas, the Party of the Democratic Revolution (PRD, by its Spanish initials). The PAN and the PRI cooperated in the elaboration of yet another electoral reform, which raised the bar for cross-party presidential candidates such as Cárdenas. Under the new law, parties nominating a common candidate for the presidential elections were required to coordinate candidacies for all congressional races taking place at the same time. This had to be done prior to the official start of the campaign, which created substantial transaction costs and therefore impeded the coordination of the anti-PRI opposition (Díaz-Cayeros & Magaloni 2001).

The two parties arrived at an agreement which stipulated that the PAN's cooperation with the regime would be rewarded with the recognition of subnational electoral victories (Haber et al. 2008: 133–134). During the state elections of Baja California, the PRI made good its promise and the *panista* Ernesto Ruffo became the first opposition candidate to compete successfully for gubernatorial office. The willingness of the PAN elite to cooperate with the PRI should also be seen in light of the experience of the 1986 gubernatorial election in Chihuahua, where a strong electoral showing of the PAN had been met with fraud and repression by the PRI. The PAN elite came to realize that the recognition of electoral victories required the goodwill of the upper echelons of the PRI hierarchy, at least until meaningful electoral reform could be achieved. Thus, while the

Salinas presidency showed the first signs of electoral democratization at the subnational level, conditions continued to be less than democratic. Electoral victories were awarded directly by the president, rather than by autonomous electoral institutions. It was the will of the president, rather than the will of voters, that determined electoral outcomes (Lujambio 2001: 70). In his efforts to reach out to the PAN, in some controversial instances Salinas went so far as to force apparently victorious PRI candidates to resign and yield to challengers from the PAN (Haber et al. 2008: 134). The informal and extra-institutional arrangements between the PRI and the PAN surrounding these elections are known as *concertacesión*.[11]

As pressure on the PRI to democratize the political system mounted, the ruling party was forced to make more and more concessions. During this period, the goal of party legislation gradually shifted. While the primary objective of legislation had been to safeguard PRI hegemony, the legitimacy crisis faced by the regime now forced the PRI to agree to reforms aimed at promoting a level playing field. Winning rigged elections was no longer sufficient. The PRI – still aiming to hold on to power – revised the rules to reduce outright procedural bias against the opposition.

The opposition had two main grievances. First, the highly unequal access to resources made it difficult for the opposition to compete successfully when the PRI, with access to the resources of the state, had so much to offer to voters. Second, electoral fraud became a focus of criticism and there was substantial pressure for more transparency in electoral processes. In both of these fields, the Federal Electoral Institute (IFE), created in 1990 by the adoption of the new federal electoral law known by its Spanish acronym COFIPE (*Código Federal de Instituciones y Procedimientos Electorales*), came to play a key role. In addition to the IFE, the 1990 reform also established the Federal Electoral Tribunal (Tribunal Electoral del Poder Judicial de la Federación, TEPJF). The TEPJF, frequently referred to as TRIFE, was created as an autonomous body to resolve electoral disputes and to certify electoral results.

In the direct aftermath of the 1988 presidential elections, opposition parties were primarily interested in putting in place mechanisms to prevent bias in the electoral institutions. This, therefore, was the aspect that received the most attention in the 1990 reform. A follow-up reform in 1993 strengthened the IFE's autonomy vis-à-vis party influence. Since the IFE was responsible for registering new parties, the process was removed from PRI-controlled authorities. The barriers for new parties, however, remained relatively high. To register as a political party an organization needed at least 65,000 members. As in previous legislation, party membership had to be geographically dispersed, with either 3,000 members in half of the states or 300 members in half of the country's electoral districts (Art. 24). The continuation of the high registration requirements is not surprising. The opposition parties that sat at the negotiation table had managed to obtain their registration despite high barriers. They had no interest in opening the field to additional challengers.

The IFE played an important part in ensuring that the presidential elections of 1994 were free and clean. Even though the election was won by the PRI, the process itself was commended for its transparency, and President Zedillo was widely perceived as the legitimate winner. Yet Zedillo himself acknowledged that the election had been clean but highly inequitable (Lujambio 2003: 382). The analysis of campaign finance reports showed that the playing field continued to be tilted in favour of the PRI, even in the absence of large-scale rigging of votes. Of all campaign resources reported to the IFE, 78.3 per cent had been spent by the PRI. The PRI had outspent the runner-up 4:1 (Iturriaga Acevedo 2007: 24).[12] Creating a more equitable distribution of financial resources between parties, therefore, became a key issue on the political and legal agenda.

The 1996 constitutional reform, which was negotiated against this background, was one of the milestones in the development of the federal public funding system. The new Article 41 explicitly states that, due to their role as entities of public interest, registered national parties are entitled to public funding, and that the distribution of such funds should be guided by the principle of equality. The COFIPE recognizes five legitimate sources of party income: 1) public funding, 2) funding provided by party members, 3) funding provided by party sympathizers, 4) income obtained from fundraising activities such as conferences, and 5) income obtained from financial investments. It also requires parties to submit income and expenditure reports on an annual basis.[13] The PRI had a stake in the new system because the lavish supply of government funds for the party had started to dry up, as the Finance Ministry was increasingly unable and unwilling to foot the bill for the party's financial needs. In the run-up to the 1994 election, the PRI's efforts to solicit financial support from business tycoons who owed their burgeoning fortunes to the privatization of state-owned corporations had landed the party in a fully fledged party-finance scandal (see Oppenheimer 1996: Ch. 5). The PRI thus shared with its competitors an interest in ensuring a stable and predictable flow of funds to the party.

While the constitutional reform of 1977 had already defined parties as entities of public interest, the electoral reform of 1996 strengthened this notion by stipulating that public funding had to account for the majority of party income. Formally, this reduced the scope for parties to raise revenue from society, even from members. While private funding accounted for about three-quarters of total party income in 1994, its share dropped to less than 10 per cent over the next three years (Lujambio 2003: 383). These federal funds were delivered directly to the central party, which had to justify the use of these funds in its annual audit reports. In case of violations, IFE could impose severe fines on parties, and it has exercised this authority to sanction several parties (Crespo 2004).

Another notable aspect of the 1996 reform was a strengthening of the Federal Electoral Tribunal (TRIFE) in terms of autonomy from political actors and in terms of authority, i.e., an increase in its responsibilities. The court was established as an important institution not only in charge of certifying federal electoral results, but also authorized to resolve complaints about federal electoral matters and competent to evaluate the constitutionality of actions taken by subnational electoral institutions. The law also puts the court in charge of protecting the political-electoral rights of citizens (*derechos político-electorales*). This rather broad formulation became important, because the court interpreted this responsibility to mean that it was competent to receive complaints about intra-party disputes. Conflicts regarding internal leadership elections and candidate selection procedures frequently ended up before the high electoral court, a development unintended by reformers and resented by party elites as judicial meddling in internal organizational matters.

Reforms during the 1990s thus played an important role in strengthening electoral institutions. Advances in the fairness of elections did not come cheap, however, and Mexico has invested massively in the development of its electoral bureaucracy. During the election years of the 1990s, funding for the IFE and TRIFE exceeded the combined cost of the legislative and judicial branches of government (Eisenstadt & Poiré 2005: 5). Nonetheless, Mexicans were "justifiably proud of their great success in converting one of the most fraudulent electoral systems in the world to one of the cleanest in less than a decade" (Eisenstadt 2007: 42). When the presidential elections of 2000 brought to office the first opposition president, many observers considered this as the final step in Mexico's transition to democracy. Yet, while the election of Vicente Fox (PAN) was certainly a milestone, the gradual nature of the transition meant that parties would remain subject to the same legal framework.

Party Regulation after 2000

The pattern of frequent electoral reforms characteristic of the transition period continued after 2000. Ironically, however, reforms during the new democratic period did not always lead to more political openness. While the trend towards increasingly detailed regulation continued, the effect of reforms on the responsiveness and responsibility of parties as organizations has been mixed at best.

This general pattern is perhaps most obvious with regard to party registration requirements. Even though there had been considerable progress in reducing bias against already registered opposition parties vis-à-vis the PRI, barriers for new political groups remained so high as effectively to deny them entry to the electoral arena. Furthermore, with the 2003 reform, the first after the election of Vicente Fox, barriers for new groups even increased. Specifically, the reform established a narrow window of time in which aspiring parties had to notify the IFE of their intention to seek formal registration. Previous laws, including the first COFIPE in 1990, required this notification as part of the registration process, but never set any specific dates or limitations on when this notification could be made. As of January 1, 2004, however, aspiring parties were restricted to a seven-month window from January 1 to July 31 following any federal election to make this notification to the IFE (COFIPE 2006, art. 28). Groups that missed the July 31 deadline would have to wait at least three more years before starting the registration process. Further, the 2003 reform increased the number of signatures required for the party formation process. With this reform the bar to the entry of new parties was raised again for the first time since 1977, as it returned to the 1973 standard of requiring signatures from two-thirds of states (20) or electoral districts (200), rather than from half. Perhaps more importantly, the 2003 law increased the minimum requirement for the total number of signatures from 65,000 to 0.26% of the list of eligible voters (*padron electoral*) used in the prior federal election. This small fraction of a percentage point may seem very low, but it amounted to approximately 200,000 people in 2011, which constitutes a 300% increase in required signatures compared with the 1990 standard. Even in the post-transition era, barriers to new entrants thus remained high and even increased, tilting the electoral landscape so as to favour the existing major parties.

Just as increased openness of the electoral arena failed to materialize, the elections of 2006 also shattered public confidence in electoral institutions, one of the major accomplishments of the democratization period. On

Sunday, July 2, 2006, after a fiercely contested campaign, the presidential election in Mexico closed without a clear winner. Adding to the unease, the two leading candidates – Felipe Calderon (PAN) and Andres Manuel Lopez Obrador (PRD) – both claimed victory (McKinley 2006). Indeed, it took the IFE five days to reach a final vote tally, declaring Calderon the winner by a margin of less than one percentage point (0.58%). That tally was immediately challenged by the PRD before the nation's high electoral court, leading to a partial recount. Two months later, after recounting 9 per cent of the votes, the court acknowledged some irregularities in the electoral process yet still affirmed the result and rejected a full recount (McKinley 2006b; 2006c). Lopez Obrador continued to lead large protests that paralysed parts of Mexico City's centre for several months, and Calderon eventually took office in early December in a highly polarized context. During the election and in its immediate aftermath, Mexico's political institutions seemed newly unstable and vulnerable, and its electoral institutions – principally the previously unimpeachable IFE – suffered from new criticisms.

Concerns in the aftermath of the 2006 elections were twofold. For one, the electoral institutions were criticized for falling short in upholding existing electoral law and regulations, specifically for failing to (a) rein in the intervention of sitting President Vicente Fox in favour of Calderon, and (b) deliver a clear and timely result. In addition, however, the run-up to the election also witnessed a high volume of attack advertisements and negative campaigning, revealing what many perceived as gaps in the regulatory capacity of electoral laws. A new reform process began as an immediate consequence of the 2006 electoral crisis. The main thrust of the reform aimed to address perceived weaknesses that generated or exacerbated the 2006 crisis, including uneven access to the media, negative campaigning, and the process of making (and resolving) legal challenges during the electoral process.

After legislative approval in the closing months of 2007, the new COFIPE was published on January 14, 2008, taking effect the following day (COFIPE 2008, Transitorio Primero). The new law kept many of the earlier features of electoral regulation, but made several notable modification or additions. The revised COFIPE continued the trend of increasingly detailed regulation, bringing new aspects of party behaviour and competition under the umbrella of the law, and even elevating several provisions to constitutional status. Particularly noteworthy in this regard were the further regulation of electoral campaigns and of the internal life of parties. Yet, the democratizing effect of the reform was mixed at best (see also Serra 2009 for a critical reading of the reform).

The first area of concern was the regulation of electoral campaigns. The new law responded to some of the perceived problems of 2006 by reducing the official campaign season, regulating campaigning during the process of candidate selection (so-called "pre-campaigns"), and restricting electoral propaganda distributed by the sitting government. In light of a tradition of using social programmes to drum up support for the incumbent party these changes may well be justified and seen as pro-democracy measures. However, the reform regulated electoral campaigns to the point of undermining the quality of public debate leading up to and during elections. This negative influence took two forms: (1) constraints on who can participate in this public debate, and (2) a sweeping prohibition against negative campaigns. First, only political parties could produce political advertisements, and they could do that for *free* – funded and supervised by the IFE. The advantage of organizing advertisement purchases through the IFE was that such control reduces the power of commercial radio and television networks and their ability to favour certain parties by selling airtime at discounted rates (see also Serra 2009). However, beyond curbing the disproportionate influence of commercial networks, the reform undermined the ability of ordinary citizens, businesses, or civic organizations to participate in the public debate, as they were barred entirely from political speech (art. 49). In short, the range of actors able to participate in the public debate regarding political issues narrowed dramatically. Moreover, given that parties still received extraordinary sums of public funding but no longer had to pay for political advertising, the free advertisements acted as a kind of informal subsidy beyond the official funding. Thus, it is unclear why such generous public financing of campaigns was necessary, how exactly the formal campaign funding was being used, or what this money was buying. Second, all negative speech was forbidden (art. 38). Parties were prohibited from "denigrating" (*denigrar*) or "slandering" (*calumniar*), even if the negative information they were communicating was true! Further, this prohibition was elevated to constitutional status (art. 41).

A second area where the new law was controversial was in its effect on the internal life of parties. On the one hand, the new law placed high burdens on existing parties. There was new regulation regarding duties of parties, including transparency and the publication of a wide range of information regarding their organization, functioning, and funding. Indeed, entirely new sections in articles 41 to 44 outlined a series of responsibilities regarding transparency. This again illustrated the degree to which parties in Mexico had ceased to be private institutions, or were moving substantially towards the public end of the public-private continuum. While the extraordinary level of public support for political parties arguably justifies far-reaching oversight to track how public funds are used and ensure accountability, it becomes harder and harder to conceive of parties as civic organizations within society. Even more than in other countries, Mexican parties have essentially become part of the state.

Yet, even though the law further regulated the internal life of parties, it also afforded considerable protection to party elites by determining that any challenges relating to internal party matters must first be addressed to review bodies within the party itself (art. 46). Further, this protection was constitutionalized (art. 116). Previously, as explained above, the high electoral court, Tribunal Electoral del Poder Judicial de la Federación (TEPJF, frequently referred to as "TRIFE"), had exceptional authority to intervene in internal party matters. While the regulation of disputes regarding the "internal life of parties" is highly unusual in comparative perspective, in Mexico it provided an effective brake on the power of party elites and therefore a way to democratize the internal life of parties. The need for an alternative is illustrated by the increasing number of challenges brought before the court. While in 1999 only four intra-party conflicts were received by the TRIFE, this number increased to 292 in 2003 and 1,100 in 2006.[14] Thus, while formally aligning with comparative standards, in the Mexican context the reform further defers to de facto authorities at the top of existing hierarchies within parties by restricting the opportunity for any challenges that may arise. Challenges must first be made to an adjudicatory mechanism inside the party. Further, party statutes can be challenged only within 14 days of the time they are first presented before the electoral authority for registration (Art. 47.2). The statute of limitations (SOL) poses an additional barrier to disputes relating to internal party life. Normally, a clock related to a SOL like this would begin to run (a) from the moment these documents are published (if abstract review is allowed) or (b) from the time an actual harm results from enforcing the provisions in these documents (in the case of concrete review). The fact that all challenges are barred beyond a very early window of time makes these documents virtually unchallengeable. Lastly, only party members can initiate these challenges. Previously, the COFIPE allowed other citizens and organizations to challenge party documents, but the standing to initiate these kinds of challenges was dramatically reduced in 2007 (see also Sáenz 2007).

As noted above, several new provisions were elevated to constitutional status. Indeed, beyond the prohibition on negative speech and the protection of internal party matters, other provisions that were constitutionalized included (a) media use by parties, (b) the funding of parties, and (c) the oversight of party funding. The constitutionalization of so much detail regarding electoral matters is highly unusual comparatively (see IFES 2009), and offers opportunities for constitutional challenges. The kind of detail seen in these provisions is usually left to ordinary legislation, which is easier to amend and adjust over time, a process that will probably be necessary. Thus, the constitutionalization of so much electoral regulation means that these regulations may lead to high-profile and resource-intensive constitutional challenges, and they will be that much harder to undo in the future.

Finally, barriers to entry for new parties, which were already high in Mexico, especially after the 2003 changes noted above, were raised even further by the 2007 reform. Prior to 2003, aspiring parties could notify electoral authorities at any stage of their intention to register. After 2003, they had a seven-month window every three years to notify the IFE of this intention. Now, under the new law, aspiring parties have only a *one-month window every six years* to make this notification. Specifically, they must notify the IFE no later than January 31 in the year following a presidential election (COFIPE 2007, art. 28). For instance, if a party wanted to register to compete in the 2018 elections, it had to notify IFE no later than January 31, 2013, more than five years ahead of time.

Reflections on Party Regulation and the Nature of Democracy in Mexico

As mentioned at the outset, Mexico stands out comparatively because of the scope of party regulation through public law and the frequency with which electoral laws have been reformed. Over the past decades, the number of areas of party behaviour legally constrained and regulated has grown steadily. The *scope of regulation* has, at least in part, been legitimized by making reference to the "engineerability of political parties", i.e., the hope that all-encompassing and "good" regulation can induce parties to behave as responsible democratic actors. Indeed, this formalist faith in the engineerability of organizations extends to other institutions in

Mexico, illustrated by the frantic pace of police reform, reforming and then re-reforming public safety agencies – especially at the federal level – for at least three decades (e.g., Sabet 2010). A specific concern regarding parties, however, is that reforms have to be agreed upon by the subjects of regulation – political parties themselves – and are therefore necessarily political. The process is unavoidably self-interested, so creating "good" regulation is only one among many motivations for reform, and in many instances not the most important one.

The explanation for the speed of reform is twofold: (1) following each election, there is a realization that the existing regulation was insufficient to promote responsible party behaviour and clean campaigns; and (2) the balance of power among the major players has shifted, allowing actors to pursue their own agendas. Both of these factors highlight the importance of the electoral calendar or cycles. Elections illuminate lacunae, and as majorities change after elections, each incoming party brings with it a new agenda for regulatory reform. The frequency of elections therefore helps to explain the frequency of regulatory reform. Against this background, the elevation of many of the controversial provisions in the 2007 reform to constitutional status may be interpreted as an attempt to anchor these provisions in public law by constraining future reformers. In the remainder of this chapter, we review the successes and achievements of party regulation in promoting democracy, as well as some of the challenges that remain.

First among the successes, parties in Mexico are well institutionalized with strong organizations. This is true especially compared to other new democracies, and is therefore no small achievement. The strength of parties is due in part no doubt to the resource-rich environment for parties since 1990, as well as the organizational legal-technical tutelage provided by the IFE and electoral courts. Yet, the financial burden on public coffers is considerable. In 2008, which was not a federal election year, the budgets of the IFE and TRIFE amounted to €588 million. The lion's share of this went to the IFE, which passed €168 million of public funding on to registered political parties and spent €330 million on its own activities, such as maintaining the voter register and auditing party finances. The TRIFE's operating budget was lower than the IFE's but still consisted of €90 million. Compared to other democracies, Mexico thus invested heavily in monitoring compliance with party regulation. Overall, the cost of funding political parties and of maintaining the IFE and TRIFE in 2008 was €8.90 per registered voter.[15] This amount is outrageously high when compared to other democracies in the region. The cost of party funding alone was 18 times the regional average.[16] This makes Mexico the most expensive democracy in Latin America (IFES 2009).

Second, the IFE (now INE) has succeeded in preventing electoral fraud. Acknowledging that no system is perfectly clean, overall the IFE had an excellent record on this account, despite the criticisms levied during the 2006 election. Nevertheless, a crucial distinction exists between establishing "clean" elections (i.e., absence of fraud) and guaranteeing "fair" elections (i.e., a level playing field), and the former is easier than the latter. Stated differently, the IFE has generally succeeded in preventing the outright stealing of votes or stuffing of ballot boxes (the infamous *urnas embarazadas*, or "pregnant urns"), but there continue to be wide disparities in the effective power and influence of different parties in the electoral landscape.

Outstanding challenges include levelling the playing field to correct for this unfairness. Even though the system has become more open over the past two decades, it still works in favour of the major parties, which limits the options available to voters. This is evident in, among other areas, the way funding is apportioned according to vote returns. Moreover, with the 2008 round of reforms, the balance of power within parties has been tilted more heavily towards party elites. Overall, party elites have been strengthened, while legal resources available to ordinary party members and citizens have weakened. A second challenge involves the extremely high cost of parties and the electoral apparatus, including the IFE (INE), a cost that undermines support for the system. An associated concern relates to the fact that, given the high levels of funding and the fact that parties can now broadcast their political advertisements for free via the IFE, it is increasingly unclear what parties are doing with their money, raising serious questions about accountability.

Third, public confidence in electoral institutions must be rebuilt. After 2006, there was widespread dissatisfaction with parties, official candidates, and electoral institutions, leading to the "voto nulo" campaign in the 2009 mid-term elections (e.g., write-in candidates like *Esperanza Marchita*, or "Hope Dashed"). The IFE itself has suffered in public opinion polls, though perhaps this is not much of a concern since it continues to enjoy – along with the military and the TEPJF – some of the highest levels of public confidence among Mexican institutions (LAPOP 2010). Still, confidence in the IFE has been steadily dropping since the 2007 reform, from 68% of the population reporting some level of positive opinion and only 18% reporting any negative opinion in 2006, to 59% positive and 25% negative in 2008, to 53% positive and 31% negative in 2010.[17] From

2006 to 2008 alone, the IFE suffered a 10-point drop, and public opinion has continued to slide. These are not good signs after more than 30 years of substantial electoral reforms.

Symptomatic of the fetish with re-designing formal institutions described here, Mexico reformed its electoral laws once again in 2014, with a constitutional reform in January of that year followed by implementing legislation in May. The legislation passed May included three federal electoral laws (see note 1), which replaced the single electoral code that had been reformed only in 2007. Further, the states were mandated to make similar, harmonizing reforms to their local electoral codes. Principal changes in the latest federal reform included the following: (1) the IFE was reformed and renamed the INE, as noted in the introduction; (2) state electoral institutions acquired greater autonomy from state legislatures; (3) for the first time in Mexico, re-election is allowed, though it will be phased in differently across different posts; senators can hold up to two consecutive terms, federal deputies can hold up to four consecutive terms, and, as long as state constitutions allow it, mayors and other municipal officials can hold up to four consecutive terms (Constitution, arts. 59, 115); and (4) the threshold of votes required to retain party registration at the national level was increased from 2% to 3%. The consequences of these and other provisions of the 2014 reform are yet to be determined, and many provisions are not set to take effect until much later. For instance, the rules regarding re-election of federal senators and deputies do not take effect until 2015 and 2018, respectively, so the real impact on the re-election of those officials will not be felt unless and until they run for their second term, which will not be until 2018 and 2024, respectively. For now, the 2014 reform is yet another example of re-engineering the electoral rules in Mexico, suggesting we can anticipate still more major formal transformations to come.

Lastly, the same process of engineering electoral codes that is at work at the federal level is filtering through the 32 territorial units at the subnational level (Harbers and Ingram 2014). Indeed, as noted above, the 2014 federal reform in Mexico requires all subnational units to re-adjust their electoral laws. Each of the federal units has its own local electoral code, electoral institute, and electoral court, and change and performance are highly uneven. This leads to great diversity in party regulation within the political system, with variation within states over time, across states, and across levels of government. This electoral federalism is perhaps one of the most exciting areas of research on public law and political parties, not just in Mexico but in other large, federal systems, including the other two such systems in Latin America – Argentina and Brazil. Future research that examines the longitudinal, spatial, and cross-level variation in party regulation identified here, along with the other challenges outlined above, should contribute important insights to our understanding of political institutions in old and new democracies alike.

Notes

1 *Ley General de Instituciones y Procedimientos Penales* (LEGIPE; 493 articles), *Ley General de Partidos Polí*ticos (97 articles), and *Ley General en Materia de Delitos Electorales* (26 articles) (all published May 23, 2014, and effective May 24, 2014).

2 Yet the multitude of offices controlled by the PRI meant that there were ample opportunities for career politicians to move between positions. Voters were, therefore, often familiar with candidates because of their previous political offices.

3 The 1946 membership requirement equals 1.2 per cent of all registered voters and 0.3 per cent of the national voting age population. The 1954 reform required support from 0.6 per cent of the voting age population. Data on the number of voters have been obtained from the website of the Institute for Democracy and Electoral Assistance (www.idea.int).

4 The PPS was established under the label *Partido Popular* in 1948. The PARM was officially registered in 1957. That the electoral authorities were favourable to some parties while discriminating against others is illustrated by the fact that they recognized the PARM while simultaneously withholding the legal registration of the much better organized Communist Party (Scott 1964: 148), or rejecting the registration of the outspokenly anti-PRI *Partido de la Revolució*n (see Navarro 2010: 224-25).

5 Parties were to receive one seat for each 0.5 per cent of the vote they obtained. The maximum number of seats that could be obtained in this way was 20. The formula for the allocation of party deputy seats was revised in 1973, when the threshold for receiving PR seats was lowered to 1.5 per cent and the cap expanded to 25 seats (Edmonds-Poli & Shirk 2009: 168–170).

6 Prior to 1977 there had been indirect financing for opposition parties, in the form of tax exemptions (since 1963) and access to electronic media (since 1973). Even though the 1977 reform of the electoral law formally introduced direct party financing, it did not specify the total amount of public funding or how resources were to be distributed between parties, which rendered the

process highly discretionary. A concrete framework for the allocation of state subsidies was not established until 1987.

7 The PAN, wary of the PRI's efforts to undermine the independence of the opposition, initially refused to accept public monies. The party's position on the issue changed only in 1989 after a change in the party leadership (Wuhs 2008: 83).

8 This reform also established the controversial "governability clause", which grants the largest party an automatic majority of seats as long as it obtains at least 35 per cent of the vote. The "governability clause" survived a series of constitutional reforms. Yet it was not applied in practice because the PRI was able to win a sufficiently large share of the vote (Díaz-Cayeros & Magaloni 2001). The 1996 reform finally capped the seat share of the majority party in the Chamber at 300 (out of 500), which meant that the largest party would lack the two-thirds majority required to amend the Constitution.

9 Note that this differs from the German system, which grants voters two votes, one for the district's direct candidate and another for the preferred party.

10 The last challenge to the party's presidential nomination had occurred in 1952, when General Henríquez Guzmán broke away only to lose by a 5:1 margin to the PRI candidate, Adolfo Ruiz Cortines. Henríquez Guzmán's attempt to face up to the PRI ended with his inglorious retirement from public life. The registration of the party that had supported him was revoked by the electoral authorities because of an alleged illegal resort to force (Scott 1964: 151).

11 The term *concertacesión* draws on the Spanish words for arrangement (*concertación*) and cession (*cesión*) (Prud'homme 1997: 1).

12 "Informe y Dictamen que rinde la Comisión de Consejeros constituida para la revisión de los informes financieros de campaña presentados por los partidos políticos", IFE, April 7, 1995. Unofficial reports suggest an even more extreme spending imbalance during the presidential race, with the PRI's campaign chest containing $700 million, compared to the PAN's $5 million and the PRD's $3 million (Oppenheimer 1996: 110).

13 During the initial years of public financing, parties had received state resources without any oversight. It is therefore unclear how much money parties received and how they spent it. The notion that parties have to justify their use of public funds was first contemplated in the 1987 reform (Art. 61VIII, *Código Federal Electoral*), and then developed further in the reform of 1993. The 1993 reform also prohibited donations from municipal, state, or federal authorities to political parties. As the electoral authorities lacked the auditing capacity to control and verify party reports, however, financial oversight was essentially a paper tiger until the reform of 1996, which granted

the IFE authority to check party bank accounts and impose sanctions in cases of violation. The reform also called for the establishment of a permanent auditing committee, rather than the temporary *ad hoc* committees that had existed previously (Lujambio 2003; Peschard 2006).

14 Data provided by the Coordinación de Jurisprudencia y Estadística Judicial, Dirección de Estadística Judicial, Tribunal Electoral del Poder Judicial de la Federación.

15 Per voter amounts are calculated on the basis of voting age population statistics, which include all citizens above the legal voting age. This information is available through the website of the International Institute for Democracy and Electoral Assistance (www.idea.int, last accessed October 19th, 20112). The exchange rate between the Mexican Peso and the Euro was 16 to 1 in January 2008.

16 The average was US$ 0.94 per vote cast in 13 Latin American countries compared to US$ 17.24 in Mexico during the 2003 mid-term election (IFES 2009: 69). Calculations are based on election years for all countries.

17 The LAPOP surveys ask respondents for scores on a scale of 1-7. Percentages are calculated by aggregating scores from 1-3 for negative opinion and 5-7 for positive opinion. Alternately, public confidence in the IFE has been dropping from a mean of 5.04 in 2006, 4.76 in 2008, and 4.44 in 2010. The AmericasBarometer by the Latin American Public Opinion Project (LAPOP), www.LapopSurveys.org.

References

AmericasBarometer, Latin American Public Opinion Project (LAPOP), www.LapopSurveys.org.

Bruhn, Kathleen (1997) *Taking on Goliath: The Emergence of a New Left Party and the Struggle for Democracy in Mexico*, University Park: Pennsylvania State University Press.

Crespo, José Antonio (2004) Party Competition in Mexico: Evolution and Prospects. In Middlebrook, Kevin J. (Ed.) *Dilemmas of Political Change in Mexico.* London, Institute of Latin American Studies, 57-81.

Crespo, José Antonio (2008) "Cofipe: la reforma insuficiente." *Excélsior* (Jan. 23).

Díaz-Cayeros, Alberto & Magaloni, Beatriz (2001) Party Dominance and the Logic of Electoral Design in Mexico's Transition to Democracy. *Journal of Theoretical Politics,* 13, 271-293.

Edmonds-Poli, Emily & Shirk, David A. (2009) *Contemporary Mexican Politics,* Lanham, Rowman & Littlefield.

Eisenstadt, Todd A. (2007) The Origins and Rationality of the Dichotomy Invoked in Mexico's 2006 Post-Electoral Conflict. *PS: Political Science & Politics,* 40, 39-43.

Eisenstadt, Todd & Poiré, Alejandro (2005) Campaign Finance and Playing Field "Levelness" Issues in the Run-up to Mexico's July 2006 Presidential Election. UC San Diego: Center for U.S.-Mexican Studies. Available at: http://escholarship.org/uc/item/30s6n73s.

González Casanova, Pablo (1995) La democracia en México. Actualidad y perspectivas. In González Casanova, Pablo & Roitman Rosenmann, Marcos (Eds.) *La democracia en América Latina: actualidad y perspectivas.* Mexico City, La Jornada/Centro de Investigaciones Interdisciplinarias en Ciencias y Humanidades (UNAM), 587-610.

Greene, Kenneth F. (2007) *Why Dominant Parties Lose: Mexico's Democratization in Comparative Perspective,* Cambridge, Cambridge University Press.

Haber, Stephen, Klein, Herbert S., Maurer, Noel & Middlebrook, Kevin J. (2008) *Mexico Since 1980,* Cambridge, Cambridge University Press.

Harbers, Imke & Ingram, Matthew C. (2014) Democratic Institutions Beyond the Nation State: Measuring Institutional Dissimilarity in Federal Countries. *Government and Opposition*, 49, 1, 24-46.

International Foundation for Electoral Systems (2009) *Aplicación de la Reforma Electoral de 2007/2008 en México desde una perspectiva internacional comparada*. Washington, DC.

Iturriaga Acevedo, Juan Cristián (2007) Financiamiento a Partidos Políticos en México. In Vázquez, Federico & Mortiz, Jürgen (Eds.) *El triángulo de la bermudas: El financiamiento de la política en México.* Mexico, Friedrich Ebert Stiftung, 15-33.

Klesner, Joseph L. (2005) Electoral Competition and the New Party System in Mexico. *Latin American Politics and Society,* 47, 103-142.

Langston, Joy (2006) The Birth and Transformation of the *Dedazo* in Mexico. In Helmke, Gretchen & Levitsky, Steven (Eds.) *Informal Institutions and Democracy: Lessons from Latin America.* Baltimore, The Johns Hopkins University Press, 143-159.

Lujambio, Alonso (2001) Democratization through Federalism? The National Action Party Strategy, 1939-2000. In Middlebrook, Kevin J. (Ed.) *Party Politics and the Struggle for Democracy in Mexico: National and State-Level Analyses of the Partido Acción Nacional.* La Jolla, Center for U.S.-Mexican Studies, University of California, San Diego, 47-94.

McKinley, James (2006a) "Electoral Crisis in Mexico as Top 2 Declare Victory." *New York Times* (Jul. 3).

McKinley, James (2006b) "Mexico Tribunal Rejects Demand for Vote Recount." *New York Times* (Aug. 6).

McKinley, James (2006c) "Court Rejects Challenges to Mexico Presidential Vote." *New York Times* (Sep. 6).

Mizrahi, Yemile (2003) *From Martyrdom to Power: The Partido Acción Nacional in Mexico,* Notre Dame, University of Notre Dame Press.

Molinar Horcasitas, Juan (1991) *El tiempo de la legitimidad: Elecciones, autoritarismo y democracia en México,* Mexico City, cal y arena.

Navarro, Aaron W. (2010) *Political Intelligence and the Creation of Modern Mexico, 1938-1954.* University Park, Pennsylvania State University.

Oppenheimer, Andres (1996) *Bordering on Chaos: Mexico's Roller-Coaster Journey Toward Prosperity,* Boston, Little, Brown & Company.

Peschard, Jacqueline (2006) Control over Party and Campaign Finance in Mexico. *Mexican Studies/Estudios Mexicanos,* 22, 83-106.

Prud'homme, Jean-François (1997) Los conflictos electorales estatales y las relaciones interpartidistas nacionales en México (1988-1994). *Documento del Trabajo del CIDE,* No. 61.

Sabet, Daniel. 2010. "Police Reform in Mexico: Advances and Persistent Obstacles." Working Paper Series on U.S.-Mexico Security Collaboration (May). Woodrow Wilson International Center for Scholars - Mexico Institute, and Trans-Border Institute at University of San Diego.

Sáenz, Liébano. 2007. "La letra chiquita del Cofipe." Dec. 8. Available at: http://liebanosaenz.wordpress.com (last accessed October 27, 2009).

Scott, Robert E. (1964) *Mexican Government in Transition,* Urbana, University of Illinois Press.

Serra, Gilles (2009) "Una lectura crítica de la reforma electoral en México a raíz de 2006." *Política y Gobierno* XVI(2): 411-427.

Shirk, David A. (2005) *Mexico's New Politics: The PAN and Democratic Change,* Boulder, Lynne Rienner.

Story, Dale (1986) *The Mexican Ruling Party: Stability and Authority,* New York, Praeger.

Valdés Zurita, Leonardo Antonio (2007) "Aplicación de la reforma constitucional." Voy y Voto (marzo), No. 181: 28-31.

Ward, Peter M., Rodríguez, Victoria E. & Cabrero Mendoza, Enrique (1999) *New Federalism and State Government in Mexico: Bringing the States Back in* Austin, TX, Lyndon B. Johnson School of Public Affairs, The University of Texas at Austin.

Wuhs, Steven T. (2008) *Savage Democracy: Institutional Change and Party Development in Mexico,* University Park, Pennsylvania, Pennsylvania State University Press.

About the authors

Tim Bale is a graduate of Cambridge, Northwestern, and Sheffield universities. He began his teaching career at Sheffield, before moving on to Victoria University of Wellington and then Sussex University, before moving to Queen Mary University of London in 2012. For four years Tim was the co-editor of the *European Journal of Political Research*'s annual *Political Data Yearbook*. In 2008 he won the Political Studies Association's Bernard Crick Prize for Outstanding Teaching and in 2011 he received its W.J.M. Mackenzie prize for his book *The Conservative Party from Thatcher to Cameron*. He has published articles on various aspects of party politics in a number of journals and is also the author of *European Politics: a Comparative Introduction*, the third edition of which was published in the spring of 2013. His latest monograph is *The Conservatives since 1945: the Drivers of Party Change*.

Ingrid van Biezen is Professor of Comparative Politics and Chair of the Institute of Political Science at Leiden University. She is a co-editor of *Acta Politica*, the official journal of the Dutch Political Science Association and a former co-editor of the *EJPR Political Data Yearbook* and the ECPR series Studies in European Political Science (Routledge). She is the author of *Political Parties in New Democracies* (Palgrave 2003) and *Financing Political Parties and Election Campaigns* (Council of Europe 2003), and the editor of *On Parties, Party Systems and Democracy: Selected Writings of Peter Mair* (ECPR Press 2014). Between 2008 and 2014 she was the Principal Investigator on two large-scale research projects on the legal regulation of political parties funded by the UK Economic and Social Research Council and the European Research Council.

Jaco van den Brink is an attorney-at-law at Bouwman Van Dommelen advocaten (The Netherlands). He completed his Bachelor's of both Law and History at Utrecht University. Afterwards, he obtained a Master's degree in Law at Leiden University, with a focus on Legal Philosophy. In 2012, he attended a Master's Programme in Political Philosophy.

In the meanwhile, he has been conducting research into philosophical approaches of constitutional rights.

Fernando Casal Bértoa is a Research Fellow and co-director of the Centre for Comparative and Political Research at the School of Politics and International Relations at the University of Nottingham (UK). Previously, he was a Post-doctoral Fellow at the University of Leiden in The Netherlands. He studied Law at the University of Navarra (Pamplona, Spain) and Political Science at the University of Salamanca (Spain). After specializing in Eastern and Central European Studies at the Jagiellonian University (Cracow, Poland), he obtained his PhD at the European University Institute (Florence, Italy). His work has been published in *Party Politics*, *Government and Opposition*, the *International Political Science Review*, *South European Society and Politics*, and *East European Politics*.

Wojciech Gagatek is Assistant Professor at the University of Warsaw. He received a PhD in Social and Political Sciences from the European University Institute in Florence, and previously an MA in Political Science and an MA in Law from the University of Warsaw. He has been a visiting fellow at the University of Zurich. His main research interests and academic publications focus on the political system of the European Union (with a particular interest in the European Parliament), democracy and political representation in the EU and comparative political parties.

Imke Harbers is assistant professor of political science at the University of Amsterdam and a research fellow at the Centre for Latin American Research and Documentation (Cedla). Her research focuses on subnational political institutions, decentralization and democracy, with a regional emphasis on Latin America. She holds a PhD from Leiden University and has been a visiting fellow at the Center for US-Mexican Studies at the University of California, San Diego. Her work has appeared in journals such as *Comparative Political Studies*, *Political Studies*, *Party Politics*, *Government & Opposition* and *Publius: The Journal of Federalism*.

Matthew Ingram is an Assistant Professor in the Department of Political Science, University at Albany, State University of New York. His research examines justice sector reforms and judicial behavior, as well as the political geography of violence, primarily in Latin America. He holds a law degree (J.D. 2006) and a Ph.D. in political science (2009), both from the University of New Mexico. His work has been published in *Comparative Politics, Government and Opposition*, and the *Journal of Law, Economics, and Organization*, as well as in edited volumes and policy reports. Prior to joining the faculty at the University at Albany, he was a post-doctoral fellow at the Center for U.S.-Mexican Studies at the University of California, San Diego, and at the Kellogg Institute for International Studies at the University of Notre Dame

Richard S. Katz is Professor and Chair of the Political Science Department at Johns Hopkins. He was co-editor of the *European Journal of Political Research* (2006-2012), and of the *EJPR Political Data Yearbook* (1996-2006). His books include *A Theory of Parties and Electoral Systems* (Johns Hopkins University Press 1980, 2006), *Democracy and Elections* (Oxford University Press 1997), *How Parties Organize: Adaptation and Change in Party Organizations in Western Democracies*, ed. with Peter Mair, (Sage 1994), *Handbook of Party Politics*, ed. with William Crotty (Sage 2006), *The Challenges of Intra-Party Democracy*, ed. with William P. Cross, (Oxford: Oxford University Press 2013). He is a member of the Executive Committee of the European Consortium for Political Research and chair of the OSCE/ODIHR Core Group of Experts on Political Parties.

Ruud Koole is full professor of political science at Leiden University (since 2006). He studied history at the University of Groningen and political science at the Institut d'Études Politiques in Paris. He wrote his thesis (1992) on the organization of Dutch political parties between 1960 and 1990. He publishes and teaches on the functioning of political parties, the legitimacy of political institutions, the constitutional and political system in the Netherlands and Dutch political history. In the past, he has been the Director of the Documentation Center on Dutch Political Parties of the University of Groningen (1981-1989) and the Chairman of the Dutch Labour Party (2001-2005). Since 2011, he is also member of the Senate of the Netherlands.

Hans-Martien ten Napel is an Associate Professor of Constitutional and Administrative Law at Leiden University in the Netherlands, where he is also Research Fellow of the Leiden Law School. Since 2008, he has also been a senior researcher at the School of Human Rights Research. Before his transfer to the Law Faculty, he taught at the Department of Political Science, and was a Post-Doctoral Fellow at the Minda de Gunzburg Center for European Studies at Harvard University. His current fields of expertise include Dutch parliamentary democracy, political rights, freedom of religion, the Dutch Constitution, and church-state relationships. Recently he has been awarded a Research Fellowship in Legal Studies at the Center of Theological Inquiry (CTI) at Princeton University, which enables him to be in full-time residence for the academic year 2014-2015.

Remco Nehmelman is full professor of Public Institutional Law, at Utrecht University, the Netherlands. His fields of interest concern Constitutional Law, more specifically Constitutional Political Law (e.g. Political Parties Law) and Law for Lower Governmental Organizations (e.g. Municipalities). He is also a member of the Dutch Council of Public Administration, an advisory body of the Dutch Government and Parliament.

Daniela R. Piccio is a post-doctoral Research Associate at Leiden University. Her research and teaching interests include political participation, political representation, comparative party politics and party (finance) regulation. She obtained her PhD at the European University Institute of Florence with a dissertation titled "Party Responses to Social Movements: A Comparative Analysis of Italy and the Netherlands". Her work has appeared in *South European Society and Politics*, *Representation*, the *International Political Science Review*, as well as in several edited book volumes.

Ekaterina R. Rashkova is an Assistant Professor of Comparative Politics at the University of Innsbruck, Austria. Her research interests lie in electoral and party systems and the strategic behaviour of political actors, including party regulation and gender equality. She is the co-founder of the Comparative Politics Research Group Innsbruck (www.cprg.at) and co-editor of *Gender Politics and Party Regulation* (special issue of *Representation*, 2013) and *Contested Legitimacy: Paradoxes in the Legal Regulation of Political Parties* (special issue of the *International Political Science Review*, forthcoming). Her work studies both new and established democracies and has appeared in *Comparative European Politics*, *Party Politics* and *Political Studies*, as well as several edited books.

Maria Spirova is Senior Lecturer of Comparative Politics and International Relations in the Institute of Political Science at Leiden University, Netherlands. She has published on issues related to party development, minority policy, ethnic politics and Europeanization in the post-communist world. She is the author of *Political Parties in*

Post-communist Societies: Formation, Persistence and Change (Palgrave McMillan, 2007) and co-editor of *Party Patronage and Party Government in European Democracies* (with Petr Kopecký and, Peter Mair, OUP, 2012). Her research has appeared in *Party Politics*, *West European Politics*, *EJPR*, *Electoral Studies*, *East European Politics*, *Comparative European Politics*, *Europe-Asia Studies* and *Communist and Post-communist Studies*.

Index

Printed and bound by CPI Group (UK) Ltd, Croydon, CR0 4YY
09/11/2026
14999538-0001